MOVING ON

MOVING ON

Reading Selections for Canadian Students

Christine Straus

Marie Clayden

Dianne Fenner

Christine McAdam

Moving On: Reading Selections for Canadian Students

Authors
Christine Straus, Marie Clayden,
Dianne Fenner, Christine McAdam

Director of Publishing
David Steele

Publisher
Mark Cressman

Program Manager
Doug Panasis, Resources.too

Developmental Editor
Susan Petersiel Berg

Copy Editor
Naomi Pascoe

Production Coordinator
Helen Locsin

ArtPlus Production Coordinator
Dana Lloyd

Cover Design
Dave Murphy/ArtPlus Ltd.

Text Design
Sandra Sled/ArtPlus Ltd.

Cover Photograph
Tim Barnett/Taxi/Getty Images

Page Layout
Barb Neri/ArtPlus Ltd.

Photo Research and Permissions
Lisa Brant

Printer
Transcontinental Printing Inc.

The authors and publisher gratefully acknowledge the contributions of the following educators:

Ken Draayer, Niagara District School Board, ON

Myra Junyk, Toronto Catholic District School Board, ON

Diana Knight, Halton District School Board, ON

Catherine Logan, Toronto District School Board, ON

Mary Lou Smitheram, Upper Canada District School Board, ON

Catherine Stasiw, Toronto Catholic District School Board, ON

As well as Arnel Fausto, Eileen McCabe, and Joanne McCabe.

National Library of Canada Cataloguing in Publication

Moving on : reading selections for Canadian students /Christine Straus ... [et al.].

A component of Making it work 12, to be used with Making it work 12: A handbook for reading, writing, language, and media, and teacher's guide.
For use in grade 12.
ISBN 0-7725-2922-1

1. Readers (Secondary) I. Straus, Christine
II. Title: Making it work 12.

PE1121.M69 2002   428.6
C2002-905465-6

We acknowledge for their financial support of our publishing program the Canada Council, the Ontario Arts Council, and the Government of Canada through the Book Publishing Industry Development Program (BPIDP).

TABLE OF CONTENTS

UNIT 3 *Working with Others*

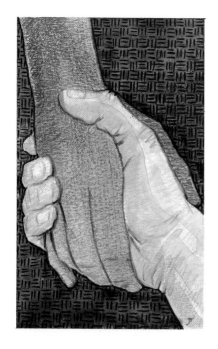

UNIT 5 *An Enterprising Spirit*

Faint as in a dream
is the voice that calls
from the belly
of the wall

Table of Contents Organized by Genre

NONFICTION

LITERATURE

Looking back, looking forward — reflections allow us to do both of those things. On our path to learning for life, we have the chance to reflect with each new thing that we learn.

In this unit, you will read people's reflections on their own lives, on how work, issues, attitudes, and the lives of others have affected them, and on what they have learned, and hope to keep learning each step of the way.

CONTENTS

Before You Read

Before you read this poem, complete one of the following statements in your reading response journal.

When I look at my face in the mirror, I see…
When I look at family photographs of me, I see…
When I look into my own eyes in the mirror, I see…

Me *as My* Grandmother

by Rosemary Aubert

Sometimes
I look up quickly
and see for an instant
her face
in my mirror,
random tightness
turns my mouth
into a facsimile of hers,
eyes caught oddly
in the glass
make me
into her
looking at me.

Now that she's dead,
I understand
that it is right
that I should age
and wrinkle into her.
It brings her back,
it puts me into
the cycle of family.
We look at all time
with just that
one same face.

Handbook Link

How to recognize
the perspectives of
authors and readers

After You Read

1. Re-read the statement you wrote. Write the response that you think the poet would have given, then note how the two responses compare.

Before You Read

This selection is a radio play. Before you read it, listen to the audio version. Then, with a partner, briefly discuss any plays you are familiar with, both stage and radio. List what you expect to find in a play that is read on the radio as opposed to one that is performed on a stage.

One Ocean

by Betty Quan

Scene 1: Narration. Inside Memory

Music: establish theme, continue under.

DAUGHTER: (*older*) A long time ago. It was my favourite. A story. No, our story. Just a Chinese folktale. Yes. About the Jingwei bird and why she is always dropping sticks and stones in the ocean. When I was small, I used to pretend I was that little bird. I would soar through our communal courtyard with arms for wings. That was when we were still allowed to enjoy our stories, to tell our stories, before, before…*Bah-bah.* Father. Do you remember like I do? Tell me about the Jingwei. Yes, like you used to do when I was small. You told me that story when I left Hong Kong for Canada. Do you remember? I was sad. We were both sad. Like a bird in your hand I was until you set me free across the sky, across the ocean. Such a long time ago, yet so close I can still see it unfolding before me. Father? Tell me a story. Like you used to do (*as if repeating what she hears in memory*) "A long time ago." It seems like yesterday. A long time ago. But that is how we begin our stories, isn't it? We begin with "a long time ago."

Scene 2: Folktale Remembered

FATHER: A long time ago there was an emperor who had a young daughter. They loved each other very much. But although his powers could touch all corners of the land, the emperor could see only as far as the shoreline that divided his kingdom with the sea.

DAUGHTER: Beyond that shoreline, his vision was limited, like a kite held high in a strong breeze—he could see the shape, but not the colours.

(Music ends. Sound effects: birds, breeze, ocean, continue under.)

DAUGHTER: Father, look at the waves, so tall they must be hiding something behind them. I will take my boat for a ride.

FATHER: (*as Emperor*) Not so far, not so far.

DAUGHTER: (*as Jingwei*) Don't worry, Father. I'll be careful.

FATHER: (*as Emperor*) Why don't you wait a while? I'll join you. We can journey to the horizon together, where the sea meets the sun.

DAUGHTER: (*as Jingwei*) When? When can we do this? (*laughing*) You're always promising such things, Father! You're too busy as Emperor. I'll go out on my own first. On my own adventure. Then, I'll show you what I've seen.

FATHER: (*as Emperor, laughing*) When?

DAUGHTER: (*as Jingwei*) What does that matter? We have all the time in the world.

DAUGHTER: (*older*) The sun was warm upon the little girl's face—

FATHER: —and the salty breeze off the water tempted her to travel farther and farther. To see what hid behind the tall waves of the sea.

DAUGHTER: (*older*) Far far far away she went, when suddenly—

(Sound effects: thunder and rainstorm)

FATHER: (*as Sea God*) Who dares come this far upon the ocean of my reign?

DAUGHTER: (*older*) The Sea God's bad temper came upon the little girl.

(Sound effects: Jingwei screams as the waves engulf her)

FATHER: The water became a blanket that covered her. And the little girl died.

(Sound effects: all suddenly end)

DAUGHTER: (*older*) Died? I don't remember her dying. Is that right? I thought the water changed her into a bird. Like magic.

FATHER: I would tell you that when you were small. When you didn't understand death.

DAUGHTER: (*older*) Like I do now.

FATHER: It is only a story. (*continues*) The little girl's soul became a small bird called Jingwei.

(Music begins)

DAUGHTER: (*older*) Father, I died that day you sent me away.

FATHER: No child, you were reborn. Now, continue the story.

DAUGHTER: Angry was the spirit in that bird, angry at the sea it was for taking her away from her beloved father. And every day the Jingwei would carry in her beak stones and twigs from the mountains of the east and flying west ahead drop her small stones and twigs into the sea. And the Sea God finally noticed what Jingwei was trying to do.

(*Music ends. Sound effects: ocean. Close: the wings of a bird in motion*)

FATHER: (*as Sea God, laughing*) Silly creature, my sea is wider and deeper than your limited imagination. You can never fill me up in a million years.

DAUGHTER: (*as Jingwei*) But I can. Every day for a million years I will do this. Every day until one day. Until one day…(*begin fade down*) Until one day…Until one day…

FATHER: And the small bird flew back to land—

FATHER & DAUGHTER: (*older*)—only to return with another small stone or twig to drop into the sea.

DAUGHTER: (*older*) And Jingwei said: "One day, there will be a bridge between me and my father. One day, even if it takes a million years to build it." (*She no longer speaks as the Jingwei.*) Soon, father. I will see you again. Soon.

(*Sound effects: fade down*)

Scene 3: Airport

(*Sound effects: airplane's acceleration and ascent. Fades into airport interior: Chinese public address system, etc. Close: a swallow singing*)

FATHER: Yes, yes, sing a goodbye song to my daughter. Here's a sunflower seed.

DAUGHTER: I don't think pets are allowed here.

FATHER: This is not just a pet, eh my little friend? Now keep your bag in full sight. Many pickpockets. There is more freedom here in Hong Kong but that doesn't mean there is less danger. Here's your ticket. Show it to that man over there. Where's your passport?

DAUGHTER: I don't want to go to Vancouver, father. Why me?

FATHER: Your big brother has a family now. You will go first, then settle down. Then we can join you.

DAUGHTER: When?

FATHER: Soon. Soon. Look at us now. We used to have a fine house and good food to eat. First the Japanese and the war, now Mao. Remember, just a few years ago, Mao decided China must have its Great Leap Forward? And the country went two steps forward and five steps back?

Scene 4: Narration. Inside Memory

(*Music fades under.*)

DAUGHTER: (*older*) Mosquitoes, flies, rats, and sparrows: Mao called these the "four pests." 1958: it was the year I turned sixteen. (*bitter laugh*) Do you remember? Mao believed grain production was down because the sparrows were feeding on the backs of the people. Families were armed with pots and pans. We were to scare the sparrows out of the trees so they would eventually drop dead from exhaustion. Six hundred million of us, running under trees, in the countryside, in the cities, making enough noise to waken the dead. Yes, the sparrows ate the grain, but they also ate the insects. Without the sparrows, no one could control the insects. The sky would rain the corpses of little birds to join the corpses of three hundred million people, dead of starvation.

Scene 5: Airport

(*Sound effects: airport interior. Close: the swallow singing*)

FATHER: You know how lucky we were to get out of China?

DAUGHTER: I know.

FATHER: How can we Chinese have luck when we are killing birds!? This is why it is good we are here now. No more death. No more hunger. No more sacrificing our own symbols of fortune and happiness. Maybe my good luck has returned right here in this cage. Maybe now we will all have good luck.

DAUGHTER: Maybe's, nothing but maybe's.

FATHER: You have a chance now, can't you see? To start a new life in a new place.

DAUGHTER: Let me finish school first.

FATHER: (*joking*) Maybe, you'll find a rich Canadian and marry him.

DAUGHTER: I'm 18 years old; I don't need a husband. I can try to find a job here, in Hong Kong.

FATHER: Just a temporary thing, you'll see. Your mother, your brother, me. We'll be a family again. We're relying on you. Work hard. Stay out of trouble. Be a citizen your new country can be proud of. When you're settled, you'll sponsor us to come. We'll join you later.

DAUGHTER: Please don't make me go, father.

FATHER: Who is the parent here? Who makes the decision?

DAUGHTER: Please, father, don't make me go all alone.

FATHER: Look, my Jingwei. Yes, you have always been like a little bird to me. If I could, I would always try to protect you, away from bad things. But this—this—is a good thing.

DAUGHTER: I don't want to go!

FATHER: Believe me, it's for the best. You'll like it in Canada.

DAUGHTER: Don't you want me to stay here, with you?

FATHER: It doesn't matter what I want. It's what I want for you.

FEMALE: (*over sound system, filtered*) Last boarding call for Flight 973 departing for Vancouver, Canada. (*The announcer repeats this in Cantonese.*)

DAUGHTER: I've never been in a plane before, Father. Have you?

FATHER: No. Not yet. But in time, no?

DAUGHTER: Yes, in time.

Scene 6: Airfield

(*Sound effects: airport exterior. Plane accelerating and ascending. Closer: the swallow's song*)

FATHER: Goodbye! (*to himself*) Goodbye.

(Sound effects: swallow singing)

FATHER: What's that? What are you singing about?

(Sound effects: swallow singing. Metal clink of the cage being opened)

FATHER: Come on, there. No, it's not a trick. Out. Yes. Fly, go on, fly. Fly.

(Sound effects: close: the acceleration of a bird's wings, heard under)

FATHER: Build a bridge between me and my daughter. Make our ocean one.

Scene 7: Narration. Inside Memory

(Music: begins and continues under)

DAUGHTER: (*older*) You broke your promise. You never came. You let me leave you behind. I waited for you, Father. For the family. A long time ago. Where are you? Are you here, with me? Did you follow on the shadow of the airplane's wings? (*voice begins to break*) Did I fly away like a kite in the breeze? So high up you can see the shape, but not the colours? Can you see me? I'm so far away but all you have to do is pull me home. Father. Father. When I finish building a bridge, will you cross it? Even if the stones are loose, and the twigs breaking. Will you cross it? Father? (*beat*) Bah-bah? How big is the ocean?

(Music ends. Sound effects: exterior: airfield. Plane's acceleration and ascent crosses into that of birds in flight, their wings in motion. Fade into ocean, water lapping on a beach. Up and out.)

After You Read

1. With a partner, discuss and explain the symbols of the Jingwei, the bridge, the ocean, and the sparrow.
2. a. Write point form notes describing what the daughter learns about herself from her memories.
   b. Describe how the daughter's memory of the story changes as she gets older.
   c. Using the symbols from the play, write a brief poem that the daughter might have written about her memories.

Handbook Link

How to write a poem

Before You Read

According to a comment written by author Margaret Atwood, and para-phrased in this essay, all of Canada's people are immigrants, even if they were born in Canada. Discuss your thoughts about this comment with a partner before you read the essay.

Who, Then, Is a "Canadian"?

by Suwanda Sugunasiri

Alien hordes. That's what the term "ethnic" came to be associated with in pre-war years. By 1930, an ethnic was, by dictionary definition, someone who was "neither Christian nor Jewish"; the implication was "a heathen."

Today sociologists define an ethnic community as "an involuntary group of people who share the same culture."

So, none of us can help it. We are—Anglo-Saxons, Jews, Francophones, Native People, Blacks, Chinese, South Asians, Arabs, Latin Americans—*all* ethnics! Just as Margaret Atwood says, we're all immigrants, even if we were born here.

No doubt some, like the Native People who were the exclusive inhabitants of Canada 10,000 years ago, and the Anglo-Saxons and Francophones who laid claim to the land 200 years ago, are "old ethnics" compared to the "new ethnics."

Who, then, is a "Canadian"?

A family friend, of English origins, highlighted the issue for me recently when he wondered out loud who in his family would be Canadian and who not. He and his wife were born and raised in England, their 20-year-old son was only a year when he came here, and their daughter was born in Canada.

By international law, of course, the daughter is "Canadian." But the brother, six years her elder, is hardly any different from her—in language, food, taste in fashion and music, etc. Naturally. They were both educated in Canadian schools. So is he not Canadian?

When it comes to the parents, they still prefer Beethoven to the Beatles, or to Gordon Lightfoot.

Their Canadianness has never been questioned. But the issue came to be raised because we have mutual friends, among both old ethnics and new ethnics, of white, black, brown, yellow skin colour, and in between, who have the same history but have had a different experience.

Indeed some of these friends have their roots among the loyalist Black Canadians of Nova Scotia. The children, whatever the ethnic origin, watch "Hockey Night in Canada" as they eat popcorn, wear Roots sweatshirts and speak Canadian English fluently. Their parents drink Canadian lager, pay $50 for a dinner with a rotating view from atop the CN Tower and attend concerts at Roy Thomson Hall in Toronto.

Some of them are Christians—Catholics, Protestants, Greek Orthodox. Others are Jewish, Rastafarian, Muslim, Hindu, Buddhist, Sikh, Zoroastrian; not to mention non-believer and Rational Humanist…and heathen.

The traditional model of the "nation-state," born of the European experience, where an entire people bounded by a national border share the same ethnicity, birth status, language, culture, etc., and believe in the same god, clearly does not fit the Canadian experience.

A country of immigrants and ethnics, old or new, calls for a more flexible definition of Canadianness. Try this one on for psychological comfort: a Canadian is someone who lives in Canada; considers Canada to be his or her permanent home, come hell or high water; is able to communicate with other Canadians, in English or French, in whatever accent and dialect, but without giving up any original language facility; respects, and is willing to share other people's values, customs, etc., in such a way as to contribute to a developing, and changing, Canadian culture; and proudly claims "*Je suis canadien*" or "I'm Canadian," not by the involuntary accident of birth but by conscious choice.

To be sure, such a definition is not neat and tidy; it may even be nebulous and slippery. But such is the nature of Canadian society. Perhaps with time, we might be able to do some tightening up.

However, what we really need is not definitions. Simply our traditional Canadian large-heartedness. The moment we stop asking the question, "Where are you from?" we will cease to see alien hordes. The moment we begin to recognize, and accept, the claims to Canadian nationality, we will see 25 million Canadians, old and new ethnics, walking through the frontiers of our hearts.

After You Read

Handbook Link

How to cite sources

How to interpret and assess information, ideas, and issues in text

1. a. Copy the author's definition of "Canadian" using a parenthetical reference and a proper citation for the quotation.
   b. What do you think it means to be Canadian? What would you change in the definition?
2. Is "frontiers of our hearts" an appropriate phrase to conclude the selection? With a partner, explain why and offer support for your answer.

Before You Read

Before you read, discuss with a partner or small group anything you know about autism. (You can also look up the definition in a dictionary.) Then make a list of things that would make life challenging for a person with autism. As you read, use self-stick notes to identify the difficulties that the author has overcome.

Adversity
by David Trupp

First of all, I'm autistic so I know all about adversity. Autism is a disorder in which withdrawal occurs and it is hard to develop relationships. Not to mention the tons of fixations that when I think about it now, are crazy. One of the downfalls is going to see the doctors all over the place from Hamilton all the way to London—from doctors to psychiatrists to workers to analysts. It drove me completely insane going from doctor to doctor and city to city and back. Growing up, I had lots of fixations; for example, dead-end streets. I absolutely hated turning in to dead-end streets or even walking into them probably because the mystery of the road wasn't there because it had ended.

I wasn't big on change either and in fact I'm still not big on change. I'm pretty sure that the slightest change set me off when I was younger. It was because I felt secure when things were just the way they were and when change did occur I didn't feel that security that I would normally have.

I was fascinated by typical ordinary things. Spinning objects were one of them, for instance, spinning tops, especially colourful ones. I was just so

fascinated by them, by the way they moved. I was into 3-D objects also. It was all the sides combined to make a 3-D object that I was fascinated with. I am still fascinated by it for some reason.

I think that my autism has made me stronger for numerous reasons. I can relate to the struggle of not knowing where I am; or of trying to advance to higher levels in things that I do. It's given me good people skills because I understand people's problems because I've had lots of them. I can understand people who feel they are lacking something and/or feel less of a person. I was like that and said to myself at one point, "I'm done, I'm quitting." Sometimes I still feel that way.

When I was younger, I had a lot of fear. The fear of reaching out to someone. The fear of falling. The fear of rejection. As a young kid, I felt like a mutant in school. I was always different from all of the other kids. I hardly had any friends because of that whole withdrawal thing. To put it bluntly, I hated being me.

I don't want to come off as feeling sorry for myself because there are people who are severely austistic or even severely disabled for that matter. And that's another thing. People will take advantage of someone with my condition or somebody disabled, or they feel bad for us, or they look down on us as "stupid" people. Let me rephrase that, some people.

I guess that's where my comedy comes in. It's like an alternative to feeling low. It's like a fire escape for me. It's a way to break loose from the downsides in my life. It's like a zone that no one else can enter. It is MY Zone.

Sometime in March 2001, I went back to Hamilton to see the doctor who diagnosed me, Dr. Peter Szatmari. It turns out he reversed the diagnosis. However, I still have some mild characteristics of autism. It blew my mind because for 15 years, all I have done was struggle with autism and now I only have a few mild characteristics of it. Trust me, it's shocking. I have come a long way from a scared three-year-old little boy with autism and lots of obstacles in his way to a young man who is almost rid of it. I am not completely rid of it, but there are some symptoms that I had five years ago that are now gone.

In the future, I would love to volunteer and work with autistic children. I feel that there is a need to spend time working with them, educating them, and above all showing them that it is okay to be different. It's okay to have a setback. I have learned that just because you have a disability, you shouldn't feel any less than someone else. Love yourself regardless of a disability. People who are different, like myself, have a gift that no one else can offer. Mine is acting and comedy. That's the gift that I was blessed with. I am a fantastic writer, too. That is also something that I can share with the world.

When I look back on my entire 15 years spent as an autistic, I think, "Wow, I did it. Autism made the challenge and I came out victorious." I've overcome this stage in my life and now I am ready for the next.

After You Read

1. Reflect in your reading response journal:
   a. What does David learn about himself through his experiences with autism?
   b. How does he plan on using his experience in his future career? What lesson can you learn from this as you plan your future career?

Handbook Link
How to interpret and assess information, ideas, and issues in text

Before You Read

As a boy, author Robert Peck lived on a farm with his parents, where his favourite pet was a pig named Pinky. Peck and his family are Shakers, part of a small Christian community in the United States. This is a chapter from a novel that Peck wrote about his life.

Skim the first four paragraphs. From the clues that you see, in what time period is the story set? How old do you think Robert is? Read the story to confirm your predictions.

A Day No PIGS Would Die

by Robert Newton Peck

June come. I sure was happy as today was the last day of school.

It was hot that afternoon. But I came racing home with my final report card all folded up in my pocket. The weather was dry as dust, and I was glad to be walking across pasture on the soft green meadowland, instead of kicking rocks the long way round which was by the dirt road.

Way off to my right side, a wagon was coming down the long hill, headed for town. I didn't know the team or the driver. As the wagon moved along the dirt road, it blowed up clouds of dust that seemed to hang in the air behind it. Looked like the wagon was chased by a long dusty-gray snake. The driver had his coat took off, riding in his shirt with his sleeves rolled up. It looked like Isadore Crookshank who sat the seat, but I couldn't tell for sure.

I watched the wagon until it went out of sight around a roadbend. And soon the snake had gone, too. It was like the wagon hadn't passed by at all.

From a quarter mile away I could see the corn cratch that Solomon moved with the capstan. And its new boards from one end to the other, like stripes, to fill in what used to be the open space between slats. Closer, I could see Pinky moving about, chasing one of the chickens.

"Pinky," I yelled. But she was too far away to hear. So I ran again. But not too far, as it sure was a hot day for June.

Now that I was near, I called to Pinky again. This time she heard, and come to meet me. Boy! She was growing. I'd had her just ten weeks and already she was about my size. I lay on my back on the grass so she could come up to me and I could see her face. It always looked to me like she was smiling. In fact, I know she was. Lots of things smile, like a flower to the sun. And one thing sure. I knew that just like I could smile to see Pinky, she sure could smile to see me.

I got up, running toward the house. Pinky followed, but not as fast as when she was tiny. Her weight gain was good, but it slowed her down some. Just as we got to the fence, I saw Mama on the front stoop, waving for me to come up to the house. I'd hoped she hadn't took notice of me rolling on the meadowgrass in my school clothes.

"Rob," she said, as I came in the house, "look who's here."

There she was, sitting in our good chair, and wearing one of her big dresses with all the

colorful flowers on it, and smelling so good with perfume that it almost made me sick. There she was, Aunt Matty.

She lived in town, in Learning. Once a month or so, she'd come to pay call on Mama. She wasn't my real aunt, like Aunt Carrie. But I guess she was a distant cousin twice moved; which to go along with my reckoning means that she used to live in two other places before she moved to Learning. Anyhow, she wasn't my real aunt. Just a friend of Mama and Aunt Carrie, so that they got out the good cups to drink tea out of. But I called her Aunt Matty. Or sometimes Auntie Matt. Her real name was Martha Plover.

"Hello, Aunt Matty."

"Well, look at the size of you. You're growing like a weed." Aunt Matty always said that, and yet it always made me feel good.

"Thank you," I said.

I should have excused myself right then and there, and changed my clothes for chores. But instead I made my big mistake of the day. And it could of been my big mistake of the whole darn summer.

Like a fool, I pulled out my report card.

I showed it to Mama and to Aunt Carrie. They couldn't read hardly at all, but they knew what an A looked like. I'd got A in geography, spelling, reading, arithmetic, and history. The only other mark I got was a D in English, which I didn't bother to point out. So when Mama and Aunt Carrie saw all them A's they said I was a good boy.

The trouble kicked up when I showed my report card to Aunt Matty. She could read. But as it turned out, she couldn't read the letter A, no matter how many she saw. All she could read was D, where I got a D in English.

"You got D in English!"

The way Aunt Matty took on, it must have been the first D anybody ever got, because it sure gave her the vapors. I thought she was going to die from the shock of it. Like she seen a ghost. There it was. A big black D, as big and black as Miss Malcolm could make it, right there on my old report card. And it was more than poor Aunt Matty could bear. She let out a gasp, and her hand went to her throat like she was spasmed.

"D in English," she said again, to make sure that there wasn't a soul who missed it.

Well, I thought to myself, I've done it. Brung disgrace on my family's house. Appeared a D in English was so dark a deed that no one could live it down.

"'Course it's not the end of the world," said Aunt Matty. "There *is* a remedy."

Remedy! There was a word that struck a fever. Mama had give me a spoonful of remedy for one thing or another almost every winter and spring. It made you go to the backhouse a lot. Morning, noon, and night. Sometimes twice each, and it was no picnic to have your butt burn like Hellfire.

"All he needs," said Aunt Matty to Mama and Aunt Carrie, "is a tutor."

At this, I heaved a breath of well being. I sure knew what a "tooter" was. Jacob Henry had one. Its real name was a cornet, and he played it in the school band. But what Jacob called it was his "tooter." So I was some relieved, now knowing that I weren't going to get marched to the kitchen, took by the ear, and forced to gag down a tablespoon of remedy. A cornet was bad, the way Jacob played it. But it sure beat a remedy that you had to swallow now and run after.

"Fact is," said Aunt Matty, "I will tutor him myself." That was when I busted out laughing fit to kill. Aunt Matty, big and round in her flower dresses and all her beads, was strange to look at as she was. But to see her blowing on a cornet, with her cheeks all puffed out the way Jacob's got, was too much to stand. A sight like that could lead the high school band in a parade. Auntie Matt and her silver cornet, highstepping down the main street of Learning every Four of July. It was more than ribs could take.

That's when I should of known better. Seeing me laugh was more than Aunt Matty could bear. Anyone who got a D in English had no right to joy. It was her next words that stopped the laughing for time to come.

"D in English! It's no laughing matter. Next thing it'll be an F, for Failure. And you know what that means. Expulsion. He'll be put back a grade. So there's no time to lose. I'll start to tutor him today, and right now. Come, Robert."

Up jumped Aunt Matty, grabbing me with one of her chubby hands and her big old floppy pocketbook with the other. I could tell she meant business. As she drug me into the parlor, all her bracelets were rattling as if to say so. Well, it was all right with me. If Aunt Matty wanted to play the cornet, I was partial to it.

"Grammar," she said, pushing me with some force into a hardwood ladderback chair. "That's where you're falling down. Before I married your Uncle Hume, I was an English teacher. And that's where we're going to start. Living in this house and all its Shaker ways, it's a wonder you can talk at all. You'd get better than a D in English if you were a fearing Baptist."

That was it! That there was the time my heart almost stopped. I'd heard about the Baptists from Jacob Henry's mother. According to her, Baptists were a strange lot. They put you in water to see how holy you were. Then they ducked you under the water three times. Didn't matter a whit if you could swim or no. If you didn't come up, you got dead and your mortal soul went to Hell. But if you did come up, it was even worse. You had to be a Baptist.

And here I was, alone with one. Bless the dear old goodness there weren't a pond in our parlor. It sure would be a painful caution to have a Baptist the size of Aunt Matty hold you under. Even to think of it made me gasp for breath, and I made a throaty noise.

"You all right?" asked Aunt Matty, digging around inside her big pocketbook. She came up with a tiny whitelace hanky, not much bigger than a stamp.

"Here," she said, "blow your nose. You can't learn English with an acting sinus."

I blew!

"Now then," said Aunt Matty, as she snatched back her hanky, giving it a sick look, "we're going to have a little test on grammar. You tell me, Robert, which sentence is correct. Ready?"

"Yes'm."

"It was I who he called. It was me who he called. It was I *whom* he called. And, it was me whom he called."

I just sat there, dumb as a post. I guessed I didn't have brains enough to dump sand out a boot. If she'd asked me if'n I was Robert Peck, I don't guess I could of answered a good stout yes or no.

"Well?"

"I don't know, Auntie Matt. They all sound fair enough to me."

"Just as I suspected from the first."

"The first what?"

"It's just an expression, Rob. But it's just as I feared. You don't know grammar, because you don't know how to *diagram.*"

"We haven't had that yet," I said.

" 'Course you haven't. Trouble with teachers today is, they don't diagram. All they think of is the Bunny Hug."

"We haven't had that either."

Aunt Matty went fishing into her big pocketbook once again. She pulled out an armload of things that she didn't want, and finally some paper and pencil.

"So," she said, writing as fast as she talked, "I am going to write out a sentence, and *you* can diagram it. Hear?"

"Yes."

"There now. *Jack hit the ball hard with Joe's yellow bat.* Let's see you diagram *that*."

"I can't, Auntie Matt."

"I know you can't. But any schoolboy who gets a D had better learn. First off, what's the subject?"

"English."

"What?"

"English is the subject I got a D in."

Aunt Matty wiped her face with the hanky I blowed my nose into. She gave a big sigh (like Solomon when he's pulling the plow and comes to the end of a furrow) and I knew that grammar sure was a tribulation.

"Rob," she said real soft, "I used to teach English, and there was one thing I never did. Know what that was?"

"Played the cornet?"

"Not exactly. I never got angry. A good teacher does not lose her temper, no matter how stupid her pupils are."

"That's good," I said, "because in our school they sure are some dull ones."

As Aunt Matty fanned herself with the hanky, I wondered what she was thinking about. I was joyful to hear that Aunt Matty didn't get mad. An angry teacher is bad aplenty, but I didn't know how good I could fend off an angry Baptist.

Picking up the pencil, Aunt Matty started to draw some lines and circles (and a few other gee-gaws that I'd never seen before and never seen since) on the sentence about Jack. She put a zig-zag here, and a crazy elbow joint there. There was ovals and squiggles all over the paper. It was the fanciest thing I ever saw. The part about Jack was still in sight, but now it had arms and legs that thrashed out in six directions. It looked to me like a hill of barbwire.

And the worse it got, the prouder Aunt Matty was of it.

"Behold!" she said at last, trying to pry loose the pencil from her own fingers. "*That* is a diagram!"

I wasn't about to make sport of it. Aunt Carrie always said that only the foolish defy the Dark Spirits. I didn't know the truth of it, but years back in the town of Learning, somebody had come across an old woman who was a witch. She'd just look at a barn and it'd burn to cinders. She could dry up a creek with one crack of her knuckles. And sour your cow's milk before it bubbled in the pail. One look from that old witch, they said, would mildew silage and peel paint. Must have been a Baptist.

"Gee, Aunt Matty," I said. "I ought to get A in English now for certain."

"Here," she said, handing me the paper that she'd sweated over like it was canning. "Take it up to your room and pin it on the wall."

She pushed the paper to my hand, and I felt the unholy touch of it all the way upstairs and down.

"Did you thank Aunt Matty?" my mama asked me. "Can't forget manners."

"Thank you, Aunt Matty. Now I got to do chores. If'n it don't get done, they'll be a nevermind of fuss 'tween I and Papa."

I was careful not to slam the door. Just outside, Pinky was waiting for me, and we raced each other to the barnyard fence. And just as I took leave of the house, I heard all of Aunt Matty's bracelets go rattling, and I heard mama say:

"How was the first lesson?"

"Next time," said Aunt Matty, "I'll teach the pig."

After You Read

1. Were your predictions about the story correct? List details from the story to support your answer.
2. This story is told from Robert's point of view, using informal language. In a small group, discuss why informal language is appropriate in this selection. How would the tone change if the language were formal?

Handbook Link

How to create your own voice in writing

Before You Read

There are some things we know are true about ourselves, but don't know why they are true. In this essay, Stephen King explores one of those truths. Do you enjoy horror movies? What does your answer tell you about yourself?

Before you read, write the title of the essay on a sheet of lined paper. As you read, look for and list some of the reasons King gives to answer the thesis he poses in the title.

Why We CRAVE Horror Movies

by Stephen King

I think that we're all mentally ill; those of us outside the asylums only hide it a little better—and maybe not all that much better, after all. We've all known people who talk to themselves, people who sometimes squinch their faces into horrible grimaces when they believe no one is watching, people who have some hysterical fear—of snakes, the dark, the tight place, the long drop ... and, of course, those final worms and grubs that are waiting so patiently underground.

When we pay our four or five bucks and seat ourselves at tenth-row center in a theater showing a horror movie, we are daring the nightmare.

Why? Some of the reasons are simple and obvious. To show that we can, that we are not afraid, that we can ride this roller coaster. Which is not to say that a really good horror movie may not surprise a scream out of us at some point, the way we may scream when the roller coaster twists through a complete 360 or plows through a lake at the bottom of the drop. And horror movies, like roller coasters, have always been the special province of the young; by the time one turns 40 or 50, one's appetite for double twists or 360-degree loops may be considerably depleted.

We also go to re-establish our feelings of essential normality; the horror movie is innately conservative, even reactionary. Freda Jackson as the horrible melting woman in *Die, Monster, Die!* confirms for us that no matter how far we may be removed from the beauty of a Robert Redford or a Diana Ross, we are still light-years from true ugliness.

And we go to have fun.

Ah, but this is where the ground starts to slope away, isn't it? Because this is a very peculiar sort of fun, indeed. The fun comes from seeing others menaced—sometimes killed. One critic has suggested that if pro football has become the voyeur's version of combat, then the horror film has become the modern version of the public lynching.

It is true that the mythic, "fairy-tale" horror film intends to take away the shades of gray ... It urges us to put away our more civilized and adult penchant for analysis and to become children again, seeing things in pure blacks and whites. It may be that horror movies provide psychic relief on this level because this invitation to lapse into simplicity, irrationality and even outright madness is extended so rarely. We are told we may allow our emotions a free rein … or no rein at all.

If we are all insane, then sanity becomes a matter of degree. If your insanity leads you to carve up women like Jack the Ripper or the Cleveland Torso Murderer, we clap you away in the funny farm (but neither of those two amateur-night surgeons was ever caught, heh-heh-heh); if, on the other hand, your insanity leads you only to talk to yourself when you're under stress or to pick your nose on the morning bus, then you are left alone to go about your business … though it is doubtful that you will ever be invited to the best parties.

The potential lyncher is in almost all of us (excluding saints, past and present; but then, most saints have been crazy in their own ways), and every now and then, he has to be let loose to scream and roll around in the grass. Our emotions and our fears form their own body, and we recognize that it demands its own exercise to maintain proper muscle tone. Certain of these emotional muscles are accepted—even exalted—in civilized society; they are, of course, the emotions that tend to maintain the status quo of civilization itself. Love, friendship, loyalty, kindness—these are all the emotions that we applaud, emotions that have been immortalized in the couplets of Hallmark cards and in the verses (I don't dare call it poetry) of Leonard Nimoy.

When we exhibit these emotions, society showers us with positive reinforcement; we learn this even before we get out of diapers. When, as children, we hug our rotten little puke of a sister and give her a kiss, all the aunts and uncles smile and twit and cry, "Isn't he the sweetest little thing?" Such coveted treats as chocolate-covered graham crackers often follow. But if we deliberately slam the rotten little puke of a sister's fingers in the door, sanctions follow—angry remonstrance from parents, aunts and uncles; instead of a chocolate-covered graham cracker, a spanking.

But anticivilization emotions don't go away, and they demand periodic exercise. We have such "sick" jokes as, "What's the difference between a truck-load of bowling balls and a truckload of dead babies?" ("You can't unload a truckload of bowling balls with a pitchfork …" a joke, by the way, that I heard originally from a ten-year-old). Such a joke may surprise a laugh or a grin out of us even as we recoil, a possibility that confirms the thesis: If we share a brotherhood of man, then we also share an insanity of man. None of which is intended as a defense of either the sick joke or insanity but merely as an explanation of why the best horror films, like the best fairy tales, manage to be reactionary, anarchistic, and revolutionary all at the same time.

The mythic horror movie, like the sick joke, has a dirty job to do. It deliberately appeals to all that is worst in us. It is morbidity unchained, our most base instincts let free, our nastiest fantasies realized … and it all happens, fittingly enough, in the dark. For those reasons, good liberals often shy away from horror films. For myself, I like to see the most aggressive of them—*Dawn of the Dead*, for instance—as lifting a trap door in the civilized forebrain and throwing a basket of raw meat to the hungry alligators swimming around in that subterranean river beneath.

Why bother? Because it keeps them from getting out, man. It keeps them down there and me up here. It was Lennon and McCartney who said that all you need is love, and I would agree with that.

As long as you keep the gators fed.

After You Read

1. With a partner, discuss some of the reasons each of you listed as you read. Do you think King's reasons are good support for his thesis? Why?
2. a. Discuss with your partner what you have learned about Stephen King. What perspective do you think he is writing from here?
   b. How does King benefit from having an audience for horror?
3. Find some examples of humour, allusion, and irony in the essay. How do they add to the essay?

Handbook Link

How to recognize the perspectives of authors and readers

How to recognize allusion and irony

Before You Read

Before you read, consider the role of television in your life. Write down the description that fits you best at this time in your life:
- I don't watch TV
- TV provides me with an escape from reality
- TV entertains me
- TV informs me
- TV educates me

As you read, note how the role of TV has changed over time in Ms. Danis's life.

My TV

Gisèle Danis: "I'll never forget growing up, joining Dad every night to watch the CBC National News"

Gisèle Danis
New Host of Guide to VRLand.
Television has always been a great form of escapism and education for me. My first memory of TV dates back to *The Mickey Mouse Club* and Sunday night's *Wonderful World of Disney*. From there, *The Flintstones*, *The Brady Bunch*, *Happy Days* and *Three's Company* dominated my junior school, day-TV watching hours.

Quickly after that I got glued to the life sagas of *Knots Landing* and *Melrose Place*. Today, shows like *Friends*, *Seinfeld*, *Frasier* and *Dharma & Greg*, help me escape my everyday life pressures, as do specialty channels. There's always something to learn, dream or just imagine on networks like Discovery, OLN, A&E, Showcase, Women's Television Network and History.

A constant in my life is TV news — I watch a lot of news — I'll never forget growing up, joining Dad every night to watch the CBC National News at 10 p.m. This complemented my interest and passion in current and world affairs, which led me to a 10-year career as a reporter/anchor with the CBC/SRC and CBC Newsworld.

So as you can see television has been at the centre of my life … it played and continues to play a huge role providing me with escapism in the early days and education in the later part of my life. And today I have the best of both worlds.

After You Read

1. In your reading response journal, answer the following:
   a. Who is the intended audience of this article?
   b. What do the editors of this article want to convey about television?
2. a. Write the statement "Television is a great source of escapism." Then write the statement "Television is a great source of education." List several reasons why you agree with each statement. Then list several reasons why you disagree with each statement. Support your reasons.
   b. Choose one of your sets of responses (either for or against either of the two statements). Deliver your responses orally to a small group, then listen as others in the group share their responses.

Handbook   Link

How to assess information from media

How to create and give effective oral presentations

How to become an effective listener

Before You Read

The cultural critic Neil Postman says that when new technology is introduced to the world, we focus on what it will do, but rarely think about what it will undo. In a small group, discuss what television as a technology allows people to do or become. Then discuss what television causes or allows people to undo.

TELEVISION VIEWING:
The Human Dimension
by Charles S. Ungerleider and Ernest Krieger

The Blind Men and the Elephant

Many, many years ago, there lived six elderly blind men. Each day after his chores were completed, a young man would visit the six blind men, offering aid and friendship.

On one occasion, the old men asked their young friend if he would lead them to the centre of the village where they could sit, enjoying the sounds of village activity. "Certainly," replied the young man. "I will take you tomorrow, as soon as I have finished my chores."

On the following afternoon, the blind men waited eagerly at the door of their house for their friend. The young man finally arrived. "I have not finished my work, but I will take you to the village now and return for you when my chores are done."

After he had taken them to the village, the young man departed to complete his work. The six blind men soon grew tired of sitting in the village square, and decided to move cautiously around the square. They formed a line. By placing their right hand on the shoulder of the man in front, each was able to follow the other.

Growing bolder with each step, the blind man at the head of the line walked more and more quickly toward the edge of the square. The men then snaked around the square's edge. The procession stopped abruptly when the first man walked into the side of an elephant. The momentum of the others propelled them in several directions around the elephant.

"Ouch," exclaimed the leader, "I have walked into a wall!"

By this time, the others were reaching out to find their companions. As they did, each man touched a different part of the elephant.

One man screamed as he touched the elephant's trunk, thinking it was a huge snake. Another, grasping the elephant's ear, thought he had taken hold of a large fan.

"Ouch," said another, touching the pointed end of the elephant's tusk.

The two remaining blind men found the elephant's leg and tail. The one who had taken hold of the elephant's leg thought he had found a tree trunk. The other who took hold of the elephant's tail was certain he had found a rope.

The elephant's driver shouted at the blind men, frightening them. "Release that elephant, you old fools!"

When they were reunited, the blind men began to talk about their experience. "An elephant is a wall," said one. "I am certain, because I have never bumped into anything so large and flat until today."

"No, no," insisted another. "An elephant is a snake. I have held it in my hand. I know."

In no time at all, the blind men were fiercely arguing. Each man was certain that the elephant was something different.

"Wall."

"Snake."

"Spear."

"Rope."

"Fan."

"Tree."

The young man, returning from his chores, could not help overhearing the argument among his blind friends. "You are all wrong," he said. "Each of you has touched a different part of the elephant. You must combine your experiences to find the truth."

With the dispute settled, the young man took his friends back to their home.

Viewing Television: The Human Dimension

Just as the blind men disagreed about the elephant, people differ in their perceptions of television programming. What people see on television and how they respond to what they see depends on many different influences. Among the strongest is the viewer's previous experiences. The same television program may be viewed very differently by people who have had different experiences.

A wide range of influences shape people's experiences and ideas, including such elements as age, education, group memberships, and political outlook. These elements become the filters through which people see the world in which they live, including television.

It is obvious, for example, that young children and people in their teens do not see things in the same way. Young children's mental abilities are not as developed as those of older people. This difference affects what young children and older people see on television.

Young children have more difficulty than older children knowing where a program ends and a commercial message begins. Older children are more capable of distinguishing what is "real" from what is "fictional" than younger children.

Education is an important influence on what people see and how they interpret what they see. For example, students who are familiar with the techniques of television production are better able to understand how certain illusions are created for the viewer than are students who have not learned about such techniques.

The groups to which people belong also help to shape their responses to the world around them. People identify more closely with the outlooks of the groups to which they belong.

Young people are more likely to view a television program about rock n' roll music than are senior citizens. Senior citizens, on the other hand, would probably be more interested in watching a television program about the problems of living in retirement communities.

People belong to many other groups in addition to their age group. Canadians who are active members of the Roman Catholic Church are more likely to seek information about changes in Catholic Church policy than are people of other religious backgrounds. Torontonians would be more interested in changes in Ontario's tax laws than people living in Vancouver. In general, people seek out messages that match their own ideas and avoid information that contradicts their viewpoints.

What people see and how they respond to what they see on television is influenced as much by their own experiences as by what is actually shown and how it is presented. Like the blind men exploring the elephant, people must combine a variety of sources of information to get a complete picture of the television experience.

After You Read

1. With your class, discuss how you think the lesson of the folk tale applies to television viewing.
2. Using supporting details from the excerpt, write a short opinion paper that explains why it is useful to an audience to view media in a critical way.

Handbook   Link

How to assess information from media

How to write a short essay

Before You Read

When we choose to help others, we say something about ourselves. One way to help is to give to a charitable organization. Brainstorm the techniques you know of that charitable organizations use to promote their work. List any examples that you have found effective, and explain why.

After You Read

1. With a partner, describe some of the design elements of the ad. How do the design and art attract the audience's attention?
2. With your partner, discuss and explain what you do and do not find effective about this ad. Compare it to other ads that you find effective and analyze the similarities and differences.

Handbook   Link
How to identify
design elements
in text

In a year when so much was taken, you still managed to give.

Thank You.

United Way of Greater Toronto

Before You Read

Sometimes we hold in our hands not only our own destinies, but the fate of others. In this magazine excerpt from her memoirs, Irene Gut Opdyke tells how she put her own life in danger by helping her Jewish friends escape from the Germans during World War II. Although she was only a young woman, she was determined "To do right; to tell you; and to remember."

Think of a time when it was difficult, and maybe even dangerous, to do the right thing. Write several paragraphs explaining the situation, the circumstances, and the outcome.

In My HANDS

By Irene Gut Opdyke with Jennifer Armstrong

Irene Gut had heard the warning over and over. It was written on posters. It was broadcast from loudspeakers on the street: "Whoever helps a Jew shall be punished by death." She decided to ignore it.

A young Polish Catholic girl, she was herself a prisoner of the Nazis, who had overrun her country. Their terrible atrocities filled her with anger and rebellion. Whatever she did might only be a drop in the ocean, but she was determined to fight back.

A Brief Reunion

I had been separated from my family for nearly two years. As we sat together, we took turns sharing our stories. The war had taken a toll on everyone. Mamusia's dark hair had turned completely grey since I last saw her. Tatus had lost his job and had been reduced to sewing black-market slippers. But he was one of the lucky ones. Other men had disappeared and were never heard from again.

There was still one person I was waiting to see: my beloved sister Janina. When she finally came home, she walked in and froze when she saw me. "Irena!" We ran into each other's arms. My other three sisters joined us, and we laughed and sobbed and clung together.

That night Tatus said a special prayer of thanksgiving for our safe reunion. Our home, all our possessions, our photographs and books—everything was gone. Food was scarce, but we were together. We were lucky.

Janina took me on a tour of Radom the next day. Everywhere we went, there were German soldiers, officers of the Wehrmacht, and SS men in grey uniforms. And pasted on the walls were posters caricaturing the Jews.

Janina led me south to Glinice, a largely Jewish section of Radom. As we approached, I saw fences topped with barbed wire, and a gate guarded by German soldiers and dogs. "Glinice ghetto," Janina murmured, glancing around. "All the Jews from Radom and the surrounding countryside have been forced to move in there, and into Walowa ghetto."

"But what does it mean?"

"We don't know."

In July we were stunned when the Germans took Tatus away to help run a ceramics factory he had designed in Kozlowa Gora. For weeks we heard nothing. Then a letter came, and Mamusia broke down weeping at his news: Old friends had

A Family Together — The young Gut sisters briefly reunited in 1941: Wladzia, Irene, Marysia, Bronia and Janina.

turned away from him because he was working for the Germans. Strangers now occupied our house.

Mamusia decided to take the three younger girls and join him. Because she had heard rumours that young Polish women were being put into brothels in Germany, she would not risk taking Janina and me. We pleaded with her, sobbing all the way to the train station, but she was adamant.

Janina and I felt we had woken from one nightmare into another. I couldn't believe this was happening so soon after I'd been reunited with my family. My sister and I grew even closer, desperate to stay together. The house was emptier now, but we continued to share a bed where we held hands each night till we fell asleep.

We soon found out, though, that the Germans had other uses for young women. One Sunday, as I knelt in church, there was a pounding of boots on the steps outside. The church doors opened, and Wehrmacht soldiers shouting "*Raus! Zur Strasse!*" herded us out at gunpoint. They separated us: children and elderly to one side, youths and middle-aged to the other.

We were crowded into troop transports to be taken away: The Germans needed workers. I was put to work packing boxes at an ammunition factory in Radom.

The plant floor was a hell of noise and chemical fumes. Often I felt faint from exhaustion, malnourishment and bad air. We were forced to work standing for hours at a time, and we were not paid. We had become slaves.

The Box Under the Fence

One morning a group of officers came to inspect us, and as they approached, I passed out. When I came to, I was on a couch in an office. A German major sat behind the desk—an older man in his 60s, wearing thick glasses. He asked my name, then said: "You're jeopardizing the efficiency of the factory. If you're too sick to work—"

"No, Herr Major, I am not too sick," I interrupted. "Please don't deport me. I will work harder."

He considered for a moment. "Your German is very good. Perhaps you would be better suited for working in the officers' mess. Do you have domestic skills?"

I nearly jumped from the couch. "Yes, Herr Major!"

He wrote out a pass for me, gave me an address and told me to go home and report for work at 7 a.m. I glanced at the name on the pass as I left: Major Eduard Rügemer.

My new job was at a stately old hotel in Radom, where I served three meals a day to German officers in the dining room. The amount of food I saw consumed—and left over—sometimes made my head spin, especially when I knew how poorly everyone else was eating.

After several weeks, I got up the courage to ask the cook, Herr Schulz, if I might take some leftovers home for my aunt and sister. Schulz had been kind to me. Now he generously prepared packages of meat, bread and vegetables for me to take home. It made my heart ache with relief when I noticed Janina

Beloved Sister — Irene (right) saved Janina from a Nazi's advances.

beginning to lose the pinched and hollow look in her face.

One morning in November, Schulz asked me to set the tables in the upstairs ballroom for a formal dinner. Opening the velvet drapes to let in some light, I glanced outside.

The ballroom was at the rear of the hotel, and I realized I had never looked out that side of the building. A wooden fence topped with barbed wire ran directly in back of the hotel. Then I understood: Beyond the barbed wire was the Glinice ghetto.

I had sometimes overheard officers talking of the "Jewish problem" during dinner, but I had always been too busy working—and, to be honest, too worried about my own problems— to think about it. Now I berated myself for the good food I had eaten and given my family, for being so lucky, so well fed.

I worked setting tables for nearly an hour, when suddenly the sound of gunfire broke into the quiet ballroom. Men, women and children were running through the streets. SS men were spilling out of trucks and shooting at the fleeing Jews. Through the glass I heard faint screams and the frenzied barking of police dogs. The snow darkened with blood. I felt a scream rising in me as though I had been shot myself.

I had just seen the Germans' answer to their Jewish problem.

When I returned to work the next day, my skin prickled constantly, as if the presence of the ghetto beyond the hotel was making itself known to me. I had to do something.

After lunch I found myself alone in the kitchen. It was the chance I had been waiting for. I grabbed a pail and stepped out into the alley, which ran alongside the hotel and dead-ended at a fence. The ghetto was on the other side. I glanced out towards the street, but nobody was looking my way.

"Whoever helps a Jew shall be punished by death" was the warning I had heard over and over. It was written on posters and was broadcast from loudspeakers on the street.

Taking a large metal spoon from my apron pocket, I dug a small hole in the frozen dirt. From the pail, I took out a tin box I had filled with cheese and apples. I wedged it in the hole and then hurried back to the kitchen.

The next morning I looked for the box. It was empty.

Every day after that, I found a chance to slip out and leave food under the fence. I knew it was a drop in the ocean, but I could not do nothing.

"I'll Look After You"

When 1942 arrived, Schulz told me the entire operation would be moving east in April, to Ternopol. I didn't know whether to laugh or cry at the irony of the change.

Still, I had one reason for happiness. I had told Schulz how skilled and capable Janina was, and he agreed to put her on the dining-hall staff with us. Together we were sent east by truck to Lvov; the new factory in Ternopol was not yet ready, but it was necessary to move our operations closer to the Soviet front.

One day after church, Janina and I met a young Polish woman named Helen Weinbaum. She told us that her husband,

Henry, had been taken to the *Arbeitslager*, the work camp for Jews. Helen was not Jewish, but she fervently swore she wished she were. At least then she would be with her beloved Henry. We parted company that day as good friends.

By August we were in the complex in Ternopol, and I had resumed serving the officers their meals. Janina and I shared a small room beside the service kitchen. Schulz also put me in charge of the laundry facility, where I would oversee the washing and mending of the officers' and secretaries' clothes.

Like the factory, the laundry used Jewish workers from the local camp. My staff of a dozen men and women was wary of me at first, assuming that I was German, but I did my best to reassure them. At last they trusted me enough to tell me about life in the Arbeitslager.

"Sometimes Sturmbannführer Rokita forces us to stand outside the barracks for hours after a full day of work," Ida Haller, a short redhead with a take-charge manner, told me. Rokita was the SS commander of the work camp in Ternopol.

"If anyone moves or makes a noise they're beaten, or sometimes shot," added her husband, Lazar, a quick-witted man of about 40.

Fanka Silberman, a pretty woman my own age, said, "At least we are better off here than in the ghetto."

They were all pale and emaciated from hunger. "I'll look after you," I said.

Moses Steiner, a stooped and gloomy man, made a small shrug. "You're only a young girl. What can you do?"

When I left the room, I thought: *Steiner is right. I am only a girl.* But that had its advantages, too. While I served dinners in the evenings, the officers talked as if I were not there, and I listened.

I listened especially when Sturmbannführer Rokita dined with Major Rügemer. When I first saw Rokita, I remember feeling a knock of surprise. He was one of the handsomest men I had ever seen. About 30 years old, he had gleaming blond hair and eyes the colour of the sky. But he had a heart of ice. The silver death's-head ring he wore on his hand mirrored his soul.

As the months passed, I would report Rokita's conversations to the workers in the laundry. "Expect trouble tomorrow," I'd tell them. "A raid or something. Spread the word."

Lazar Haller had become their spokesman. He decided how best to communicate with the ghetto. Despite brutal security, some prisoners from the Arbeitslager were allowed to visit their families in the ghetto. This enabled them to pass on messages. When we knew of a planned Aktion, some people escaped to the forests or hid out before the raid. We were able to save a number of Rokita's potential victims from him.

A Nightmare of Worry

In town, Helen Weinbaum and I crossed paths one bitterly cold day [in 1943] and quickly brought each other up to date. Helen had learned that her husband, Henry, was Rokita's valet. As a sophisticated, cultured young man, Henry was indispensable to someone like Rokita. He tended bar at his headquarters and, like me, sent word of the Sturmbannführer's plans to the ghetto when he was able. Helen and I promised to keep in touch if we could manage it.

There was reason for concern. With increasing security problems in mind, the Nazis continued their speedup of Aktionen against the Jews in the spring of 1943. Rokita and his Sturmbann made forays to "thin" the ghetto and the Arbeitslager with increasing frequency.

"Many people are choosing to hide in the *puszcza* [forest]," Herschl Morks, one of my laundry workers, told me one day. "My brother and I have decided that we will go, too. Irene, you must help us to get there."

Helen had moved to a farm outside Ternopol, and I was soon making plans to borrow a *dorozka* (wagon) from her, and to transport in secret Herschl and Nathan Morks and their wives, Pola and Miriam, to the black-shadowed forest of Janowka.

I knew that what I was doing could bring me a bullet in the head, but as the saying went, I might as well be hanged for a sheep as for a lamb. The Nazis did not distinguish between leaving food under a fence and smuggling four people in a *dorozka*, so neither did I.

One morning, late in May, I secured a pass to take the day off. Somehow the four Morkses had managed to escape from the Arbeitslager. They hid out by the roadside overnight. A kilometre outside Ternopol, I picked them up, covered them with hay and drove them safely to the forest.

The following Sunday, I took two more of my friends to the same spot. Then all my plans unravelled when Major Rügemer called me to his office. "Irene, I have decided to take a villa in town, and I will need a housekeeper," he said, facing away from me. "I can't think of anyone better suited than you."

All I could think of were my friends still in the laundry… How could I help them if I moved?

I stared at the back of his head, suddenly furious. All I could think of were my friends still in the laundry: Ida and Lazar Haller, Clara and Thomas Bauer, Moses Steiner and Fanka Silberman. How could I help them if I moved?

"Oh, that is very good, Herr Major," I forced myself to say. "I'm glad you think I can do the job."

Defeated, I returned to the kitchen, avoiding the laundry room. I could not tell my friends how futile their faith in me had been.

Later that day, Schulz and I went to see the new house. As I followed the cook down to the basement, I felt a stirring of excitement. The place had apparently been set up for servants' quarters, with a kitchenette, a bathroom, storage rooms and a boiler room with a coal chute leading in from outdoors. Several people could easily live down here.

In the laundry room that afternoon, I described the house and its basement. Clara Bauer was pressing her hands together. "Maybe God meant it to do us some good. Do you think we could hide there?"

"I'm sure of it," I said.

It would take a few weeks before the house was painted and ready to move into. In the meantime, however, I could not forget that

Unlikely Sanctuary — At Major Rugemer's villa (from left), his secretary with Helen Weinbaum, Helen's mother and Irene.

Rokita's fatal work was speeding up. On July 15 he turned up at dinnertime and took a seat at Major Rügemer's table. "We'll all be celebrating soon," he announced to the major.

"Why is that?" Rügemer asked.

Rokita grinned. "Because by the 22nd of this month, Ternopol will be *judenrein* [Jew-free]."

I picked up my tray and began walking away. I felt lightheaded. There was so little time left to save my friends.

The next day, I went to tell them my plan. On the 21st, I said, they should stay in the laundry room after work. I would lock them in for the night and smuggle them to the villa the next day.

"We are in God's hands," Lazar said. "And in Irene's." Their faith put me to shame.

The next five days were a nightmare of worry. On the 21st, Helen sent word that she was waiting for me at the guardhouse. I brought her back to my little bedroom, where she promptly broke down. Henry had been ordered to report back to the ghetto from Rokita's quarters at the end of the day.

"What will I do, Irene?" she groaned, banging her forehead with her fists as the tears spilled down her face. "I can't hide him. There's no room! He'll be discovered."

I slid close to her and spoke in her ear, my skin crawling at the thought of German officers passing in the hall. "Helen, I have a house. By tomorrow evening it will be safe for Henry to go there. He must hide tonight and tomorrow, and then when it is dark, he must go through the coal chute. Can you get to him and tell him?"

Silently she nodded yes. I whispered the address. "Go now. Tell him." She nearly ran down the hall. So little time left.

A Midnight Escape

Later that afternoon I nervously crammed some towels into a basket and crossed the compound to the laundry room. Jewish workers from the factory were being loaded into trucks to return to the Arbeitslager.

"Now," I told my friends. Without a word, they crawled into a space behind some shelves that they had rigged up as a false front. We heard more trucks arriving. I rearranged the boxes and bottles on the shelves to make things look natural, but I knew the hiding place would never foil a determined search.

By six o'clock, most of the officers and secretaries had left for a concert in town. The hotel, warm with the lingering summer heat, was filled with an unfamiliar silence. Soon—I did not know when—the SS teams would arrive. I had to think of a new hiding place for six people before then.

I went up to Major Rügemer's suite and began to tidy up his bathroom. Glancing up, I noticed, high on the wall above the toilet, a grating that was about one metre square. Curious, I pulled off the screen.

It was a tunnel, an air duct perhaps. I guessed that it was big enough to fit six people. I would not find a better hiding place than the commanding officer's bathroom.

By 9:30 p.m. the hotel was mine. I made my way across the compound, unlocked the laundry-room door and slipped inside. I whispered the news to my friends about the air duct. Lazar and Thomas offered to investigate it, so I led them wordlessly across the compound. When we reached the bathroom on the third floor, Lazar boosted Thomas up into the opening.

"Is there room for all?" Lazar asked.

Thomas stuck his head back out. "Yes, just barely."

"I'll get the others," I whispered. It was midnight when I finally got them safely stowed away with food and blankets and crept back to my own room.

After breakfast the next day, I went to the villa. I still had one unanswered question: How was I going to get those people out of Rügemer's bathroom and out of the compound?

In the end, after [a] close call with [an] SS trooper, I decided simply to steal the major's keys. That night, when I heard him snoring, I stepped into his room, closed my hand carefully over the keys and backed out, locking the door behind me. I could not have him walk into the bathroom until I'd got my friends out.

I urged them to hurry, and we went single file down the staircase as fast as their stiff legs would allow. They stood behind me, watching anxiously while I found the right key and unlocked the door to the street.

"You know the address," I whispered. "Go through the coal chute on the left side of the house and wait in the basement. I'll be over first thing in the morning. Stay in the shadows, and God bless you."

In a moment they had disappeared into the darkness.

As I fell asleep that night, I felt a surge of triumph: The Nazis thought Ternopol was judenrein tonight. But I had taken action myself. There were at least six Jews left in town. As long as I could help it, Ternopol would never be judenrein.

A New Hiding Place

The next day at the villa, I was almost fearful of what I might find, but when I clattered downstairs and opened the door to the furnace room, I breathed in relief as seven figures emerged from the shadows: my six friends and a young, handsome fellow I knew must be Henry Weinbaum.

I was overcome with emotion. They were all there, safe and alive. Then, to my surprise, I discovered three strangers—Joseph Weiss, Marian Wilner and Alex Rosen—who greeted me with an odd mixture of sheepishness and defiance. Henry had told them, they said.

For a moment I was at a loss. I had ten lives in my hands now. But there wasn't time to worry; the workmen were due any minute to start painting. I hurried everyone up to the attic, where they would have to stay until the work was done, and locked them in.

When the basement was ready, I waited until dark and triumphantly escorted my friends to their new quarters, fresh with the smell of sawdust and new paint.

It was the start of a new way of life for all of us. We rigged up a warning system. A button was installed in the floor of the front entry foyer, under a rug. From it, a wire led to a light in the basement, which flickered on and off when I stepped on the button.

We had also found a new hiding place: a tunnel that led from behind the furnace to a bunker beneath a gazebo. If there was serious danger, everyone could scramble into the hole and wait for me to give the all-clear.

The basement was cool even in the intense summer heat; there was a bathroom and newspapers that I brought home after the major was finished with them. All in all, the residents of the basement enjoyed quite a luxurious hiding place. And yet it almost fell apart when the major moved in at last.

"The basement is finished, isn't it?" he asked me when he arrived.

The hairs on my arms prickled with alarm. "Do you have some plans for it, Herr Major?" I asked, keeping my voice calm.

"I'm sure it will do very well for my orderly."

I did not have to fake the tears that sprang to my eyes. "Please don't move him in here," I pleaded. My mind raced with explanations, and I quickly came up with the excuse that I was afraid to have a young man alone here with me, since I had terrible memories of being attacked by Soviet soldiers.

The major put his hand on my shoulder. "Of course, Irene. I would not dream of making you unhappy."

We quickly fell into a routine. Every day when the major left the house, I locked the front door and left the key in the lock so that he couldn't come back in unexpectedly.

Every evening I returned to the factory to serve dinner, but I always went home before the major.

Survivors — (From left) Marian Wilner, Fanka Silberman, Henry Weinbaum, Alex Rosen, Pola Morks, Irene and Moses Steiner.

I got in touch with Helen when I could, and we arranged a day when she could come to visit Henry. We agreed that she would arrive in her farm wagon, and I would then take it to bring supplies to my friends hiding in the forest.

Early one morning, with the major on his way to Lvov, Helen drove up in the farm wagon. I led her through the basement door, closing it behind her. I smiled as the sound of Henry's shout of joy reached me through the door.

A Close Call

Meanwhile, the Germans continued to spread their terror. One afternoon, as I was coming home from the *Warenhais* (supply store) laden with soap and toilet paper, I took a shortcut that led through a square. A crowd was blocking my way and SS men were herding it in a jostling cluster around a gallows. While we watched, a Polish couple carrying two small children in their arms were forced up onto the platform, and behind them, another couple with a toddler were prodded up at gunpoint. Even from a distance, the yellow stars on the coats of the second group showed plainly. There were nooses for all.

Their crimes were announced. The Jews were enemies of the Reich, and the Poles had been caught harbouring them. It took no time to hang them. No time at all.

I cannot remember finding my way back to the villa. My limbs were frozen with the cold and the brutality I had seen. Without thinking, I walked through the front door, forgetting to lock it behind me. With a shaking hand I shoved the key into my pocket.

As always, I opened the cellar door, but turned away without speaking. In a few moments Fanka and Clara came upstairs and found me standing in the kitchen, staring at my packages.

"Irene, what is it? What's wrong?" Clara asked, immediately coming to my side, as Fanka took my cold hands and rubbed them between hers. Then, as if through a fog, I noticed a sound from the hallway, and before I could speak, the kitchen door swung open and the major came in.

Clara and Fanka and I stood facing Major Rügemer like statues, and the major stared at each of us in utter astonishment. His face began to tremble with emotion, but without a word he turned on his heel and walked out. The library door slammed shut across the hall.

"Holy God," Fanka whispered.

I banged through the kitchen door and ran across the hallway and into the library. "Herr Major!" I cried.

He stopped his pacing and whirled around at me. "Irene! What in God's name have you done to me?" he shouted.

"They are innocent people!" I stumbled over my words in a panic, and began to cry. "They've done nothing! Do not turn them in, I beg you. I know you are a good man! This war will soon be—"

"Enough!" he interrupted. He was red with fury—and fear. I grabbed at his hand and kissed it, but he yanked it away and strode out of the house.

My faint hope that the major would be merciful kept me from running to the forest then and there. The group downstairs was ashen with fear, but I told them to get in the bunker under the gazebo and wait for three days. "If I don't come back for you," I said, "get out through the coal chute at night and try to get to Janowka."

At last the major came home. I stood up when I heard the door bang open. His footsteps were shuffling and uneven; it was obvious that he was drunk.

"Would you like some coffee, Herr Major?" I asked.

He stared at me. "No."

I began to grow uneasy. I made a movement towards the door, but he stepped in front of me. I knew what was coming, but I could not believe it. He grabbed my arms, pulling me towards him. "I won't keep your secret for nothing, Irene," he said.

I felt a wave of panic. "Major Rügemer, please—"

"I want you willingly. That is my price."

Tears spilled over my cheeks. I was lost. He took my hand and led me up the stairs.

The next morning, I lay in bed filled with shame and humiliation. The major came in and sat down on the edge of the bed. It was all I could do not to fling myself away from him.

"I'll protect you, Irene," he said. "I love you; you must have realized that before now. I couldn't let any harm come to you."

I forced myself to nod.

"And your friends will be safe here. I won't turn those women in, although I risk my own life. You understand that, don't you?"

I nodded again, and he left the room.

Liberation

As 1944 arrived, there was renewed fighting on the Soviet front. The battles were moving closer to our position all the time, and on some nights we could hear the faint, distant detonations of shelling to the east. People were beginning to leave Ternopol … My friends would have to leave.

My only choice was to smuggle them to the forest, where they could join the others. I got a sleigh and took the men first, along with shovels, picks, blankets and as much building material as we could scavenge to make an adequate shelter.

Henry Weinbaum had the same build as the major and wore his extra hat and coat as a disguise so he could sit beside me. We passed two patrols on our way to Janowka, but the silhouette of Henry's uniform showed clearly against the snowy landscape. We were never stopped, though it was after curfew.

Once we reached the forest, the other three men slid out from under cover and then tramped among the trees carrying their unwieldy burdens. "God go with you," Henry said as he followed the others.

In early March, Helen brought the farm wagon to transport the women. When we reached the forest, we unloaded food and equipment, and then Helen kissed me goodbye. I knew I would never see her again.

It was winter. My friends would be wet and uncomfortable. But the Germans were retreating, and my friends were alive and free. When Rügemer returned a week later, he announced we were leaving for Kielce to escape the advancing Soviets. But I had other plans. A Polish friend living in the forest urged me to join the partisans. He told me to go to his brother-in-law's house in Kielce, where I could join the resistance.

Brave Lady — Irene Gut Opdyke has never forgotten the horrors of war.

To my surprise, escape was easy. Rügemer drove me to Kielce and then told me he would leave me alone in a hotel room while he reported to superiors. He was haggard and anxious. In spite of everything, I was already forgiving him for what he put me through because he had helped me save many lives.

I left the hotel, armed with my friend's information, and made contact with the resistance. In the spring and summer of 1944, I delivered messages between the partisans and their spies who worked for the Germans. Sometimes I carried packages of money smuggled in from England to be used for guns or sent farther up the line to another group. I threw myself into the work with a passion, but by December, I succumbed to pneumonia. I was very ill for three months, and when I finally recovered, the Red Army was pouring like a lava flow towards the heart of Germany. The Battle of Berlin pounded that city into ruins, and on April 30, 1945, Hitler killed himself.

Poland was "free" but had been turned over to the Soviets. I was tired. I had no more strength for fighting. I wanted my mother. It was time to start looking for my family.

Irene Gut emigrated to the United States in late 1949, and in November 1956, she and William Opdyke were married. Her mother died the next year, but Irene, Janina and their three sisters were finally reunited in 1985.

In 1982 Israel's Yad Vashem Holocaust memorial honoured Irene Gut Opdyke as one of the Righteous Among the Nations.

Reflecting back on her experiences, she now says: "The war was a series of choices made by many people. Some of those choices were as wicked and shameful to humanity as anything in history. But some of us made other choices. I made mine.

"This is my will: to do right; to tell you; and to remember."

After You Read

1. a. What is the highest point of interest in the story?
   b. How does the author build suspense?
   c. How does description help to build the suspense?
2. What did Irene Gut learn about herself from her experiences in the war? Discuss your answer with a partner, and provide examples from the selection to support your points. How do you think the things she learned made a difference to how she lived the rest of her life?

Handbook Link
How to analyze the role of suspense

We make decisions every day. They can be as small as what to eat for lunch, or as big as what we think we can do to make the world a better place.

In this unit you will read about decisions that people make about where they live, how they work, how they treat others, how they act, and more. The selections you read will help you see how the decisions we make help us to keep learning about ourselves and the world around us.

CONTENTS

Before You Read

In this excerpt from Tomson Highway's play *The Rez Sisters*, we meet Philomena Moosetail and Pelajia Rosella Patchnose. These sisters live on a reserve in Wasaychigan Hill in Northern Ontario, but Pelajia wants to leave the reserve to go to Toronto. Read Pelajia's first speech. Why is she discontented with her life? What do you think Toronto represents to someone in her situation? Do you think she will ever leave the reservation? Why or why not?

The REZ Sisters

by Tomson Highway

Act One

It is mid-morning of a beautiful late August day on the Wasaychigan Hill Indian Reserve, Manitoulin Island, Ontario. Pelajia Patchnose is alone on the roof of her house, nailing shingles on. She wears faded blue denim men's cover-alls and a baseball cap to shade her eyes from the sun. A brightly-colored square cushion belonging to her sister, Philomena Moosetail, rests on the roof beside her. The ladder to the roof is off-stage.

PELAJIA
Philomena. I wanna go to Toronto.

PHILOMENA
From offstage.

Oh, go on.

PELAJIA
Sure as I'm sitting away up here on the roof of this old house. I kind of like it up here, though. From here, I can see half of Manitoulin Island on a clear day. I can see the chimneys, the tops of apple trees, the garbage heap behind Big

Joey's dumpy little house. I can see the seagulls circling over Marie-Adele Starblanket's white picket fence. Boats on the North Channel I wish I was on, sailing away somewhere. The mill at Espanola, a hundred miles away … and that's with just a bit of squinting. See? If I had binoculars, I could see the superstack in Sudbury. And if I were Superwoman, I could see the CN Tower in Toronto. Ah, but I'm just plain old Pelajia Rosella Patchnose and I'm here in plain, dusty, boring old Wasaychigan Hill … Wasy … waiting … waiting … nailing shining shingles with my trusty silver hammer on the roof of Pelajia Rosella Patchnose's little two-bedroom welfare house. Philomena. I wanna go to Toronto.

Philomena Moosetail comes up the ladder to the roof with one shingle and obviously hating it. She is very well-dressed, with a skirt, nylons, even heels, completely impractical for the roof.

PHILOMENA
Oh, go on.

PELAJIA
I'm tired, Philomena, tired of this place. There's days I wanna leave so bad.

PHILOMENA
But you were born here. All your poop's on this reserve.

PELAJIA
Oh, go on.

PHILOMENA
You'll never leave.

PELAJIA
Yes, I will. When I'm old.

PHILOMENA
You're old right now.

PELAJIA
I got a good 30 years to go …

PHILOMENA
… and you're gonna live every one of them right here beside me …

PELAJIA
… maybe 40 …

PHILOMENA
… here in Wasy.

Tickles Pelajia on the breasts.

Chiga-chiga-chiga.

PELAJIA
Yelps and slaps Philomena's hand away.

Oh, go on. It's not like it used to be.

PHILOMENA

Oh, go on. people change, places change, time changes things. You expect to be young and gorgeous forever?

PELAJIA

See? I told you I'm not old.

PHILOMENA

Oh, go on. You.

PELAJIA

"Oh, go on. You." You bug me like hell when you say that.

PHILOMENA

You say it, too. And don't give me none of this "I don't like this place. I'm tired of it." This place is too much inside your blood. You can't get rid of it. And it can't get rid of you.

PELAJIA

Four thirty this morning, I was woken by …

PHILOMENA

Here we go again.

PELAJIA

… Andrew Starblanket and his brother, Matthew. Drunk. Again. Or sounded like …

PHILOMENA

Nothing better to do.

PELAJIA

… fighting over some girl. Heard what sounded like a baseball bat landing on somebody's back. My lawn looks like the shits this morning.

PHILOMENA

Well, I like it here. Myself, I'm gonna go to every bingo and I'm gonna hit every jackpot between here and Espanola and I'm gonna buy me that toilet I'm dreaming about at night … big and wide and very white …

PELAJIA

Aw-ni-gi-naw-ee-dick.[1]

PHILOMENA

I'm good at bingo.

PELAJIA

So what! And the old stories, the old language. Almost all gone … was a time Nanabush and Windigo and everyone here could rattle away in Indian fast as Bingo Betty could lay her bingo chips down on a hot night.

PHILOMENA

Pelajia Rosella Patchnose. The sun's gonna drive you crazy.

And she descends the ladder.

PELAJIA

Everyone here's crazy. No jobs. Nothing to do but drink and screw each other's wives and husbands and forget about our Nanabush.

From offstage Philomena screams. She fell down the ladder.

Philomena!

As she looks over the edge of the roof.

What are you doing down there?

---

[1] Oh, go on. (Ojibway)

PHILOMENA

What do you think? I fell.

PELAJIA

Bring me some of them nails while you're down there.

PHILOMENA

Whining and still from offstage, from behind the house.

You think I can race up and down this ladder? You think I got wings?

PELAJIA

You gotta wear pants when you're doing a man's job. See? You got your skirt ripped on a nail and now you can see your thighs. People gonna think you just came from Big Joey's house.

PHILOMENA

She comes up the ladder in a state of disarray.

Let them think what they want. That old cow Gazelle Nataways … always acting like she thinks she's still a spring chicken. She's got them legs of hers wrapped around Big Joey day and night …

PELAJIA

Philomena. Park your tongue. My old man has to go the hundred miles to Espanola just to get a job. My boys. Gone to Toronto. Only place educated Indian boys can find decent jobs these days. And here I sit all broken-hearted.

PHILOMENA

Paid a dime and only farted.

PELAJIA

Look at you. You got dirt all over your backside.

Turning her attention to the road in front of her house and standing up for the first and only time.

And dirt roads! Years now that old chief's been making speeches about getting paved roads "for my people" and still we got dirt roads all over.

PHILOMENA

Oh, go on.

PELAJIA

When I win me that jackpot next time we play bingo in Espanola …

PHILOMENA

Examining her torn skirt, her general state of disarray, and fretting over it.

Look at this! Will you look at this! Ohhh!

PELAJIA

… I'm gonna put that old chief to shame and build me a nice paved road right here in front of my house. Jet black. Shiny. Make my lawn look real nice.

PHILOMENA

My rib-cage!

PELAJIA

And if that old chief don't wanna make paved roads for all my sisters around here …

PHILOMENA

There's something rattling around inside me!

PELAJIA

… I'm packing my bags and moving to Toronto.

Sits down again.

PHILOMENA

Oh, go on.

She spies Annie Cook's approach a distance up the hill.

Why, I do believe that cloud of dust over there is Annie Cook racing down the hill, Pelajia.

PELAJIA

Philomena. I wanna go to Toronto.

PHILOMENA

She's walking mighty fast. Must be excited about something.

PELAJIA

Never seen Annie Cook walk slow since the day she finally lost Eugene to Marie-Adele at the church 19 years ago. And even then she was walking a little too fast for a girl who was supposed to be broken-heart … *Stopping just in time and laughing.* … heart-broken.

Annie Cook pops up the top of the ladder to the roof.

ANNIE

All cheery and fast and perky.

Halloooo! Whatchyou doing up here?

PELAJIA

There's room for only so much weight up here before we go crashing into my kitchen, so what do you want?

ANNIE
Just popped up to say hi.

PELAJIA
And see what we're doing?

ANNIE
Well …

PELAJIA
Couldn't you see what we're doing from up where you were?

ANNIE
Confidentially, to Philomena.

Is it true Gazelle Nataways won the bingo last night?

PHILOMENA
Annie Cook, first you say you're gonna come with me and then you don't even bother showing up. If you were sitting beside me at that bingo table last night you would have seen Gazelle Nataways win that big pot again with your own two eyes.

ANNIE
Emily Dictionary and I went to Little Current to listen to Fritz the Katz.

PELAJIA
What in God's name kind of a band might that be?

ANNIE
Country rock. My favorite. Fritz the Katz is from Toronto.

PELAJIA
Fritzy … ritzy … Philomena! Say something.

PHILOMENA
My record player is in Espanola getting fixed.

ANNIE
That's nice.

PHILOMENA
Good.

ANNIE
Is it true Gazelle Nataways plans to spend her bingo money to go to Toronto with … with Big Joey?

PHILOMENA
Who wants to know? Emily Dictionary?

ANNIE
I guess so.

PELAJIA
That Gazelle Nataways gonna leave all her babies behind and let them starve to death?

ANNIE
I guess so. I don't know. I'm asking you.

PELAJIA and PHILOMENA
We don't know.

ANNIE
I'm on my way to Marie-Adele's to pick her up.

PELAJIA
Why? Where you gonna put her down?

Pelajia and Philomena laugh.

ANNIE
I mean, we're going to the store together. To the post office. We're going to pick up a parcel. They say there's a parcel for me. They say it's shaped

like a record. And they say it's from Sudbury. So it must be from my daughter, Ellen …

PELAJIA and PHILOMENA
… "who lives with this white guy in Sudbury"…

ANNIE
How did you know?

PHILOMENA
Everybody knows.

ANNIE
His name is Ray<u>mond</u>. Not <u>Ray</u>mond. But Ray<u>mond</u>. Like in Bon Bon.

Philomena tries out "bon bon" to herself.

He's French.

PELAJIA
Oh?

ANNIE
Garage mechanic. He fixes cars. And you know, talking about Frenchmen, that old priest is holding another bingo next week and when I win …

To Philomena.

Are you going?

PELAJIA
Does a bear shit in the woods?

ANNIE
… when I win, I'm going to Espanola and play the bingo there. Emily Dictionary says that Fire Minklater can give us a ride in her new car. She got it through Ray<u>mond</u>'s garage. The bingo in Espanola is bigger. And it's better. And I'll win. And then I'll go to Sudbury, where the bingos are even bigger and better. And then I can visit my daughter, Ellen …

PELAJIA
… "who lives with this white guy in Sudbury"…

ANNIE
… and go shopping in the record stores and go to the hotel and drink beer quietly — not noisy and crazy like here — and listen to the live bands. It will be so much fun. I hope Emily Dictionary can come with me.

PHILOMENA
It's true. I've been thinking …

PELAJIA
You don't say.

PHILOMENA
It's true. The bingos here are getting kind of boring …

ANNIE
That old priest is too slow and sometimes he gets the numbers all mixed up and the pot's not big enough.

PHILOMENA
And I don't like the way he calls the numbers. *Nasally.* B 12, O 64.

ANNIE
When Little Girl Manitowabi won last month …

PHILOMENA
She won just enough to take a taxi back to Buzwah.

ANNIE
That's all.

Both Annie and Philomena pause to give a quick sigh of yearning.

PHILOMENA
Annie Cook, I want that big pot.

ANNIE
We all want big pots.

PELAJIA
Start a revolution!

PHILOMENA and ANNIE
Yes!

ANNIE
All us Wasy women. We'll march up the hill, burn the church hall down, scare the priest to death, and then we'll march all the way to Espanola, where the bingos are bigger and better …

PHILOMENA
We'll hold big placards!

ANNIE
They'll say: "Wasy women want bigger bingos!"

PELAJIA
And one will say: "Annie Cook Wants Big Pot!"

PHILOMENA
… and the numbers at those bingos in Espanola go faster and the pots get bigger by the week. Oh, Pelajia Patchnose, I'm getting excited just thinking about it!

ANNIE
I'm going.

PELAJIA
You are, are you?

ANNIE
Yes. I'm going. I'm running out of time. I'm going to Marie-Adele's house and then we'll walk to the store together to pick up the parcel — I'm sure there'll be a letter in it, and Marie-Adele is expecting mail, too — and we'll see if Emily Dictionary is working today and we'll ask her if Fire Minklater has her new car yet so we can go to Espanola for that big pot.

She begins to descend the ladder.

PELAJIA
Well, you don't have much to do today, do you?

ANNIE
Well. Toodle-oo!

And she pops down the ladder and is gone.

After You Read

1. The playwright refers to boats on the North Channel, Wasy, the CN Tower, and paved roads. Write a paragraph to explain the meaning of these references, and how they work together to describe a common theme in this part of the play.

Handbook Link
How to recognize allusion and irony

How to understand themes in literature

Before You Read

Think about a person who has had a positive influence on you. Write a paragraph that describes the person and his/her qualities, character, and struggles, and tell briefly the impact the person has made on your life. Then read about Lesra Martin, whose life was changed forever because of his relationship with an extraordinary person.

The Metamorphosis
of LESRA MARTIN

by Lynne Schuyler

Lesra and Cheryl — Her compassion made him realize how much he loved her.

L esra Martin lived in Bushwick, N.Y., a Brooklyn neighbourhood rife with gangs and drug dealing. At 15, he met some Canadians who saw promise in the youth and invited him to Toronto to further his education. But soon they discovered that Lesra, near the top of his class back home, could barely read or write. So they undertook to reverse the damage done by his neighbourhood and in the process discovered a remarkable young man.

Life in Hell

Sticky, humid heat clung to Lesra Martin as he sat next to his father, Earl, on the subway. Neither spoke as the grimy train clattered and swayed, rushing towards Greenpoint, a white section of Brooklyn north of their home in Bushwick. This July 1979 morning would be Lesra's first day at his summer job in an environmental lab, part of a government-sponsored project for inner-city kids whose families were on welfare.

Lesra, 15, stared at the unfamiliar cityscape rolling past. He was anxious, but not about his new job.

The skinny, malnourished tenth grader knew only the world of his neighbourhood, a few city blocks that more resembled a war zone than a community. Bushwick, one of Brooklyn's poorest areas, was a tough district of boarded-up storefronts, mounds of garbage, rusting car shells and burned-out tenement buildings. Bursts of gunfire were common.

Even walking to school was perilous. At the first sound of shots, Lesra had learned to duck behind the tires of the nearest parked car or flatten himself in a doorway. He had some protection: His older brother Fru, a gang member already in trouble with the law, told others that Lesra was off-limits. But rival gangs staked out entire city blocks; it was a place where blacks like Lesra lived on one side, and poor whites and Hispanics on the other.

Now, crossing into Greenpoint, unfamiliar territory, Lesra was nervous. "You mind your p's and q's," Earl cautioned in his low, raspy voice.

Lesra stared at his father's shaking hands. Their lives hadn't always been like this. He had dim memories of a different life, of a house in Queens with a green lawn. His parents had been different, too.

In the 1960s Earl had worked as a factory foreman. The family shared lots of special times. Alma, Lesra's mother, used to crank their living-room stereo to full volume, grabbing her babies by the hand and dancing with them. Sometimes they went up to the Apollo Theatre to see performers like James Brown scorch the stage.

But overnight, it seemed, their lives abruptly shifted due to a series of humiliating setbacks. A severe back injury left Earl disabled. They lost their house in a fire; at times, they were homeless, stranded in shelters or with relatives. The Martins slid into poverty, ending up in Bushwick. By then, both Earl and Alma had severe drinking problems, and their lives disintegrated into endless late-night arguments that disturbed their hungry children's sleep.

Lesra pushed his fears aside and tried to listen as his father pointed out the stops he'd have to remember to return home. The 15-year-old willingly shouldered a heavy responsibility. Five of his seven siblings had left home, but the rest of his family, housed in a decaying tenement, depended on every cent he earned. The family's welfare cheque was exhausted long before month's end, and it wasn't unusual for the household of five to go a week with very little food.

Lesra had been nearly 11 when their lives hit rock bottom. Hungry, wanting to help out, he walked into a local store one day and, uninvited, began bagging groceries. The manager shooed him out, but the feisty kid kept returning until they let him stay. Customers took to the good-natured, pint-size boy who lugged their groceries home. On good days he pocketed $2 or $3 in tips, enough to buy rice and beans for his family.

A likable kid with a bright smile, Lesra had a knack for drawing people to him. Still, it wasn't enough to protect him from the random violence always at hand. His mother feared Lesra would not survive the streets if he didn't toughen up. "Men aren't allowed to cry," she constantly told him. Yet Lesra hated fighting; it was a last resort when nothing else worked. In the neighbourhood he earned the moniker The Diplomat for his ability to talk his way out of trouble.

By the time he was 13, Lesra was fast becoming hardened. Repeated harassment from gang members forced him to tuck an unloaded gun into his pants one day. He fanned it around at school, hoping it would make the others back off. By 15, he was feeling the pressure to join a gang.

Now, as the subway train screeched into the station, Lesra had no way of knowing how profoundly his life was about to change.

The Canadians

In the middle of that July 1979, Canadians Terry Swinton, 32, Sam Chaiton, 28, and several housemates had travelled to the Greenpoint Environmental Protection Agency (EPA) lab to research a gas-saving pollution device. They were part of a group of eight university friends who, in the 1960s, joined resources and became successful entrepreneurs. All shared a strong social conscience, mixing business with activism and compassion for anyone less fortunate. They owned a house in Toronto and ran a profitable business importing batiks from Malaysia. Living and working together, they had become family.

At the EPA lab, Lesra's infectious grin and raw energy soon caught the attention of Chaiton and Swinton. Lesra and William Fuller, another ghetto youth hired at the lab, spent their workdays playfully punching, chasing and spraying each other with water instead of the taxis they were supposed to wash. Whenever Lesra saw the Canadians, his face would light up. "Yo, Canada!" he would loudly chortle. They loved his quick wit, his curiosity and his good nature.

"I'm gonna be a lawyer," Lesra cheerfully told them one day, confiding his ambitions. "Lawyers make lots of money from people in trouble, and where I live, someone's always in trouble."

Listening, Swinton and Chaiton sensed Lesra didn't have the faintest idea what a lawyer actually did. Privately, they speculated that he was more likely to need a lawyer than to become one.

The Canadians returned to Toronto but couldn't get Lesra and William out of their minds. They purchased plane tickets for the pair, inviting them to Toronto for a long weekend at the beginning of August.

In Toronto, the two Brooklyn youths were shocked by the ordinary: clean streets, clipped lawns, graffiti-free subway cars. In turn, the Canadians were stunned at how little the boys seemed to know outside of their own neighbourhoods.

"New York's a country, right?" Lesra asked them one day. The Canadians exchanged bewildered looks. Lesra was set to enter Grade 11 that fall. How could he not know what country he lived in?

In mid-August, Terry and Sam returned to Brooklyn for more research at the lab. With them was Lisa Peters, 34, another of the group's members. They spent time with both boys and met their families. One night, as Lesra horsed around with Sam and Terry in their hotel room, he noticed Lisa tucked away in the corner, deeply absorbed in a book.

What could be more interesting than the fun we're having? he wondered.

Lisa began reading to him from Claude Brown's *Manchild in the Promised Land*. Lesra stopped goofing around and sank into a chair, mesmerized by the story of a New York ghetto youth who survived desperate poverty to become a lawyer and a writer. The book was a revelation, one that filled him with hope.

Lesra was euphoric when the Canadians invited him to spend ten days with them later in the month. This time, Lesra's return to Bushwick was even more difficult: In Toronto, for the first time in his life, he had felt safe.

For their part, the Canadians had formed a close emotional bond with the boy. They were deeply troubled by the gaps in his schooling and worried for his survival in a neighbourhood where drugs, jail or gangs were the only options.

A bold plan took hold: Why not bring Lesra to Canada? Maybe they could help him reach university. They had the financial means and plenty of room in their large Edwardian-style house on nearly a hectare of land.

The eight members of the group wrestled with the idea. Was it fair to take Lesra from his family, who loved and depended on him? "Once he leaves, it'll be hard for him to go back," Peters pointed out. If he came, they agreed, the entire household would invest their energy and resources in helping him realize his potential.

One afternoon in September, African-American poet James McRae, a co-worker at the EPA lab and a friend of the group, sat in the Martins' tiny living room. Lesra nervously watched as McRae explained the Canadians' proposal. McRae reassured the Martins that the Canadians weren't taking Lesra away; he would be back for summers and holidays. "It would be a shame to pass up an opportunity like this," he said. "Nothing is more vital than access to a decent education."

His parents were perplexed by this generous offer. Lesra saw the pain in his mother's eyes, yet he desperately wanted to go. Agitated, uncertain, Alma hopped up from the couch. "I can't make that decision; you can't ask me to give up my son," she said. Still, she wanted something better for her boy. She turned to her husband. "Earl, you decide."

A few days after McRae's visit, the Canadians flew Earl Martin to Toronto to check out their home and to discuss Lesra's education. He returned a day later. Lesra met him at the subway station, anxious to hear his decision. "What do you think—can I go?" he asked.

"Well, boy, you can if you want to," his father said, clearly satisfied that his son would be in good hands.

A Different World

Lesra arrived in Toronto in October 1979. Apprehensive, excited, he had no idea what to expect but was overjoyed to be with the people he affectionately dubbed The Canadians.

Carefully they drew him into a larger world by reading books and newspapers out loud, by watching TV news, by asking his opinion during business discussions. Everything provided fodder for learning.

One day they sat on the grass at the Ontario legislature, Queen's Park, across the street from the University of Toronto. Sam pointed out the university's law school. "That's where you'll be going to school one day," he told Lesra. Lesra hadn't the vaguest idea of the enormous obstacles he faced in reaching such a goal.

At first the Canadians guessed that Lesra was no more than a few grades behind. They talked about enrolling him in Grade 9, perhaps with some extra tutoring.

"Read this," Sam said one day, sliding a book into Lesra's hands.

Lesra fumbled to pronounce the words. Sam watched as his eyes skittered over the page, desperately searching for words he recognized, like "cat."

"What's this word, and this?" Sam repeatedly asked, pointing to the text.

Stumped and unwilling to admit it, Lesra searched his memory for words he knew or made up the words as he went along, growing more frustrated and angry.

Suddenly it dawned on Sam that Lesra could neither read nor write; they had greatly overestimated his level of education. A subsequent reading test placed him at a Grade 2 level. Lesra was shattered. He had attended school faithfully, easily passing from grade to grade. If he couldn't read or write, what had been the point of his going?

Chaiton had tutored Lisa Peters' son Marty, who was severely dyslexic. It seemed natural that he could teach Lesra as well. Lesra was bright, but his lack of Standard English—the key to learning everything else—was a huge obstacle. Lesra's speech was a complicated mix of street slang, broken English, even triple negatives. He pronounced words like "beauty" as "bruty."

The first year, Sam stripped everything down to the basics, tackling phonetic skills first. None of it made sense to Lesra. "That's not the way I was taught in school," he argued. Once proud of his class standing, he soon became convinced that he was incapable of learning.

"I'm stupid. There must be something wrong with me," he frequently told Sam, tears streaming down his face. Such moments were heartbreaking for Sam. "No, Lesra, it's not your fault," he said. Often their lessons veered off into discussions of personal issues as Lesra battled deeply ingrained feelings of inferiority.

For Lesra, school had been a safe haven where he could sleep, get warm, have something to eat. Tests that challenged a student's knowledge were almost nonexistent. Kids played cards at the back of the class while teachers read newspapers. Lesra had never been assigned homework or asked to write an essay or to read a book. "That's why you didn't learn," Sam explained.

Many days ended with both of them physically and emotionally exhausted. "I can't do this!" Lesra would shout, storming up to his room and throwing his clothes into a bag. He wanted to quit, go home. Sam and the others would leave him alone to cool down. Then a couple of them would go up to his room to talk and to ask him how he'd explain to his family that he'd given up. So Lesra would calm down and begin the struggle to learn all over again.

In truth, Lesra enjoyed learning and didn't want to leave. The household was a stimulating bustle of activity, a place where learning never stopped.

Trips home, however, were a painful reminder of the staggering extremes between his two worlds. On one visit to Bushwick, he was strolling down the block with his younger brother Elston when police cars screeched to a halt near them. Trunks popped open, guns were yanked out, and the police stormed a nearby building. Lesra, 16, and Elston, 14, hit the ground as bullets whizzed over their heads. Lesra reached for his brother's hand, certain they wouldn't survive. The siege ended as abruptly as it started, but Lesra was furious that anyone had to live like this.

On every flight back to Toronto, Lesra cried. For weeks after his return, he'd be distracted and miserable, unable to study. He lashed out at the Canadians, trying to pick fights. Everyone knew that he was hurting. Eventually Lesra began taking the train, a 12-hour ride, allowing him time to adjust as he travelled between his two very different worlds.

Yet he couldn't forget his family. Lesra cut lawns, raked leaves, shovelled snow—all to earn money to send home. His family's hardships were harsh reminders of his need to become educated, to stay out of the ghetto.

Revelation

When he'd first moved to Toronto, Lesra had been struck by its peacefulness compared to the chaos of Bushwick. "Do white people ever fight and argue?" he asked the Canadians. Exposed to little else, he quickly drew the conclusion that the violence he understood so well was limited to African-Americans.

To dispel Lesra's misconceptions, the Canadians encouraged Lesra to study the past, emphasizing black heroes and black American history. One summer day in 1980, Sam handed Lesra a thick book by Frederick Douglass, a brilliant black American human-rights leader. "You can read this out loud to us," Sam said.

"It's like a foam [phone] book!" Lesra retorted. The dense volume, written in 1857, was laced with difficult words and Victorian phrases but told of Douglass's own struggle with literacy.

Terrified, Lesra flipped it open, his eyes raking over the text. Haltingly, he stumbled over the words. Tears welled up in his eyes. He slammed the book shut and glared at Sam and Terry.

"You can do it," Sam insisted. "You've got the skills to handle this. This is where the payoff is for all the work you've been doing."

Lesra remembered his mentors telling him not to stop at troublesome words, but to read the whole sentence and paragraph so that the meaning would become clear. He sounded out the words, working his way though the text. A flicker of recognition crossed his face. The words, the paragraphs, everything suddenly made sense to him.

Not long afterwards, at a used-book sale, Lesra's eyes fell on *The Sixteenth Round: From Number 1 Contender to #45472*. The fierce looking man on its cover was the author, Rubin "Hurricane" Carter. The famous middleweight boxer had been tried and imprisoned for the 1966 murders of three white people in Paterson, N.J. Intrigued, Lesra bought the book.

Hungrily he read Carter's story, published in 1974. The passion behind Carter's words and the force of his language bore into Lesra's mind and heart. The book was filled with profanity, language he had heard every day on the streets of Bushwick. That in itself was a revelation: He didn't know anyone could write as they spoke or felt in real, everyday life. As Carter's story unfolded, Lesra experienced the anger, frustration and helplessness the boxer felt over his wrongful conviction.

Until then, Lesra had looked at life as one insurmountable hurdle after another. Yet here was Carter, after years of insufferable conditions, never wavering in his resolve to prove his innocence.

Lesra thought about Carter all the time, resolving to work harder at his studies. If Carter could not be broken, then surely he could overcome his own fear of reading and writing.

One day he carefully smoothed out some paper on his desk, then picked up a pen to write Carter a letter. He struggled to find the words to express his thoughts and feelings. Soon, balls of crumpled-up paper surrounded the wastebasket as he scratched out his thoughts. Finally he folded a letter and slipped it into an envelope.

A Single Letter

At New Jersey's Trenton State Prison in September 1980, Rubin Carter barely glanced up when a guard propped a single letter between his cell's bars. Every day, mail arrived from people begging for autographs or asking to write his story. Appalled, he never opened them.

After his second trial and imprisonment in 1976, continuing to steadfastly maintain his innocence, Carter kept himself apart from the routine of prison life. *I'm not a criminal, and I'm not participating in this system*, he thought bitterly, refusing to wear prison garb and eating only food shipped in by a friend. Disillusioned, forgotten by the politicians and celebrities who had once rallied to his cause, he shunned visitors for nearly five years, refusing to let anyone but his lawyers see him in the "lowest pits of hell."

Now, the solitary letter nagged at him for hours until he finally ripped it open.

"Dear Mr. Carter," it began. It was the first letter Lesra Martin had ever written, and in it he told Carter about his home in Bushwick, his new life with the Canadians and his belief in Carter's innocence. Weeks after he'd mailed his letter, Lesra haunted the front-door mail slot, waiting for a reply. Finally, a white envelope with U.S. postage arrived. He stared in disbelief, then whooped and hollered for the others to come see.

The innocence and energy in Lesra's letter had touched a profound chord in Carter. Through Lesra, he felt a pure joy that he hadn't known in years. Soon letters flowed back and forth between Carter and Lesra and the Canadians.

On the last Sunday in December 1980, while home visiting his family, Lesra set out for Trenton State Prison. At the forbidding stone walls, lined with gun towers and barbed wire, Lesra's heart pounded with excitement over seeing Carter and with sheer terror over entering the ominous structure. *Fru's been in jail*, he thought, *and I'd probably be here too if not for the Canadians.*

It took more than an hour for him to pass through a series of screenings, sign-ins and security checks. Finally he stood in the prison's former death house, now used as a visiting area and still showing the braces where the prison's electric chair once stood.

The other visitors and prisoners paired off until Carter and Lesra, who was shaking with fear, were the only two people left standing.

"You must be Lesra!" Carter boomed in a deep, rich voice. He'd known of Lesra's intention to visit, but had not encouraged it. The death house was a degrading place for prisoners and those who came to see them.

Lesra had expected to find the Carter of his photos: the formidable, shaven-head boxer with the ferocious stare. Instead, Carter, not much taller than Lesra, greeted him with a broad grin. Sensing Lesra's fear, Carter crushed the teenager to him in a protective, fatherly hug. Lesra immediately felt safe.

As they sat laughing and talking, Lesra turned over the contradictions in his mind. From Carter's own book, Lesra knew he was no choir boy; Carter had been in and out of trouble before his murder conviction.

Still, that was no reason for him to be in jail for something he didn't do. *He's survived this place and yet he's so gentle*, Lesra thought in amazement. His every instinct told him that Carter was innocent.

Their visit drew to an end, and both sat in silence, Carter's warm hand resting on top of Lesra's. It was the first outside human contact Carter had had in years.

They both looked up as another prisoner approached.

"Mr. Carter, would you like a picture of you and your son?" the man asked, noticing the affection between the two. Pleased, and not bothering to correct him, Carter nodded. The pair stood, arms clasped around each other, and Lesra beamed.

Miscarriage of Justice

Arriving back in Toronto, Lesra couldn't stop talking about Carter. Over the next two years, through letters, lengthy phone calls and numerous visits to the prison, the entire household forged a strong friendship with Carter, slowly drawing him out of his shell.

As they learned more about his case, the Canadians were convinced there'd been a terrible miscarriage of justice. They sent him gifts of food and clothing, but they could provide little more than moral support as Carter's lawyers pushed through legal appeals on his conviction.

"How's your schooling going?" Carter asked in every phone call to Lesra. Learning, he patiently told Lesra, was not only a way to express himself but a means to take control of his life. Carter was intensely proud of Lesra and showed his school essays to other prisoners.

Inspired by Carter, Lesra worked hard, earning high marks in his correspondence courses and, later, in an English night-school course. He routinely sent his marks to Carter. "What happened to the other two points?" Carter queried when Lesra received 98 percent on one of his papers. Lesra chuckled. Like Sam Chaiton, Carter expected him to do well. Yet for every step forward, another crisis always pulled him back.

In the fall of 1981, he picked up the phone one day to hear his father's voice, dejected, slurred. "I have some bad news," Earl said. Listening, Lesra sank into a chair sobbing. Devastated, he passed the phone to Terry.

The gifts he regularly sent home were prized by his family. But a knitted cap sent to Elston had been stolen, resulting in a fight that had gone too far: Fru accidentally killed another man while trying to get it back. Guilt ridden and in shock, he had waited for the police to arrive.

Today, Lesra Martin inspires others with the story of his struggle, as Rubin Carter inspired him.

Lesra wanted to go back and help his family, but the Canadians convinced him it was better to stay. Unable to concentrate on his work, he was sick at heart for weeks afterwards, anguished that his gift had caused someone's death. Fru would later be sentenced to five to 15 years for manslaughter.

Throughout 1982 the Canadians spent months studying Carter's case, reviewing court transcripts, tracking every detail in testimony. They tacked papers to the walls, sorting and analyzing the mountain of information. Aided by Carter, they compiled a one-by-three-metre chart of witnesses, noting every discrepancy in their testimony, then sent it to Carter's lawyers, hoping it would somehow be useful in an appeal in U.S. Federal Court.

Then in November there came another blow: Carter cut off all contact with the Canadian household. He had lost another round of appeals, and in despair of ever being released, he stopped writing and phoning.

For Lesra, it was torturous to think of Carter lost in despair. To ease his mind and heart, Lesra focused on his studies, finishing Grade 13, while preparing to enter the University of Toronto. He graduated high school that spring of 1983 with straight A's and was honoured as an Ontario scholar for his superior academic performance. The Canadians surprised him one day with his diploma, beautifully framed and wrapped.

Smiling, Sam proudly told him, "The next one you frame will be your university degree!"

Lesra carefully packaged copies of his diploma and the acceptance letter from the University of Toronto, mailing a set to his parents. They were very proud; he was the first in his family to attend university. Lesra quietly sent the other copies to Carter, the only way he could say "thanks" for the role Carter had played in his success.

Renewed Effort

Eight months after Carter had cut off contact with the group, he phoned the Toronto house again.

This time his call, in late summer 1983, was to ask for help. The Canadians, inspired by Carter's continued fight, told him that no matter how long it took, they would fight alongside him to help secure his release from prison.

To finance their efforts, the friends sold their Toronto house and moved into a smaller place. Chaiton, Swinton and Peters even moved to New Jersey to be closer to Carter, while Lesra stayed behind to attend school and help with the group's home-renovation business. The trio would devote the next five years, and contribute hundreds of hours of time and energy, to Carter's case.

They researched more than 15 years worth of legal documents and evidence, and helped draft legal briefs that would be used to seek a writ of habeas corpus from a Federal Court judge, demanding that authorities justify the incarceration. In Carter's case, the writ alleged prosecutorial misconduct, suppressing evidence and improperly introducing a theory of racial revenge into the trial. If it failed, all avenues of freedom would be closed and Carter would spend the rest of his life in prison.

In September 1983 Lesra entered the University of Toronto. He had dropped the idea of becoming a lawyer, soured on a system that would allow Carter to be imprisoned unjustly.

He decided instead to major in anthropology and sociology. Listening to the other students, he was secretly pleased that he could speak and write as well as they did. Chaiton had taught him well.

By 1985 Lesra was working full-time in the renovation business, rising at 6:30 a.m., putting in a full day, then rushing off to night-school courses and doing homework. He longed to be in New Jersey, helping his friends work on Carter's case. When he could, he researched trial transcripts, often dashing down to New Jersey for weekend visits.

Freedom

Years of exhaustive work by Carter, his lawyers and the Canadians paid off in November 1985 when Federal Court Judge Lee Sarokin overturned the 1976 convictions, citing grave "constitutional violations." He ruled that Carter's conviction, and that of his codefendant John Artis, was based on "racism rather than reason, and concealment rather than disclosure" by New Jersey prosecutors.

After 20 years in prison, Rubin Carter was at last set free. The miraculous outcome left Lesra overwhelmed with joy.

Emotional upheavals at home, however, continually tugged at his heart. Both of his parents had developed cancer, and Earl suffered seizures from a brain tumor. Lesra saved his money and, in the summer of 1986, brought them to Canada on a rare visit. He bought a new suit for his father and new shoes and a white chiffon dress for his mother on her birthday.

Struck by Lesra's self-assurance, Alma proudly gazed at her son. "You've become a real man," she told him. She had been tough on him while he was growing up, preparing him for the world she thought he would have to live in, but it had created a gulf between them that had hurt Lesra deeply. Now, though, he finally understood his mother. His leaving had brought them closer together.

One night at the house, Lesra tucked his frail parents into bed. Shortly afterwards, Earl reappeared. "I want to give you something," he said quietly, motioning his son to follow him upstairs. Curious, Lesra followed, then sat on the edge of his parents' bed.

Earl cleared his throat, then slowly, gently hummed and sang a song he'd written for his son. It was called "The End Is Near."

Lesra felt his eyes brimming with tears. His father had rarely talked about his long-lost hopes for a singing career, and Lesra sensed that he was deeply ashamed of how his life had turned out. This was a truly special gift from Earl.

That fall of 1986, Lesra, now 23, took stock of his life. Carter, along with Chaiton, Swinton and Peters, was living in New York, responding to legal appeals that would drag on for another 26 months. Like the rest of the household, Lesra had carried a big load, going to school and working in the group's business to help finance Carter's case. He felt drained and wanted some time for himself.

So Lesra struck out on his own, moving into an apartment near the university.

Lesra Martin eventually did go to law school. He was called to the bar in Vancouver in 1999, as his wife, Cheryl, and Rubin Carter looked on. Today, he lectures, as he says, "about the importance of education, the freedom I found in reading, and the value of learning."

After You Read

1. Write the subheadings from the article in your notebook. Under each subheading, summarize the main events that occur.
2. Why is the story called "Metamorphosis"? Discuss with a partner how Lesra Martin changes.
3. What influence does reading have in Lesra's life? What does he learn from reading? How does the Hurricane benefit from Lesra's reading? Respond in your reading response journal.

Handbook Link

How to interpret and assess information, ideas, and issues in text

Before You Read

Work with a partner. One partner should role-play someone who is dissatisfied with his or her job and give reasons. The other partner should offer advice and give at least three strategies to help the first person. Switch roles and repeat. Then read the article.

CAREERS

Finding and keeping a sense of

For some people, the difficult thing about knowing it's time to change jobs, is believing that there are really any jobs they can get excited about doing. This is the case for Jonathon, who has been working at the same job for the past 15 years. It's not that he hates his job, in fact there are lots of things about it he enjoys. He likes the people he works with and he is good at what he does. And he even gets paid well. So on the outside he looks pretty successful. The problem is what he knows is on the inside: a sense that something is missing.

This sense of dissatisfaction started about two years ago when he returned to work after a three-week summer vacation with his family. Jonathon and his wife and three kids hopped in the van and just drove. They didn't really have a plan, other than knowing they wanted to head West. Not having a plan was a new thing for Jonathon. He remembers wondering if they'd just waste a lot of time and gas. But they had a blast! He grew closer to his kids and learned to appreciate the lively spontaneity of his wife — it usually drove him nuts! He remembers feeling really overworked that year, so three weeks off was a real treat.

But something happened on that trip. He came back feeling different somehow. And fitting back into the role he'd created for himself at the company didn't seem to work anymore.

Lately some of his co-workers had started to ask him if something was bothering him. He seemed pre-occupied, one of them remarked. His administrative assistant wondered if he was feeling burned out because of some of the large projects he had led lately. No, he wasn't feeling burned out, that would be too strong to describe what he was feeling. He reassured her that things were fine.

Things weren't fine, though and he knew it. But it wasn't burn out, it was more like he was rusting out. Yeah, that was it. He felt like a good car that could go somewhere, but it had been left sitting out in a dull constant rain for so long that it just started to rust. The funny thing was, he couldn't remember the last time he felt like he did want to go somewhere, anywhere. He had no goals or aspirations.

It's unfortunate when somebody like Jonathon feels like their work has lost a sense of purpose. They end up just going to work, doing their job and trying to keep that nagging sense of futility from surfacing too often. What's missing for Jonathon is a sense of being alive at work. Joseph Campbell said it well: "What we are seeking is an experience of being alive, so that we actually feel the rapture of being alive."

That aliveness and certainly the rapture of it all had somehow disappeared from the work scene for Jonathon. The question was what to do about it. He certainly wasn't the kind of person to make a rash move like quitting his job without a plan of where to head next. The only thing he knew for certain was that he couldn't continue like this — certainly not for another 15 years until he could even contemplate retirement.

WEEKLY

accomplishment and worth

For someone in Jonathon's situation, the first thing to figure out is: if his current job leaves him cold and unenthusiastic, what is it that does move him? If "anything worth doing is worth doing well," what does he consider is worth doing? And if there's nothing that he finds currently interesting, what used to grab his interest?

Another thing that someone like Jonathon probably has not allowed himself to do in a long time is to dream. In fact, the following is a good exercise for Jonathon to do before he even contemplates sending out any resumes:

– Take a few minutes one evening and sit in his favourite chair — and turn off the TV!

– Place a large piece of paper and some coloured markers on a table next to him.

– Close his eyes and relax.

– Allow himself to dream: dream about what he would do if he knew he could not fail. If money and time, education and skills, geography and even being married and having three kids were not an issue, what would Jonathon like to do? Maybe at first he wouldn't

be able to be specific. In the very least, though, he would probably come up with a vague sense of some way he'd like to spend his working hours.

– After about 5 or 10 minutes of dreaming, open his eyes and start to draw his dream — even if it's abstract or vague. This exercise isn't about proving his skills as an artist, so Jonathon need not worry about how it looks. The point is to just let the dream spill onto the paper.

– When he is finished, Jonathon could place that drawing somewhere where he can see it often, to remind him that he does have a dream, maybe even a goal. As it becomes clearer, he can start filling in the details and eventually make a plan of how to make his dream into a reality.

We spend so much of our life at work, it's really a shame if we don't feel like we get anything out of it except a paycheque. Getting in touch with what it is that we'd really like to be doing, is a first step on the way to actually doing it.

Cheryl Nafziger-Leis

After You Read

1. Think of the strategies that you and your partner suggested for being satisfied with a job. Were any of them addressed in the article? Do you think that any of the author's suggestions would help you?

Handbook Link

How to interpret and assess information, ideas, and issues

Before You Read

In a paragraph, reflect about the volunteering experiences you have had — the challenges, the benefits for you, and the benefits for others. Then read "I Volunteer."

I Volunteer

Experience matters

Global Youth Service Day
Canadian Youth Making a Difference

Global Youth Service Day (GYSD) celebrates, recognizes and mobilizes youth volunteers; it is an annual event celebrated by 32 international organizations in over 100 nations. In Canada, GYSD falls during **National Volunteer Week** *(April 21–27) and offers us a special opportunity to shine a spotlight on the spirit and energy of Canada's youth.*

On April 26–28, youth volunteers will be busy. Food drives, car washes, choir performances, and habitat clean-ups are just some of the activities we can expect to hear about. And there will be new projects launched—new community service projects that herald the involvement of greater numbers of youth volunteers.

Why get involved in Global Youth Service Day?

By getting involved in hands-on ways, Canadian youth help to shape the world around them. Statistics from the 2000 National Survey of Giving, Volunteering and Participating show that 29% of all young Canadians between the ages of 15 and 24 volunteer. The same survey also indicates that volunteering in adulthood is closely linked to early life experiences that teach young people about civic participation. Encouraging youth to volunteer is an investment in our nation's future. It is in all our best interest that the voice of Canadian youth be heard in our communities, institutions, organizations, and governments.

GYSD is an opportunity for young people to be recognized for their contribution. Whether four friends get together to clean up a stretch of riverbank or 14 young people canvass for a local charity, the message is clear. Canadian youth make a difference in their communities.

Through volunteering, I have met and learned from fascinating people of all ages and backgrounds, from all over the world. These individuals have opened my eyes to perspectives and knowledge beyond the scope of my own experiences.

Jill Andres Johnson,
Calgary, AB

Recognizing the power of youth volunteers

If you currently provide services for young people, consider celebrating GYSD with an activity that includes them as participants. Perhaps they can paint or clean the organization's premises, host an event, or launch a new project. Existing youth programs and activities are also valuable examples of youth participation.

If you involve larger groups of young people, think about community-wide projects that can be started during GYSD: a park or other environmental clean-up, a food drive or a fundraising campaign. If your organizations doesn't normally involve young people as volunteers, why not consider a special project to mark GYSD?

How youth volunteers make a difference

Here is a selection of youth-led volunteer project ideas that can be developed for young participants:

1. Organize a non-perishable food drive to support a local food bank.
2. Set up a bike safety presentation in your community.
3. Collect and create personal care kits for an emergency shelter.
4. Set up a toy collection for a hospital.
5. Clean up a park or roadway.
6. Provide a craft demonstration at a nursing home.
7. Paint a mural for a community centre.
8. Arrange a CPR training course for young people.
9. Organize a sport event for young players.
10. Offer art tours for young people.
11. Organize a blood clinic at school.
12. Organize a read-a-thon, walk-a-thon, or dance-a-thon to raise funds for a youth-related charity.
13. Draw up a roster of young people to visit shut-ins.
14. Set up a babysitting service for single parents and parents of children with disabilities.

Connecting with youth volunteers

For more information on youth volunteering and community service please consult the following sources:

www.gysd.net
The lead site for the international co-ordination of GYSD. Find out about youth service projects all over the world.

www.volunteer.ca
Get information on volunteering in Canada, the volunteer centre movement, volunteer management and more. The site links to:

- Volunteer Opportunities Exchange
  A great place to recruit volunteers or find volunteer positions.
- Volunteering Works!
  Dedicated to helping Canadian youth make the most of volunteering, the site features tips, exercises, and downloadable resources.
- Helping Out is Cool
  A virtual book that shows six-to nine-year-olds the fun of volunteering.

www.pch.gc.ca/cyberstation
At the youth cyberstation, Canadian Heritage provides youth with the necessary information on volunteering for skills development, employment experience, and the opportunity to connect with their communities. The interactive cyberstation contains useful checklists, quizzes and questions to help youth assess their interests and ensure they get the most from volunteer opportunities.

Produced during International Year of Volunteers 2001, the following manuals can be ordered from Volunteer Canada by visiting www.volunteer.ca or calling 1-800-670-0401.

- *Youth Works! Creating and developing youth-led volunteers projects*
  A guide to help get a youth-run community project or volunteer activity off the ground. All the components for a successful project are included-project ideas, practical tips, teambuilding, winning support from community partners and tried and true promotions.
- *Volunteers Connections: New strategies for involving youth* offers samples and suggestions on how to improve organizational structures to better involve youth volunteers. It is an important reference for any agency that involves young people.

My best friends, my role models and my employers are all people I have met through volunteering.
Irfhan Rawji,
Coquitlam, BC

Count youth volunteers in

The recent Statistics Canada 2000 National Survey of Giving,
Volunteering and Participating reveals that

- there are 6.5 million volunteers in Canada
- 29% of all volunteers are between the ages of 15 and 24
- youth volunteers contribute an average of 130 hours a year
- 78% of youth volunteers believe that volunteering is a way to improve job prospects
- 24% of youth volunteers believe that volunteering helped them get a job
- 18% of youth volunteers participate because of a school, employer or government requirement
- the key causes that Canadian youth volunteers support are education and research, social services, and arts, culture, and recreation (including sports)
- Canadian youth volunteers are involved in organizing and supervising events (53%); canvassing, campaigning and fundraising (39%); teaching or coaching (34%); providing care, support or counselling (29%); and serving as unpaid members of boards or committees (26%).

Volunteering gave me the opportunity to discover my real personality and my abilities. I've learned to lead discussion groups, to give presentations in the classroom, to take part in a board meeting, to write a press release, to establish links with business people, to design a community plan, and to launch a funding campaign ...

Bruno Larivière,
Montréal, QC

Canada's youth volunteers: time to take a bow

Global Youth Service Day provides Canadians with an opportunity to recognize and honour youth volunteers, it is a time to applaud and encourage the efforts of young people making a difference in our communities.

The following appreciation item can be ordered from Volunteer Canada at **www.volunteer.ca** or **1-800-670-0401.**

I Volunteer Bandanas
I Volunteer Lanyards
I Volunteer Pencils
I Volunteer Lapel Pins

After You Read

1. Describe the design choices used in this brochure by discussing the following questions with a partner: Who is the audience? How do you know? What language appeals to the audience? Why is the colour green an appropriate choice? What is effective about the font, headlines, visuals, organization, subheads, and balance of white space?

Handbook Link
How to describe design and production choices in media

Before You Read

Well-known Canadian journalist Peter Gzowski died in January 2002, of complications from lung disease. In this excerpt from an essay about addictions, Gzowski, a smoker for 50 years, reflects on how he got started smoking, and how hard it was to stop.

Before you read the essay, consider why people start smoking, and why they continue to smoke even though they know it could kill them. Make a list of all of reasons that make it easy to start and hard to quit.

HOW TO QUIT SMOKING
in Fifty Years or Less

by Peter Gzowski

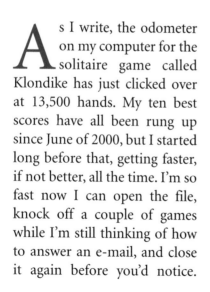

As I write, the odometer on my computer for the solitaire game called Klondike has just clicked over at 13,500 hands. My ten best scores have all been rung up since June of 2000, but I started long before that, getting faster, if not better, all the time. I'm so fast now I can open the file, knock off a couple of games while I'm still thinking of how to answer an e-mail, and close it again before you'd notice.

But let's say every game takes a minute. That's 13,500 minutes: 225 hours. Six thirty-five-hour weeks. Not counting research, I once wrote a book in not much more time than that.

Klondike is classic solitaire: red nine on black ten, black ten on red jack. The number of decisions you make is minuscule, and if you take a wrong turn you can have what golfers call a mulligan, press UNDO and go back. So what's the point? I

have no idea. Yet without warning, I'll find myself stopping in mid-paragraph to … There, dammit, I've done it again. Opened the file while you weren't looking. 13,504. And if I hadn't stopped then, I might have played all morning. Many days it's as if I can't get going at the keyboard if I don't play a little Klondike first.

I'm the same with *The Globe and Mail* cryptic crossword. I'm convinced I need it to kick-start my mind. When *Morningside* went on the road in the years I was hosting it, I'd get someone to fax me the *Globe* puzzle as soon as it hit the streets in Toronto. Which would confuse my colleagues in, say, Inuvik, but keep me from twitching. At least I can understand the appeal of the cryptic — it's a contest between you and the usually anonymous puzzle-setter, and there's a pleasure in winning. There's even a kind of brother- (and sister-) hood of crypticians who nod to each other across the aisles of airplanes when they see a *Globe* opened at the appropriate page, although the quickest way to lose your membership is to dare to give someone an answer he hasn't asked you for.

And, oh, hell, I watch *Frasier* too — every week night, on a channel that seems to have archived his every move since he left *Cheers*. His program comes on at 6:30 in Toronto, right after a CBC hybrid called *Canada Now*. There are worse routines of TV watching, I'm sure, and lots of less worthy expressions of U.S. popular culture than sitcoms. But I still feel out of control as I slouch deeper into my favourite chair, wave farewell to Ian Hanomansing, and tune in to the latest misadventures of a self-centred snob and his clearly unbalanced younger brother, whose nose bleeds when he fibs. If these guys are psychiatrists, no wonder we're all a little nuts. 13,506, 07, 08, 0…

Klondyke, cryptics, *Frasier*. Coffee (though I'll come back to that). Ritz crackers with peanut butter, going sockless until December, correcting other people's grammar, writing down phone numbers but not the names of their owners, saying "gonna," flicking mindlessly through the channels at three in the morning — all things I do but am convinced, rightly or wrongly, I could stop any time I set my mind to it. The difference between those habits, if habits they are, and what I think we mean by addictions is at least three-fold, the folds being:

1. With the possible exception of my compulsive channel hopping, I'm not hurting anyone else when I indulge in them;
2. If I were to stop playing Klondike or doing morning cryptics or baring my bony white ankles to the autumnal breezes, I would almost certainly not start shaking and retching from withdrawal; and
3. The price of continuing with these pastimes would not be death.

Considering what smoking came to mean to me — there are almost no photographs of me after the age of 17 in which I do not have a cigarette either in my hand or dangling from my lips, and no stories written about my times on radio or television without at least a mention of my lighting-one-after-the other habit — not to mention what it means to me now, when I am pretty well confined to barracks with an oxygen tube up my nose and a four-wheeled buggy, like a baby's pram without the baby, that enables me to walk from one end of the apartment to the other … considering that, and all the other ways smoking and its effects have taken over my existence, it is perhaps surprising that I can't remember my first cigarette.

• • • •

A lifetime later, when people who loved me or were worried about me or, in some cases, were paid a lot of money to figure out why I persisted in a habit that was so clearly shortening my days among them, would ask me why I didn't quit, I could sometimes do no better than "I smoke because I smoke." In the absence of a reason not to — a municipal bylaw, a coughing child, a disapproving hostess, the knowledge that an open flame might blow me and everyone in the room to kingdom come — it was simply a lot easier to light up than to

Holding a cigarette while working at the CBC. "I smoke because I smoke."

forebear. Unless I consciously stopped myself from doing so, I smoked. Even when I was sucking back three large packages a day — seventy-five cigarettes, which is about as many as you can get through if you're still going to sleep a few hours — there were very few that I actually decided to smoke. The first one in the morning, sure, though that was more a reflex than an act of free will, my hand reaching across the alarm clock before my feet were ready to hit the floor, and the last one at night. A cigarette after each meal or task completed, and certain others through the day — to pick myself up, to relax, to sharpen my appetite or ease the pangs of hunger. But most of the time, I smoked without thinking, often not realizing I had lit a cigarette until I noticed it burning in the ashtray. Would I have gone into withdrawal if I'd stopped then? Absolutely. Even the first hour of a transcontinental flight would have me drumming my fingers and looking at my watch, and on the rare occasions I could be talked into going to a non-smoking restaurant or accepting an invitation to a house with no ashtrays, I seldom made it to dessert without having to go for a walk. Over the years, I never really gave the storm clouds of abstinence time to gather. I just lit another cigarette.

• • • •

Does anyone honestly believe we didn't know smoking was bad for us? We may not have realized it would eventually kill us, or suspected it could rock us back on our heels the way I'm now rocked — I have what the health care system, bless its heart, calls COPD, for Chronic Obstructive Pulmonary Disease, but which everyone knows really means emphysema, just as acne really means boils and pimples. We probably hadn't heard of lung cancer or considered the devil's catalogue of other afflictions the world now understands are caused by smoking. But everyone knew that cigarettes did something different to your body than, say, asparagus. "That'll stunt your growth," people would say. Or "Sounds like a smoker's cough to me." Danger? If we'd even admitted there was any — a difficult concession to pry from a teenager about anything — it would only have added to the allure.

• • • •

By the time smoking had fallen out of fashion — in what has been, surely, one of the revolutionary social changes of our day — nearly all of my friends had quit. One by one, they fell by the wayside, driven not only by the now unavoidable realization that it was going to kill them but by a variation of the peer pressure that had got so many of us started in the first place. If smoking had once been smart, it was now stupid. You didn't brag about it; you were, if anything, ashamed. And what with constantly trying to figure out where you could go and when, depending on whether you could smoke or not, it was becoming more trouble than it was worth. It was, not to put too fine a point on it, a pain the ass.

Yet still I smoked. My teeth were yellow and my fingers brown. My clothes stank and so, I'm sure, did my breath.

There were holes in my sweaters and scars on my furniture. My computer keyboard was regularly choked with ashes. My car looked and smelled as if there'd been an all-night poker game in the front seat. Once, sheltering a cigarette in my pocket, I set fire to a favourite windbreaker, and more than once, holding a phone to my ear, I caught the acrid smell of burning hair. In 1996, now in my sixties, I went into hospital for surgery to fix an abdominal aortic aneurysm. About four days into my recovery, a night nurse, the one who used to prowl the halls on in-line skates, asked if I'd like to get out of bed and go downstairs with her for a cigarette, joining that sorry gaggle of people outside every hospital who lean on their IVs, bare bums exposed to the winds, as they suck on the toxin that put them there in the first place. "Are you kidding?" I snorted. But my first day home, with the physical craving presumably under control, I pawed through my cupboards until I found a half-full package of stale Rothmans and lit up in the living room.

Why? I still can't answer. If anyone asked, and they did, all the time, I'd say I hated my habit. It's hard to duck the fact that I probably hated myself for being such a slave to it. The reasons may well be buried in the childhood I've sketched so roughly here, but if they are, it will take a sharper brain than mine to ferret them. Whatever pleasure had once been associated with pulling the little red tab to remove the cellophane wrapping, taking out the layer of silver paper over half the package (we used to save that paper during the war so the RCAF could foil the enemy radar), pushing out the first cigarette, tapping it lightly on a table, lighting it, and then sucking that first, biting, all-engulfing, twitch-stopping drag of the day deep, deep into your lungs: whatever pleasure had once been there had long since gone. I smoked, as always, because I smoked.

At 9:30 on the morning of February 7, 2000, I pulled into the parking lot of a four-storey building in the suburbs of Toronto, rolled down the window of my ashtray on wheels, and flicked the butt of my last Rothmans into a snowbank.

After half a century of smoking, I had elected to incarcerate myself where I might find help. I'd signed on at a privately funded institution that had begun by working with alcoholics and, over the years, had grown into a treatment centre for people with addictions that varied from gambling to hard drugs to eating disorders. I'm preserving its anonymity because privacy is what the Slammer, as I came to call it, provided me, as it did all its patrons, and I feel I owe it that in return. As well, perhaps, as my life.

I'd sort of tried to quit before. Under the guidance of a wise and caring GP, into whose hands I'd been lucky enough to fall after my surgery, I experimented with Zyban, the patch, hypnosis, audio-tapes, acupuncture, therapy — whatever was going. Everything worked and

On the air

nothing worked. My guardian GP looked up the patch in the literature, saw how many people were having heart attacks caused by smoking while they were on it, and warned me never, ever to light up while I was attached; I ripped the patch off and had a cigarette. Hypnosis, for all my skepticism (or arrogance, if you want to be picky — of course I could never be hypnotized) actually took hold momentarily; I nodded off in the subject's chair while the doctor murmured soothing words and came awake to find my hand rising involuntarily at his command. But I lit up in the car on the way home and never went back. And so on. I foiled every attack. The truth was my heart wasn't in it, and the more I danced around, kidding myself and others, the better I understood the essential truth of smoking cessation: you can spend thousands on personal therapy and professional guidance, or you can stick a carrot in your ear and whistle *Four Strong Winds* — if you still have enough breath. The method makes no difference. If you've decided to quit, you will; if you haven't, you should get your affairs in order.

I was in pretty rough shape as I climbed out of my car that February morning. My drinking, another family trait, had been heavy enough for the last couple of years that it probably would have qualified me for the Slammer on its own. I was wobbly of stride, red of eye and shaky of hand. When I was introduced to the physician who would later turn out to be of particular help with my various demons, I shook his hand and, settling into the chair beside his desk, asked if he preferred to be called "Michael" or "Doctor."

"Steven will do," he said, "since that's my name."

I cannot say enough about the help — physiological as well as spiritual — I received in the Slammer, nor about the support of the people and systems I have leaned on since. I stayed inside my suburban minitower for most of a month, tranquilized through the worst of the physical withdrawal, a fresh strong patch glued daily to my flesh, making it through the nights with sleeping pills. I tried meditation and wished I were better at it, attended lectures on dependency, and went to AA meetings, where, though I resisted the air of evangelism, I found strength in facing my own weaknesses — yes, I was an addict, powerless without help. Some of the wisdom, I think, began to seep through. I made friends with a sprightly menagerie of other addicts in the Slammer, not only the pre-

dictable range of problem drinkers but also teenage druggies (some of whom, I'm sad to say, seemed to know more about the chemistry of artificial euphoria than the professionals who gave us our lectures), disarming gamblers and a bevy of extraordinarily attractive young women, who would eat with us in the dining hall, a dietitian at their side, and then, if no one stayed with them, go upstairs and purge themselves to starvation.

I liked all my fellow passengers, although some of my affection may just have been the companionship of shared frailties. However stupid their behaviour, I came to think, drunks and hopheads are often clever people. A 20-year-old heroin addict, a promising athlete who'd been the apple of her father's eye until she wrecked her knees and lost an American university scholarship, beat me at chess the first time she played me. A burly NCO from the Armed Forces, whom I initially had to coach on the finer points of Scrabble, scored two triple-triples on me in a single game.

My favourite fellow inmate was a jolly woman who had gambled away both her career and her house at the video terminals of the casinos. Hitting bottom, she'd reached such a state of despair that she staged an "armed robbery" on her local convenience store with a toy pistol, hoping that the cops would come and gun her down. But when I met her she was full of the strength she'd found in the Slammer, a dedicated Scrabble enthusiast, a passionate reader and the soul of kindness. She still faced a charge of armed robbery (it was later dismissed), but her real fear was that she'd wander one day into a provincial gambling den and be seduced not by the chance of winning her losses back — she was far too intelligent to think that was possible — but by the flashing lights and the unadulterated lure of excitement.

I had a special feeling, too, for the kids with eating disorders. Almost everyone else in the Slammer could be separated from their temptations — there were no cards in the common room, lest the gamblers succumb to pinochle for quarters, and anyone out on a day pass was liable to face a blood test on return — but everyone, including the young bulimics, had to face food every day. I would think of them after breakfast, as I watched my Scrabble partners and companions in group therapy step outside the swinging doors to smoke in the winter air, while I stayed inside.

Yet something worked. Gradually, and with a lot of help, I realized that I really did want to quit. By the time I was ready to retrieve my car from the parking lot (friends had arranged to have it taken away, vacuumed and returned ash-free), I felt like an ex-smoker. I'm still paying the price for my years of transgression. The emphysema — sorry, COPD — that now dominates my life didn't really strike until I'd been out for a few months and was hit by a chest infection. I've had rehab for that, too, in a different kind of institution, and I work on getting better every day. It's a long haul. But a year and many thousands of games of Klondike after I tossed out that last cigarette butt, I haven't smoked again.

Oh, yes, I said I had a point to make about coffee. It's something else I learned in the Slammer. I'd been drinking coffee at least as long as I'd been smoking when I checked in. I knew I was addicted to caffeine, that I couldn't possibly start the day without a jolt, the stronger the better. When, as my recovery began, my hands finally stopped shaking enough for me to get a cup of coffee to my lips, all I could say was, "Thank God, now I feel human again." I kept that up every day till I got paroled. I was on my way out the door before someone told me it had been decaf all along.

After You Read

1. Write a letter to the publisher of this essay to explain how you reacted to the essay. State why you think people smoke, if, as Gzowski does, they know that it is bad for them. Describe what you learned from his efforts to stop smoking.
2. With a small group, discuss how this selection relates to the theme of making decisions. What decisions did Gzowski make? How did they affect the rest of his life?

Handbook Link
How to write a letter

Before You Read

In a small group, discuss the characteristics of the "tweens" (young people between the ages of 8 and 12) that you know, and their tastes in television and movie programming, music, and clothing. Make a list of the ways you think the media might use this information to influence young people.

Analyzing the "Tween" Market

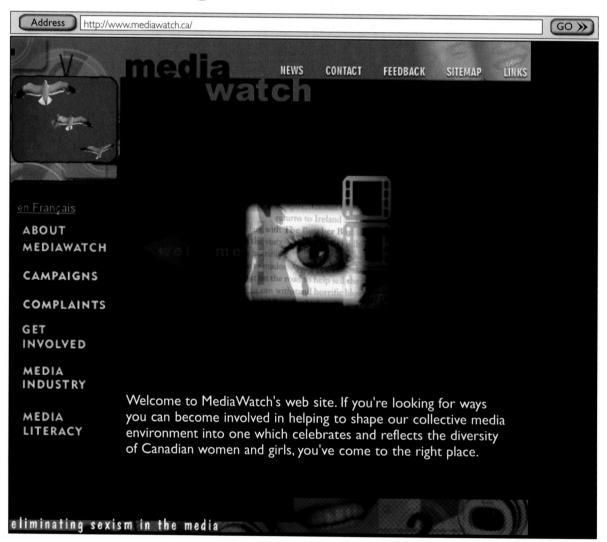

Address http://www.mediawatch.ca/   GO »

media watch

NEWS   CONTACT   FEEDBACK   SITEMAP   LINKS

en Français

ABOUT MEDIAWATCH

CAMPAIGNS

COMPLAINTS

GET INVOLVED

MEDIA INDUSTRY

MEDIA LITERACY

Welcome to MediaWatch's web site. If you're looking for ways you can become involved in helping to shape our collective media environment into one which celebrates and reflects the diversity of Canadian women and girls, you've come to the right place.

eliminating sexism in the media

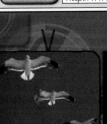

Address http://www.mediawatch.ca/about/   GO »

NEWS   CONTACT   FEEDBACK   SITEMAP   LINKS

About Mediawatch: Herstory | Media Images of Women
Educational Society | National Committee | Action Bulletin |
Lobbying Activities | View Media Watch Clip | Awards |

en Français

ABOUT MEDIAWATCH

CAMPAIGNS

COMPLAINTS

GET INVOLVED

MEDIA INDUSTRY

MEDIA LITERACY

About MEDIAWATCH

MediaWatch is a national, not for profit feminist organization working to eliminate sexism in the media. We seek to transform the media environment from one in which women are either invisible or stereotyped, to one in which women are realistically portrayed and equitably represented in all our physical, economic, racial and cultural diversity.

These changes are fundamental to altering the current social climate in which gender inequality and violence against women are pervasive. We promote change by educating media industries, government and the public, conducting research and encouraging consumer advocacy.

Over the years, MediaWatch has produced many educational print and video resources related to the media's portrayal of women and girls. We also offer a range of interactive media literacy workshops suitable for schools and community groups. If you would like more information about speakers' fees or ordering print or video resources please check out the resource list on this site or e-mail us your name and address and we will mail you more information.

WE WANT MEDIA TO

Portray Women Positively

Women are dehumanized and objectified when our body parts are used irrelevantly to attract attention and when only our sexuality is emphasized. These negative portrayals help to create a climate where violence against women is tolerated.

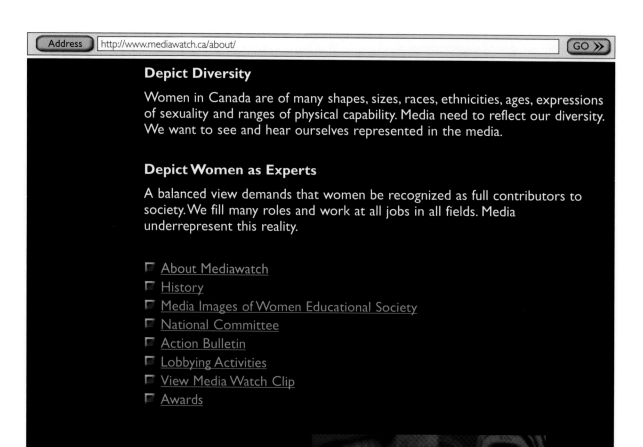

Address | http://www.mediawatch.ca/about/ | GO »

Depict Diversity

Women in Canada are of many shapes, sizes, races, ethnicities, ages, expressions of sexuality and ranges of physical capability. Media need to reflect our diversity. We want to see and hear ourselves represented in the media.

Depict Women as Experts

A balanced view demands that women be recognized as full contributors to society. We fill many roles and work at all jobs in all fields. Media underrepresent this reality.

- About Mediawatch
- History
- Media Images of Women Educational Society
- National Committee
- Action Bulletin
- Lobbying Activities
- View Media Watch Clip
- Awards

eliminating sexism in the media

Address | http://www.mediawatch.ca/research/ | GO »

NEWS   CONTACT   FEEDBACK   SITEMAP   LINKS

Research: Analyzing the "Tween" Market | Global Media Monitoring Project | Front and Centre | Cover to Cover | Please Adjust Our Sets | Women Strike Out | Bibliographies | Watching the Watchers 2001

en Français

ABOUT
MEDIAWATCH

CAMPAIGNS

COMPLAINTS

GET
INVOLVED

MEDIA
INDUSTRY

MEDIA
LITERACY

RESEARCH

RESOURCES

YOUTH

HOME

RESEARCH

MediaWatch believes that it is important to study media trends and to analyze the representation and portrayal of women in the media. The following are some of MediaWatch's most recent studies.

- Analyzing the "Tween" Market

- Global Media Monitoring Project: Women Participating in the News

- Front and Centre: Minority Representation on Television

- Cover to Cover: Magazine Analysis

- Please Adjust Our Sets: Canadian Women Watching Television - Habits, Preferences and Concerns

- Women Strike Out - 1998 Newspaper Survey

- Bibliographies

- Watching the Watchers 2001

eliminating sexism in the media

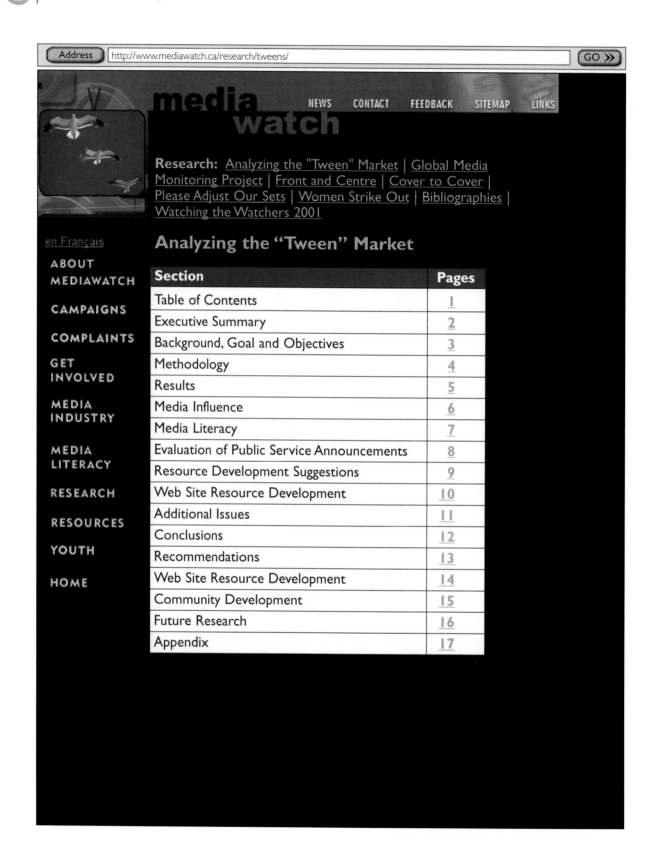

Address | http://www.mediawatch.ca/research/tweens/Default.asp?pg=2 | GO »

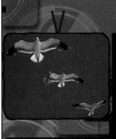

media watch

NEWS   CONTACT   FEEDBACK   SITEMAP   LINKS

Research: Analyzing the "Tween" Market | Global Media Monitoring Project | Front and Centre | Cover to Cover | Please Adjust Our Sets | Women Strike Out | Bibliographies | Watching the Watchers 2001

en Français

ABOUT
MEDIAWATCH

CAMPAIGNS

COMPLAINTS

GET
INVOLVED

MEDIA
INDUSTRY

MEDIA
LITERACY

RESEARCH

RESOURCES

YOUTH

HOME

Analyzing the "Tween" Market | **Executive Summary**

"Dear Diary:
I was looking at my Seventeen magazine today. (It took me about an hour to finish) and I caught myself feeling absolutely miserable about myself looking at the poems.
I flip the glossy pages looking at beautiful women. People I want to be. I learn make-up tips and read articles all judging me, telling me who I am, who I want to be. I'm angry and depressed as I close the magazine and place it by my side. I hate it. I never hated anything more. But I still read it. I still subscribe. I still can't wait for another issue to arrive in my mailbox and I won't stop... Until I'm perfect."

(Written by a 14-year-old female)
A Report by The Health Communication Unit (THCU),
at the Centre for Health Promotion, University of Toronto

May, 2000

Background

MediaWatch is a national, not for profit feminist organization that seeks to transform the media environment from one in which women are either invisible or stereotyped, to one in which women are realistically portrayed and equitably represented in all their physical, economic, racial and cultural diversity. The organization's roots go back to 1978 when the Minister of Communications and the Canadian Radio-television and Telecommunications Commission (CRTC) established a task force on Sex-role Stereotyping in the Broadcast Media. In 1981, following the two-year study by the task force that found sexism in the broadcast media, MediaWatch was formed as a subcommittee of the National Action Committee on the Status of Women. MediaWatch became autonomous in 1983 with its national office based in Vancouver. In 1991 the office relocated to Toronto.

Address | http://www.mediawatch.ca/research/tweens/Default.asp?pg=2 | GO »

Methodology

The recent "girl power" phenomenon has illustrated the substantial and growing buying power of 11-14-year-old females, also known as "tweens". Consequently marketing strategies increasingly single out tweens as their desired target. MediaWatch is interested in creating a web-based resource and presentation on Media Literacy for this segment. Accordingly, the goal of this project is to explore if media affects the self-esteem and body image of "tweens" and to produce a resource to inform others of the results.

Four focus groups were conducted in November 1999: two in Toronto and two in Burnaby. A community centre in Burnaby and a public school in Toronto assisted with the recruitment of a convenience sample of young women aged 11-14. Respondents were selected from youth groups and performing arts programs as potential leaders among their peers. The participants were divided into two groups: 11 & 12 year olds and 13 & 14 year olds to create comfort and facilitate discussion. The atmosphere during the focus groups supported this decision, as there were differences between the age groups.

Participants

There were striking differences between some segments of the respondents.

In general, the differences between the two Burnaby groups supported findings in the literature of a dramatic shift in self-esteem in early adolescence (Pipher, 1994; Gilligan & Brown, 1992). The younger participants were very animated, vocal and forthcoming whereas the older tweens were reserved, self-conscious and cautious - seemingly lacking in confidence. In contrast, there appeared to be little differentiation between the younger and older Toronto groups. Although the older tweens had more knowledge and personal experience than the younger tweens, both groups voiced their opinions in a straightforward and confident manner.

The researchers noted socio-economic differences between the Burnaby and Toronto groups. The Burnaby students were from working class families, living in an economically disadvantaged area. In contrast, the Toronto participants were highly motivated, high achieving students attending a school for the arts.

Address | http://www.mediawatch.ca/research/tweens/Default.asp?pg=2 | GO »

Results

Media Consumption

The tweens reported that they regularly engage in a variety of media. The majority of the young women reported that they enjoy television, magazines, radio, movies, music and the Internet. Many cited specific television programs such as "Ally McBeal," "Friends" and "Dawson's Creek" as favourites. Participants reported reading and enjoying magazines such as "Seventeen," "YM" and "People." Many of the tweens listed popular bands such as Mariah Carey, Destiny's Child and Lauryn Hill as musical favourites. The respondents reported that they spend a significant amount of their leisure time engaged with the media. The large majority of the tweens indicated that they also spend time engaged in organized sports or artistic endeavours such as dance or music lessons and that they value time with their friends.

Participants were asked to discuss images they have seen in the media that attracted their attention. Many of the tweens raised the issue of role models. These young women placed a high value on sincere, genuine women who have overcome challenges in their lives. The respondents listed Hillary Clinton and actress Drew Barrymore as examples of positive role models because both had overcome adversity in their lives and both were perceived to be women of integrity who remained true to themselves. Conversely, the young women described negative role models as women who exploited their sexuality for profit, women who demonstrate they are not true to themselves by wearing "too much" makeup or women who had cosmetic surgery. The participants listed Britney Spears, Mariah Carey and women who are in the profession of prostitution as examples of negative role models.

The majority of the tweens agreed that appealing images should be bright and colourful. Models should be athletic and should not be extremely thin.

Media Influence

The Power of Media

Although debates about media effects abound, several studies point to changes in behaviour following media exposure (Levine, 1994: 472, Graydon, 1996: 37).

A minority of respondents reported that the media influence their perceptions of their self-image. These young women reported that they try to emulate images in the media or celebrities. The large

Address http://www.mediawatch.ca/research/tweens/Default.asp?pg=2   GO >>

majority of the participants indicated a belief that while other people may be influenced by the media, their own goals or concerns were not influenced by images they witness in the media. To illustrate their point, many of the respondents pointed to a long running awareness campaign for milk that features celebrities with milk moustaches. This advertising campaign is extremely popular with this age group. However, most reported that their consumption of milk, or lack thereof, was not altered by their enjoyment of this marketing campaign.

Body Image, Weight Preoccupation and Self-Esteem

Comments about body image, weight preoccupation and self-esteem permeated throughout the discussions. These issues occupy a central place in the lives of these young women as they sort out identity issues and navigate their way through relationships with their peers and adult authority figures.

Without exception, all of the respondents appeared to be within the normal weight range for their age and height. Notwithstanding this, almost all of these young women expressed concern about their weight, the shape of their body or expressed dissatisfaction with specific body parts such as their thighs, hips, breasts or nose. Many participants expressed an awareness that preoccupation with their appearance has a negative impact on their self-esteem. Others commented that a subtle form of peer pressure in the form of looks and "comments behind [their] backs" contributed to self-criticism.

Male Relationships

The influence of media on relationships with male peers was clearly demonstrated in the older Burnaby group. This group reported that they believe the majority of fashion advertisements featuring women's clothing was intended for a male audience. The Burnaby teens reported that their male peers hang these advertising images in their lockers and regularly comment on the physical attributes of the models. The young women said that their male counterparts compared them to these models and that they did not compare favourably. The younger Burnaby group highlighted their perception of the influence of the media on teenage boys, but not to the extent or with the emotion of the older Burnaby group. In stark contrast, neither of the Toronto groups discussed this issue with respect to the males in their lives.

Media Literacy

Media Literacy Education

None of the participants had received media literacy training in school. Similarly, the participants reported that they do not have media literacy discussions with family or friends.

http://www.mediawatch.ca/research/tweens/Default.asp?pg=2

Regardless of the lack of formal media literacy education, the participants have excellent critical thinking skills with regard to messages in the media. Their comments ranged from skepticism of proposed product results to identification of contradictory messages. The variety, quantity and depth of comments clearly reveal the desire and ability of tweens to critically analyze the messages that surround them.

Social Action

The young women were asked to brainstorm potential social action techniques to respond to offensive or negative media material. Regardless of their keen critical thinking skills, many of these young women felt powerless. They did not perceive that they could do anything about offensive images or, if they did take action, they believed there would be no result.

Despite their perception of being powerless to act as agents of change, the participants developed an impressive list of suggestions for action including: petitions; telephoning the media outlet; writing letters; boycotting the product; forming discussion groups; writing opinion columns; protesting; and raising awareness. Further investigation is required to examine if they would take action or, if they did, whether unhealthy images in the media would inspire them to take action.

Resource Development Suggestions

Public Service Announcements

In order to assist with the development of resources and campaigns aimed at this age group, the respondents were asked to comment on elements of two television public service announcements (We are Girls-1997 and Boutique-1998) and one draft print advertisement (Feel Free to Puke on this Ad-1998) produced by Concerned Children's Advertisers.

Overall, the respondents are receptive to the idea of social messaging about self-esteem and body image aimed specifically at them. The young women reported that realistic models representing "average" people their age should be used. They suggested that groups should be diverse in terms of ethnicity, size and age.

The respondents reacted negatively to resources aimed at "girls only." The majority of the young women reported that they support the goals of feminism for equality between the sexes. However according to their definition of feminism, boys should be included. As such, many participants suggested that a meaningful advertisement

Address http://www.mediawatch.ca/research/tweens/Default.asp?pg=2 GO

would promote equality by including boys. Respondents clearly articulated a desire to see concrete examples of how to implement strategies for change.

The young people clearly enjoyed creative elements that used "counter culture" as part of the message. Thus, they reacted positively to seeing "hip" looking young people resisting pressure to conform to a standard not their own in "Boutique" and they clearly enjoyed the headline "Feel Free to Puke on this Ad" as a message that pushes acceptable social boundaries.

Health Resources

The respondents were able to generate a list of resources that could be available for someone wanting to discuss some of the issues raised during the present research. However, most appeared to favour using an anonymous resource such as The Kids Help Phone or look to a friend or family for assistance rather than seek help from a counselor.

Media

Participants were asked to recommend ways to communicate information about body image or to advertise resources aimed at them. Magazine advertisements, regular sections in magazines, phone lines and counter advertisements were most often mentioned.

Web Site Resource Development

All of the respondents reported that they have access to the Internet at home and/or at school. Tweens who have home access to the Internet are more likely to use this resource for pleasure than others are. Most of the older Burnaby tweens reported that they do not have home computers and do not use the Internet on a regular basis; consequently another medium would be needed to reach this group.

Respondents were asked about web site elements that would be appropriate for their age group. The majority emphasized an interest in engaging or active components. These elements would include chat rooms, colourful pictures, games, quizzes and sound bits.

The large majority reported that a web-based resource aimed at their age group should include people their age as opposed to adult celebrities or experts. Most said they prefer a strong message to a subtle one and positive messages to negative. The content of a web site should include a range of opinions, preferably in the form of personal testimonials from young people and be provided with a range of strategies in order to decide the best approach for themselves.

Additional Issues

In some of the focus groups, a number of the tweens spontaneously raised some unforeseen issues that generated a fair amount of discussion. These issues will be of interest to professionals working with young women.

Some participants raised issues and concerns about the implications of women working in the professions of prostitution, pornography and wrestling and the impact that these professions have on young women. Several of the younger participants expressed strong anti-smoking views, focussing their comments on cigarette ads and smoking prevention programs. The young women also made salient comments about guest speakers. The respondents reported that they felt effective speakers would encourage and facilitate tweens to participate in presentations by allowing the youth to voice their opinions. Finally, it was clear that some tweens in this age group are knowledgeable about social issues. It appears that young people who are actively involved in social issues often gain positive self-esteem and confidence through sharing their knowledge of the issues and what action they have taken.

Conclusions and Recommendations

The tweens in the present research are avid consumers of a variety of media. Despite their stated enjoyment of television programs, magazines, music and web sites, the young people experience negative effects on their self-esteem partly due to exposure to these images. The large majority of the participants express dissatisfaction with their bodies and compare themselves negatively to images of beauty portrayed in the media.

The respondents have excellent critical thinking skills despite a lack of formal media literacy training. The tweens are aware of many strategies to effect social change. However, the young people in this sample do not believe that they could be effective agents for social change in the current media environment.

The 11 to 14 year olds expressed an interest in Public Service Announcements and web-based resources aimed at them. They indicated an interest to be active participants in the development of such resources and identified specific creative elements that are appealing to this age group.

Address http://www.mediawatch.ca/research/tweens/Default.asp?pg=2 GO »

In order to provide media literacy training to this segment of the population, it is recommended that MediaWatch:

* Establish a Youth Advisory Committee to guide future work with young people.

* Develop an archive of current images relevant to this age group using images from youth-oriented media products. These images should be incorporated into media literacy resources aimed at this group.

* All media literacy material should include strategies for social action.

* Consider developing a train-the-trainer-resource aimed at youth in order to meet the needs of young people for peer education.

* Create Public Service Announcements (PSAs) that promote media literacy information, for youth. PSAs should include males and females, should address issues of diversity, and ideally would have a "counter culture" component as part of the creative.

* Develop a web-based resource aimed specifically at youth incorporating personal testimonials from youth, colourful graphics and active components such as chat rooms and games.

eliminating sexism in the media

Address | http://www.mediawatch.ca/research/tweens/Default.asp?pg=4 | GO »

media watch

NEWS   CONTACT   FEEDBACK   SITEMAP   LINKS

Research: Analyzing the "Tween" Market | Global Media Monitoring Project | Front and Centre | Cover to Cover | Please Adjust Our Sets | Women Strike Out | Bibliographies | Watching the Watchers 2001

en Français

ABOUT MEDIAWATCH

CAMPAIGNS

COMPLAINTS

GET INVOLVED

MEDIA INDUSTRY

MEDIA LITERACY

RESEARCH

RESOURCES

YOUTH

HOME

Analyzing the "Tween" Market | Methodology

Four focus groups were conducted in November 1999: two in Toronto and two in Burnaby. The same groups were repeated four weeks later in December. Attendance is noted below.

Table 1. Attendance at focus group sessions

	First Session	Second Session
Burnaby-11-12 Yrs.	10	9
Burnaby-13-14 Yrs.	8	4
Toronto-11-12 Yrs.	11	10
Toronto-13-14 Yrs.	8	8
TOTAL	37	31

Recruitment

The research model called for a convenience sample, in order to address safety concerns and financial considerations. Participants were recruited from Burnaby, British Columbia and Toronto, Ontario. MediaWatch sent out approach letters to community centres and schools with which they had professional associations. The first organizations to respond, a community centre in Burnaby and a public school in Toronto, assisted with the recruitment of this convenience sample of young women aged 11-14. It was requested that the teacher/community worker select participants who varied in socio-economic status and ethnic heritage.

Participants

The participants were divided into two groups: 11 & 12 year olds and 13 & 14 year olds to create comfort and facilitate discussion. The atmosphere during the focus groups supported this decision, as there were distinct differences between the age groups.

Address | http://www.mediawatch.ca/research/tweens/Default.asp?pg=4 | GO

The younger Burnaby group was very animated, vocal and forthcoming. These participants attended the same school, were at the top of the social totem pole at their school and were familiar with each other. The older Burnaby group was very reserved, self-conscious and cautious. These 13 and 14 year olds seemed to lack confidence and were hesitant in voicing their opinions. The older participants lived in an economically disadvantaged area, were not familiar with each other and many of them had just started attending a secondary school that is the largest in Canada.

The Toronto participants were unique in that they attend a school for the arts. Securing a position at this school is very competitive and consequently the students are articulate, confident and bright. These individuals will likely have more than average resources available to them as they have studied or trained in their area of specialty for a number of years. These participants do not represent the average tween, but they do represent the opinion leaders for this segment. As a result, these young teenagers may be particularly interested in issues relevant to this study and instrumental in disseminating the results among their peers. In contrast to the Burnaby groups, the differences between the Toronto age groups were subtle. The older group had moderately better verbal communication skills and knowledge of social issues. Both groups conducted themselves in a similar manner: confident and communicative.

Procedures

The format of the discussion was informal and all participants were encouraged to share their comments and respect the opinions of others. Participants were assured their identities would be kept confidential. The discussion was recorded on a laptop computer, on an audiotape recorder and a note taker was present. Participants were provided notepads and pens to take notes throughout the project.

Prior to the first session, respondents were asked to bring in images from the media that caught their attention. During the first session they were asked to comment on:

* Their free time activities
* The images they brought in
* Their experience with media literacy
* Their experience with social action
* Some images collected by the researchers

Address | http://www.mediawatch.ca/research/tweens/Default.asp?pg=4 | GO »

During the four-week interval between sessions the young teens were asked to review notes they took during the session and to use the notebook as a media diary to record images that caught their attention and explore what issues those images raised for them.

The discussion from the first session influenced the development of the discussion for the next session. The research team looked at issues that arose out of the first session and identified those which required more exploration. The second session addressed:

* Positive and negative images and their perceived effect(s)
* Social action options
* Suggestions for resource design and development
* Evaluation of public service announcements

Participants were provided incentives (food coupons, T-shirts) after both sessions. Copies of both moderator guides are located in the Appendix.

Analysis

The focus group audiotapes were transcribed verbatim and verified with notes taken during the sessions. The content of the transcripts was categorized into themes and sub themes. Comments were sorted according to themes and sub themes and analyzed.

eliminating sexism in the media

Address http://www.mediawatch.ca/involved/ GO »

NEWS   CONTACT   FEEDBACK   SITEMAP   LINKS

media watch

Get Involved: Join | Your Opinion | Comment Board | Feedback | Members Only | Letter Writing Guide |

Get INVOLVED

en Français

ABOUT MEDIAWATCH

CAMPAIGNS

COMPLAINTS

GET INVOLVED

MEDIA INDUSTRY

MEDIA LITERACY

This section will give you information on a range of topics, such as how to voice your concerns about offensive media, how to become more involved with MediaWatch, how to conduct a media literacy presentation, how to write a news release, and how to celebrate women in Canadian media who have served as mentors to young women and catalysts for change in the communications field. Get involved...get clicking.

☐ Join

eliminating sexism in the media

Address   http://www.mediawatch.ca/involved/join/   GO »

media
watch   NEWS   CONTACT   FEEDBACK   SITEMAP   LINKS

Get Involved: Join | Your Opinion | Comment Board | Feedback | Members Only | Letter Writing Guide |

Support the Work of Mediawatch

Be Active

You can make a difference. Contact MediaWatch when you see offensive media and we will support you in making change. When we hear from a number of consumers about a negative advertisement, we can call upon our supporters to create a campaign. Make your voice heard by writing letters which pressure media producers to improve their portrayals of women and girls.

Working together can make a difference.

Visit This Web Site

Visit the MediaWatch site regularly to stay up-to-date on issues and current campaigns.

en Français

ABOUT
MEDIAWATCH

CAMPAIGNS

COMPLAINTS

GET
INVOLVED

MEDIA
INDUSTRY

MEDIA
LITERACY

eliminating sexism in the media

After You Read

1. The respondents said that they don't discuss media literacy with their family or friends. In a group of three, list some hints that you could give to a younger sibling or friend to help her become a critical thinker about media. Then brainstorm social action techniques that would teach her how to respond to offensive or negative media material.

Handbook   Link
How to assess
information from media

Before You Read

A decision to shop in a large retail outlet or in a small, family-owned store has an impact on the shopper, the retailer, and the community, as Stephen Leacock details in this short story.

Consider any experiences you have as a customer or as a worker in a large retail outlet. Compare these to any experiences you have as a customer or as a worker in a small retail store. What are the advantages and disadvantages of shopping or working in each? As a customer, which do you prefer: the big or the small retailers? Why?

The Survival of the Fittest

by Stephen Leacock

A bell tinkled over the door of the little drug store as I entered it; which seemed strange in a lighted street of a great city.

But the little store itself, dim even in the centre and dark in the corners, was gloomy enough for country cross roads.

"I have to have the bell," said the man behind the counter, reading my thought, "I'm alone here just now."

"A tooth-brush?" he said in answer to my question. "Yes, I guess I've got some somewhere round here." He was stooping under and behind his counter and his voice came up from below. "I've got some somewhere —" And then as if talking to himself he murmured from behind a pile of cardboard boxes, "I saw some Tuesday."

Had I gone across the street to the brilliant premises of the Cut Rate Pharmaceutical where they burn electric light by the meterful I should no sooner have said "tooth-brush," than one of the ten clerks in white hospital

jackets would have poured a glittering assortment over the counter —
prophylactic, lactic and every other sort.

But I had turned in, I don't know why, to the little store across the way.

"Here, I guess these must be tooth-brushes," he said, reappearing at the
level of the counter with a flat box in his hand.

They must have been presumably, or have once been — at some time
long ago.

"They're tooth-brushes all right," he said, and started looking over them
with an owner's interest.

"What is the price of them?" I asked.

"W — ell," the man said musingly, "I don't — jest — know. I guess it's
written on them likely," and he began to look at the handles.

Over at the Pharmaceutical across the way the words "what price?" would
have precipitated a ready avalanche of figures.

"This one seems to be seventy-five cents," he said and handed me one.

"Is it a good tooth-brush?" I asked.

"It ought to be," he said, "you'd think, at that price."

He had no shop talk, no patter whatever.

Then he looked at the brush again, more closely.

"I don't believe it *is* seventy-five," he muttered. "I think it must be fifteen,
don't you?"

I took it from his hand and looked and said — for it is well to take an occasional step towards the Kingdom of Heaven — that I was certain it was seventy-five.

"Well," said the man, "perhaps it is, my sight is not so good now. I've had too much to do here and the work's been using me up some."

I noticed now as he said this how frail he looked as he bent over his counter wrapping up the tooth-brush.

"I've no sealing wax," he said, "or not handy."

"That doesn't matter," I answered, "just put it in the paper."

Over the way, of course, the tooth-brush would have been done up almost instantaneously, in white enamelled paper, sealed at the end and stamped with a label, as fast as the money paid for it went rattling along an automatic carrier to a cashier.

"You've been very busy, eh?" I asked.

"Well, not so much with customers," he said, "but with fixing up the place." He glanced about him. Heaven only knows what he had fixed. There were no visible signs of it. "You see I've only been in here a couple of months. It was a pretty tough looking place when I came to it. But I've been getting things fixed. First thing I did I put those two carboys in the window with the lights behind them. They show up fine, don't they?"

"Fine!" I repeated.

So fine indeed that the dim yellow light in them reached three or four feet from the jar. But for the streaming light from the great store across the street, the windows of the little shop would have been invisible.

"It's a good location here," he said.

Anyone could have told him that it was the worst location within two miles.

"I'll get it going presently," he went on. "Of course it's uphill just at first. Being such a good location the rent is high. The first two weeks I was here I was losing five dollars a day. But I got those lights in the window and got the stock overhauled a little to make it attractive and last month I reckon I was only losing three dollars a day."

"That's better," I said.

"Oh, yes," he went on, and there was a clear glint of purpose in his eye that contrasted with his sunken cheeks. "I'll get it going. This last two weeks I'm not losing more than, say, two and a half a day, or something like that. The custom is bound to come. You get a place fixed up and made attractive like this and people are sure to come sooner or later."

What it was that was fixed up, and wherein lay the attractiveness I do not know. It could not be seen with the outward eye. Perhaps after two months' work of piling dusty boxes now this way, now that, and putting little candles behind the yellow carboys to try the effect, some inward vision came that lighted the place up with an attractiveness wanting even in the glass and marble glitter of the pharmacy across the way.

"Yes, sir," continued the man, "I mean to stay with it. I'll get things into shape here, fix it up a little more and soon I'll have it" — here his face radiated with a vision of hope — "so that I won't lose a single cent."

I looked at him in surprise. So humble an ambition it had never been my lot to encounter.

"All that bothers me," he went on, "is my health. It's a nice business the drug business: I like it, but it takes it out of you. You've got to be alert and keen all the time, thinking out plans to please the custom when it comes. Often I don't sleep well nights for the rush of it."

I looked about the little shop, as gloomy and sleepful as the mausoleum of an Eastern king, and wondered by what alchemy of the mind the little druggist found it a very vortex of activity.

"But I can fix my health," he returned. "I may have to get someone in here and go away for a spell. Perhaps I'll do it. The doctor was saying he thought I might take a spell off and think out a few more wrinkles while I'm away."

At the word "doctor" I looked at him more closely, and I saw then what was plain enough to see but for the dim light of the little place — the thin flush on the cheek, the hopeful mind, the contrast of the will to live and the need to die, God's little irony on man, it was all there plain enough to read. The "spell" for which the little druggist was going is that which is written in letters of sorrow over the sunlit desolation of Arizona and the mountains of Colorado.

A month went by before I passed that way again. I looked across at the little store and I read the story in its drawn blinds and the padlock on its door.

The little druggist had gone away for a spell. And they told me, on inquiry, that his journey had been no further than to the cemetery behind the town where he lies now, musing, if he still can, on the law of the survival of the fittest in this well-adjusted world.

And they say that the shock of the addition of his whole business to the great pharmacy across the way scarcely disturbed a soda-siphon.

After You Read

Handbook Link
How to understand themes in literature

How to recognize allusion and irony

1. Create a chart with three sections. Label the first "Categories," the second "Cut Rate Pharmaceuticals," and the third "The Little Drug Store." Compare how the two stores are different, using such categories as location, price, service, and goals. Write to explain where you would prefer to work.
2. With your class, discuss the title of the story. Why do you think Leacock chose it? Do you think it is an appropriate title? Why?

Before You Read

According to David Chilton, who specializes in financial planning, saving your money takes simple common sense. Chilton wrote a fictional book, based on fact, to explain his theories. Before you read this excerpt from his book, make a list of any rules you follow (or would like to be able to follow) to save your money.

The Wealthy Barber

THE COMMON SENSE GUIDE TO SUCCESSFUL FINANCIAL PLANNING

by David Chilton

Trust me … Good financial planning is nothing more than common sense. The old KISS philosophy at its best. Keep It Simple … Sarnians.

"We all share pretty much the same goals — an annual vacation, a nice car, a comfortable home, a cottage, early retirement, the ability to give our children what they need and want … and baseball season's tickets. These are the average Canadian's goals.

"And I'll tell you right now, they're easily attainable … easily. Especially if you start young. Time is your greatest ally. If you three start now, I guarantee you that you will exceed all your goals — dramatically.

"Look at me. I'm a barber, for crying out loud! I'm proud of my business, but I'm the first to admit that I'm not pulling in a doctor's salary. Far from it. Yet you'd be hard-pressed to find many professionals with better financial statements than mine. I hope it doesn't sound like I'm bragging. It's just that it's important for you to know that if someone as simple as me can become wealthy, it's certainly possible for you geniuses."

"You're not simple, Roy. Maybe a bit slow, but not simple," Tom wisecracked.

"I don't want to seem cynical, Roy, but if it's so easy, why isn't everyone doing it?" I asked.

"Lack of knowledge. Your dad and I talk about this all the time. Our schools don't teach money skills. Our family members don't talk money. And just as important, there are very few places for an aspiring learner to turn. Our financial industry is geared toward product sales, not toward dispensing well-rounded financial planning advice.

"Most insurance agents sell cash-value policies; mutual fund salespeople sell funds and tax shelters; brokers sell stocks and bonds; bankers sell guaranteed investment certificates, and so on and so on. You can't blame them. Product sales are where the money is, so very few of them are true *financial planners.*"

"Are there any good product-oriented financial planners?" I asked.

"Sure there are, but none can do as well for you as you can do for yourself if you're well-informed."

Tom looked quizzical. "What about fee-only planners?"

"Don't depend too much on financial planners," Roy replied emphatically. "Learn for yourself. Nobody cares as much about your money as you do. You have to take responsibility for your own future. As I said earlier, the great thing is, it's not hard."

"Dad said last night that some old guy taught you a golden secret when you were young. What is it?" I probed.

"Oh, no. I'm saving that for next month. If you only pay attention once in the next seven months, let it be next month. If you follow that lesson, even if you do everything else poorly, I guarantee you that someday you'll be rich."

"Can't we start today?" I implored.

"No," to my chagrin, was his firm answer. "My granddaughter's going to be here in five minutes. I'm taking care of her for the afternoon. Cathy can stay, but I want you two out of here ASAP. Emily's only three years old, and I don't want to scare her off men for the rest of her life."

Never before had I been tempted to get my hair cut two consecutive weeks. Roy had really piqued my interest. I've known him all my life and he has always come across as a very modest man. The matter-of-fact confidence he displayed when discussing Tom's, Cathy's and my financial futures was out of character — and contagious. There was no doubt in my mind that I had taken the first step along the road to financial prosperity.

The Ten-Percent Solution

I can't remember a rainstorm worse than the one that occurred on the third Saturday in May. A north wind had come up and was blowing at seventy kilometres an hour. That, combined with a torrential downpour, had caused most Sarnians to stay inside. Most smart Sarnians, that is.

There was no way Tom, Cathy and I were going to miss out on the golden secret. We had been looking forward to it for a month. We were so excited that we even skipped breakfast.

As usual, I drove. My parents' house has indoor access to the garage and both Tom and Cathy have underground parking, so, surprisingly, it was possible to remain perfectly dry until we arrived at the shop. On the way there, Cathy suggested that Roy might be closed because of the weather. Tom and I just laughed. Roy hasn't missed an entire day of work in thirty-seven years for any reason. He had even opened on the morning of his daughter's wedding.

With so few people venturing out, we were able to get the parking spot right in front of Miller's. Between our umbrellas and his awning, we managed to get from the car to the shop door relatively undrenched.

It was locked.

Clyde, with his Florida tan, was standing on the other side peering out through the glass. "All you have to do is say 'We love the Blue Jays,' and I'll let you in. We've got coffee brewing," he chirped in his reedy voice.

By this time, we were starting to get pretty wet. And annoyed. The angle of the rain was

such that it was impossible to protect ourselves anymore, even with the help of the awning and umbrellas.

"I love the Blue Jays!" Cathy cried, not amused.

Traitor. Tom and I stood stoically.

Clyde shook his head and let all of us in. "You boys really are die-hards. You should seek professional help."

"You telling us we need a psychiatrist is like Karl Malden telling someone she needs a nose job," Tom murmured, as he towelled off.

"I thought you three might not show. It's terrible out there," Roy commented.

"What? And miss our long-awaited, eagerly anticipated first lesson? You've got to be kidding!" I retorted. "What I can't believe is that these three have shown up in this weather," I added, motioning toward Clyde, Jimmy, and James Murray. I'm not sure why I always use James Murray's given and family names. Perhaps it's because when I was young

I thought his name was James-Murray, like Billy-Bob or Bobby-Joe.

"They wouldn't miss free coffee and doughnuts if we had a tornado. You should know that by now," Roy replied, as he straightened up the counter.

"Roy, I've been looking forward to today for a month. My financial situation is getting worse instead of better," Cathy began impatiently. "I can hardly wait to hear what you have to say."

"Okay, let's get started. As your father has probably told you, I took over this shop thirty-odd years ago when my dad died. I got lucky and a few of my ideas paid off. After a couple of years, I was making a pretty good income. Very good for a barber. I added a couple of chairs in the other room, and all in all, things were moving along well.

"I decided to make barbering my life's work. I knew my income from the shop was respectable, but it was never going to make me a rich man. That bothered me because, frankly, I wanted to be wealthy. I grew up poor, and believe me, poverty is something you don't acquire a taste for. I didn't want to live in town in a tiny one-bedroom home — I wanted to live on the lake. I wanted to own this building, too. I wanted a nice car, trips to Europe, and some of the other fine things life has to offer.

"The only way I could accomplish all that on my income was to budget and save like a madman. Or at least that's what I thought. So I developed a budget — so much for rent, so much for food, so much for clothes, so much for savings … you know. Two years after starting to budget, I had very little to show for it. Sure enough, at the end of each month I'd end up saying, 'So much for savings,' but unfortunately it didn't mean what I had hoped it would mean. It was pretty depressing.

"Like you, Dave, I realized I didn't know anything about financial planning, and it was high time to learn. I didn't have a father to turn to, so I went to a person who I figured must know a lot about money, he had so much — old Mr. White.

"I explained my situation to him. I told him what I wanted to achieve. 'Is it possible?' I asked.

"He told me, 'Wealth beyond your wildest dreams is possible if you learn the golden secret: *Invest ten percent of all you make for long-term growth.* If you follow that one simple guideline, someday you'll be a very rich man.'"

"That's it?" asked Tom. "I could have gotten that from a Bank of Nova Scotia commercial!"

"Patience, Tom," replied Roy. "Patience. I felt the same way myself. I wasn't very impressed when Mr. White told me, either. My budget was already designed to save even more than ten percent, and at that point, it wasn't working and I was far from wealthy. But Mr. White went on to explain a few things that I'll tell you now, things that turn a seemingly simple sentence into an extremely powerful thought.

"Cathy, if you invested $2,400 a year, say $200 a month, for the next thirty years, and averaged a fifteen percent return a year, how much money do you think you'd end up with?" challenged Roy.

"Well, $2,400 times thirty is $72,000."

"I'm impressed," I interrupted.

" ... plus growth ... I don't know ... I'd say $200,000. Maybe not quite that much," Cathy concluded.

"Wrong. The answer is $1.4 million," Roy declared.

"Get real!" was Tom's initial reaction. When he realized that Roy was serious, he paled. "What about inflation? And where am I going to get fifteen percent? For that matter, where am I going to get $200 a month?" he stammered.

"All good questions, Tom, and we'll get to them in due course. Dave, you try one. If you had started putting thirty dollars a month away, the equivalent of a dollar a day, at age eighteen and you continued until age sixty-five, averaging a fifteen percent annual return, how much would you end up with?"

"I hate math, Roy, but I'll give it a shot. Thirty dollars a month is $360 a year, times forty-seven years ... Anybody have a calculator?"

"It's just under $17,000," injected Roy.

"Plus growth. I'll say abut $70,000."

"Close," responded Roy. "The answer is approximately $2,000,000!"

"Bull," scoffed Tom, as if he had read my mind.

"No, not bull ... magic. The magic of compound interest — interest on principal and interest, not just simple interest on principal. The eighth wonder of the world. Thirty dollars a month, a dollar a day, will magically turn into around two million. And do you know what's even more impressive? You know someone who has done it," Roy said proudly

"Thirty-five years ago, I started my savings with thirty dollars a month, which was approximately ten percent of my earnings. I have achieved just under a fifteen percent average annual return. In addition, as my income rose, my ten percent saving component rose accordingly. Thirty dollars a month became sixty dollars, then a hundred, and eventually hundreds of dollars a month.

"You three are looking at a very wealthy man."

"Are you trying to tell us that by saving ten percent of every pay cheque you've turned yourself into a millionaire?" an intense Tom demanded.

"Precisely" was the incredible response.

Roy Miller, a millionaire! I sat stunned. I knew he had done well, but a millionaire? To the best of my knowledge, I'd never met a millionaire, and I sure didn't expect my first to be my barber. Roy was clearly deriving great pleasure from the disbelief on our three faces.

After You Read

1. In your reading response journal, summarize what Roy says are the goals of the average Canadian. Explain, giving reasons, how your goals are the same or different.

2. Roy says that in order to attain your goals, "you have to take responsibility for your own future." With a partner, summarize the advice that Roy gives to help his clients take responsibility for achieving their goals and becoming wealthy.

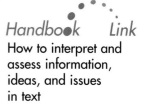

Handbook Link
How to interpret and assess information, ideas, and issues in text

Before You Read

Think of a person whom you think has vision, determination, faith, and courage. What difficulties has this person overcome in life? What has this person taught you by example?

MOTHER *to Son*

by Langston Hughes

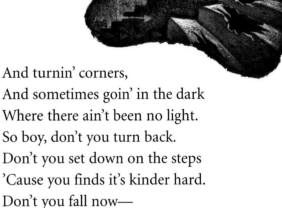

Well, son, I'll tell you:
Life for me ain't been no crystal stair.
It's had tacks in it,
And splinters,
And boards torn up,
And places with no carpet on the floor—
Bare.
But all the time
I'se been a-climbin' on,
And reachin' landin's,
And turnin' corners,
And sometimes goin' in the dark
Where there ain't been no light.
So boy, don't you turn back.
Don't you set down on the steps
'Cause you finds it's kinder hard.
Don't you fall now—
For I'se still goin', honey,
I'se still climbin',
And life for me ain't been no crystal stair.

After You Read

1. Write a paragraph to describe how the poet believes that wooden stairs are like life. Think of other ways that stairs are like life, and write a second paragraph to describe them.
2. List the metaphors that the poet uses to describe the decisions that people make on the stairway of their life. Reflect, in writing, on the meaning of each. Give examples from your own life to support your responses.

Handbook   Link
How to analyze
the role of description

From our earliest days, we learn that other people impact our life. Learning to work with others, sharing our strengths, knowing their strengths — these skills make us better in life and on the job.

This unit begins with rules for working together that are so simple they last a lifetime. It continues with a variety of texts that describe how people work together, why people work together, and the challenges and rewards of teamwork.

CONTENTS

Before You Read

According to Robert Fulghum, we all learned some of life's most important lessons when we were very young. Make a list of three or four important but simple lessons about life that you learned as a child. As you read, compare your life lessons to the author's.

ALL I REALLY NEED TO KNOW I LEARNED IN KINDERGARTEN

by Robert Fulghum

All I really need to know about how to live and what to do and how to be I learned in kindergarten. Wisdom was not at the top of the graduate-school mountain, but there in the sandpile at Sunday School. These are the things I learned:

Share everything.

Play fair.

Don't hit people.

Put things back where you found them.

Clean up your own mess.

Don't take things that aren't yours.

Say you're sorry when you hurt somebody.

Wash your hands before you eat.

Flush.

Warm cookies and cold milk are good for you.

Live a balanced life—learn some and think some and draw and paint and sing and dance and play and work every day some.

Take a nap every afternoon.

When you go out into the world, watch out for traffic, hold hands, and stick together.

Be aware of wonder. Remember the little seed in the Styrofoam cup: The roots go down and the plant goes up and nobody really knows how or why, but we are all like that.

Goldfish and hamsters and white mice and even the little seed in the Styrofoam cup—they all die. So do we.

And then remember the Dick-and-Jane books and the first word you learned—the biggest word of all—**LOOK**.

Everything you need to know is in there somewhere. The Golden Rule and love and basic sanitation. Ecology and politics and equality and sane living.

Take any one of those items and extrapolate it into sophisticated adult terms and apply it to your family life or your work or your government or your world and it holds true and clear and firm. Think what a better world it would be if we all—the whole world—had cookies and milk about three o'clock every afternoon and then lay down with our blankies for a nap. Or if all governments had as a basic policy to always put things back where they found them and to clean up their own mess.

And it is still true, no matter how old you are—when you go out into the world, it is best to hold hands and stick together.

After You Read

1. Think about how this advice could be applied to the workplace. Discuss with a partner how these lessons would help to create a pleasant workplace environment. If you have had a job, think of how the advice would have helped to resolve any workplace conflicts you witnessed. Together, summarize your ideas in your notebooks.

2. Think about how different situations, people, places, and experiences have taught you lessons about life. Following the format of the selection, write a piece called "All I Really Need to Know I Learned _____."

Handbook   Link
How to interpret and assess information, ideas, and issues in text

Before You Read

Most of the communicating we do is through talking with other people. The rules about how we talk to one another are mostly unwritten, but each of us knows that we wouldn't talk to a community leader with exactly the same language we'd use to talk to our friends.

In Internet chat rooms, we don't know the real people behind the names. So do we need written rules for chatting on the Internet? What should they be? Discuss this issue with your small group. Then scan the screen below and read the Chat Room Policy. What are the advantages and disadvantages of following each of these rules?

Making It Work Chat Room

ASSERTIVE JEANS Hey, you. Yes, you. Buy these jeans. Now!

SEARCH | http://www.makingitwork.com | GO »

○ Live Home Page   ○ Support   ○ Office   ○ Font Manager

Making It Work Chat Room

HISTORY   FAVOURITES   SEARCH   PAGE HOLDER

Welcome to the Making It Work Chat Room. This public chat room is the place where teens can help one another to "make it work" by exchanging information and views about employment. Please join in! The chat room is open and moderated from 9:00a.m to 12:00p.m and 5:00p.m to 11:00p.m every day. If you have a suggestion or tip for a fellow teen job-seeker, this is the place to share it!

CHAT ROOM POLICY

No swearing, insults, intolerant or sexual chat.

No advertising products or services. No get-rich-quick, multilevel marketing, or other scams.

No flooding or repeating.

No posting of images.

Be polite and respectful.

If you agree with these chat room policies, click here to join the discussion.

Ready to Chat

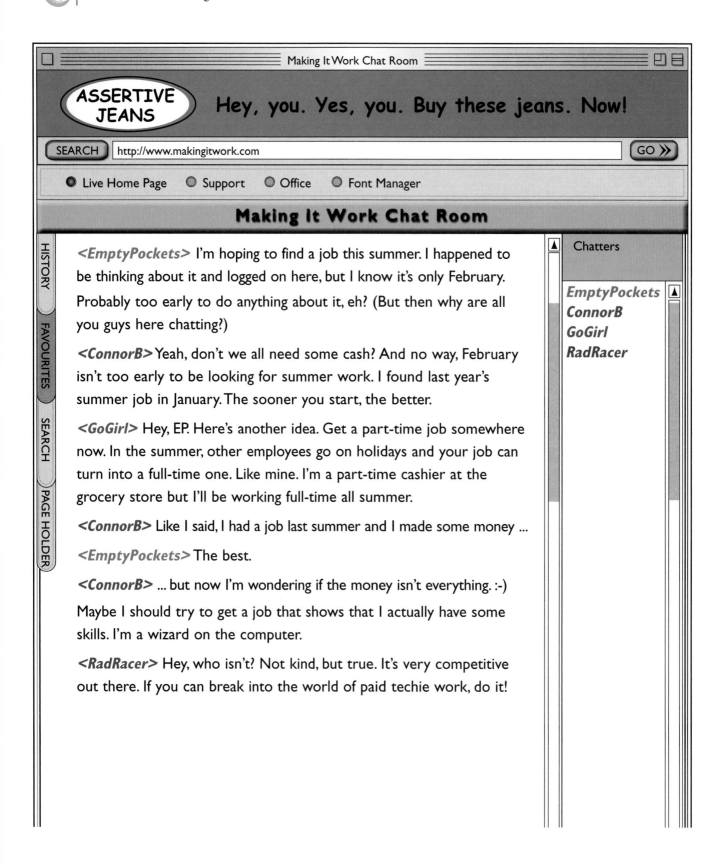

Making It Work Chat Room

ASSERTIVE JEANS

Hey, you. Yes, you. Buy these jeans. Now!

SEARCH | http://www.makingitwork.com | GO »

● Live Home Page   ○ Support   ○ Office   ○ Font Manager

Making It Work Chat Room

HISTORY FAVOURITES SEARCH PAGE HOLDER

Chatters

EmptyPockets
ConnorB
GoGirl
RadRacer

<EmptyPockets> I'm hoping to find a job this summer. I happened to be thinking about it and logged on here, but I know it's only February. Probably too early to do anything about it, eh? (But then why are all you guys here chatting?)

<ConnorB> Yeah, don't we all need some cash? And no way, February isn't too early to be looking for summer work. I found last year's summer job in January. The sooner you start, the better.

<GoGirl> Hey, EP. Here's another idea. Get a part-time job somewhere now. In the summer, other employees go on holidays and your job can turn into a full-time one. Like mine. I'm a part-time cashier at the grocery store but I'll be working full-time all summer.

<ConnorB> Like I said, I had a job last summer and I made some money ...

<EmptyPockets> The best.

<ConnorB> ... but now I'm wondering if the money isn't everything. :-) Maybe I should try to get a job that shows that I actually have some skills. I'm a wizard on the computer.

<RadRacer> Hey, who isn't? Not kind, but true. It's very competitive out there. If you can break into the world of paid techie work, do it!

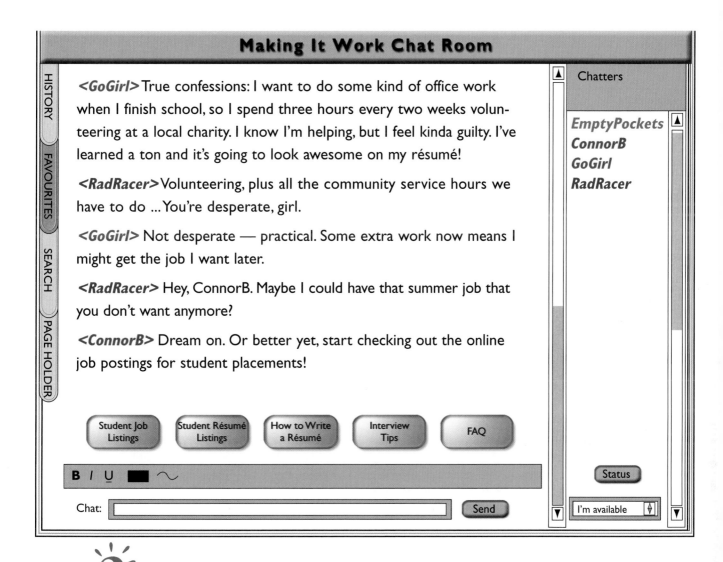

Making It Work Chat Room

<GoGirl> True confessions: I want to do some kind of office work when I finish school, so I spend three hours every two weeks volunteering at a local charity. I know I'm helping, but I feel kinda guilty. I've learned a ton and it's going to look awesome on my résumé!

<RadRacer> Volunteering, plus all the community service hours we have to do ... You're desperate, girl.

<GoGirl> Not desperate — practical. Some extra work now means I might get the job I want later.

<RadRacer> Hey, ConnorB. Maybe I could have that summer job that you don't want anymore?

<ConnorB> Dream on. Or better yet, start checking out the online job postings for student placements!

Chatters

EmptyPockets
ConnorB
GoGirl
RadRacer

Student Job Listings | Student Résumé Listings | How to Write a Résumé | Interview Tips | FAQ

B / U ■ ～

Chat: [   ]   Send

Status

I'm available

After You Read

1. Write a short analysis of this chat room by answering several questions: Who is the target audience of the chat room? What is the purpose of the chat room? Comment on the organization and ease of use of the chat room. If you have visited other chat rooms, include a comparison between this one and others you have seen.

2. Share your analysis with a small group, and discuss why people's responses may differ. Then discuss the accuracy of chat rooms and create a list of simple rules to follow when visiting and getting information from a chat room.

Handbook   Link

How to understand and analyze audience reaction

How to assess information from media

Before You Read

Scan the text for four important "short-cuts" to finding a job. How is the print designed to help you find the main points? When you find the short-cuts, discuss with a small group what helpful hints you think the writer will share. Then read the article.

Pros, peers share youth job-search secrets

By Barbara B. Simmons
SPECIAL TO THE STAR

"I wish there was a short-cut to getting a job," lamented Roberto, a student attending my résumé preparation workshop. He was expressing the sentiment of many time-pressured students facing the realities that come with doing a job search.

There are short-cuts, and some are close at hand — as close as the staff expertise and all the resources at your school's career centre, and as close as today's careers column, a compilation of tips from experts and the wisdom of students who landed jobs.

■ **Know thy self.** Most employment experts believe personal awareness is the cornerstone of marketing yourself in résumés and letters to employers and in interviews.

To gain that clarity, Bev Heim-Myers, manager of recruitment at TD Canada Trust, suggests people confer with former employers who can help identify examples of your valued contributions, with co-workers to identify your best attributes, and with your peers to gain insight into other skills, such as team-playing or leadership skills.

Orden Braham, a graduate of George Brown College's desktop publishing program, assessed his strengths as a prelude to planning his new business, "epromotions." His tip to budding entrepreneurs is to know what you're good at and enjoy doing. If you don't have the skills nec-

essary to start your new venture, develop them by getting relevant training and experience in existing businesses.

Ryerson Polytechnic University student Owen Field has obtained many interviews and landed jobs. As a result of his information technology co-op experiences, he has developed confidence in applying for positions even if they seem out of reach. Owen's approach could work for you: He suggests that if you have at least 50 per cent of the experience listed in the job description, apply for the job and present other experience or skills that will be a benefit, in the long term, to the position or company.

For an online self-assessment exercise, visit: *www.adm.uwaterloo.ca/infocecs/CRC* and click the Career Development Manual link.

■ **Do your homework.** Maintain a database of information and contacts collected from the Internet, the company, career fairs, libraries, career and employment centres and professional associations.

According to Kevin Makra, a University of Toronto graduate and editor/publisher of *The Canada Student Employment Guide 2001* and *The Canadian Job Directory*, gathering information about targeted industries and companies will help you in many ways.

You will find employers and positions you never knew existed. You can decide if a company is a good match for you and your skills. Your knowledge can make a positive impression on the employer in the interview.

Heim-Myers suggests this next tip for expanding and learning from your network.

Seek out alumni from your university or college who are working for organizations in which you are interested. They will be happy to share inside information and insights to help you prepare for interviews.

Marci Katz, 17, works part-time, volunteers in her community, and is on her high school student council. Her brand of research is easy, informal and also applies to obtaining summer jobs.

She urges young people to talk to friends who are working — you'll quickly learn what their employers are like and which places are hiring. You can also find out the types of interviews and questions to expect.

To review hundreds of online job opportunities, obtain Campus WorkLink's password from your school's career centre; for Internships visit *www.careeredge.org*.

■ **Act like a pro.** First impressions are lasting and the telephone is often the first contact with prospective employers. Catherine Allen, assistant director of human resources at Hilton Toronto, offers these tips:

When leaving a message on voice mail, avoid repetitive 'ums' or phrases with 'like' and 'is that OK?.'

Avoid using a cell phone when leaving a message for an employer. Often the sound is unclear and what the employer hears is garbled.

Kevin Makra says students can handle interviews more skillfully by being prepared with strategies to apply before, during and after the competition. He suggests that, prior to the real thing, conduct practice interviews with a friend playing the role of interviewer. It's a low-stress way to learn and become comfortable in interviews.

In interviews, be yourself, smile sincerely, make eye contact and shake hands confidently with the interviewer.

Heim-Myers has an easy tip to remember: follow and practice the S.H.A.R.P. approach. Speak to the gaps in the résumé; Honesty is best; Articulate your strengths; Relax; and Passion sells, so be passionate about yourself and about the job.

And also, stay focused. To get in the right frame of mind, arrive a bit early, turn off your cell phone or pager, visualize staying confident. Use positive language, be prepared with relevant questions to ask, and request business cards to gather correct names, titles, and addresses.

Following the interview, send a thank-you note (it may be hand-written, word processed or electronic). Refer to something applicable to help the interviewer recall you.

■ **Follow up.** If you are not the successful candidate, Heim-Myers urges you to learn from the experience.

Phone the interviewer and ask for feedback. Keep an open mind as you hear the comments. Your goal is to be better-prepared next time around. And ask the interviewer if it is possible for you to reapply and seek his/her input as to a good time to do so.

Finally, remember to be good to yourself. This is the beginning of a journey, not the end. Keep trying — the right job and the right fit will happen. Best of luck, everyone!

Barbara B. Simmons is a counsellor in the career and employment services of George Brown College.

After You Read

1. Write "job search" in the centre of a sheet of paper. Branching out from the centre, list each of Simmon's four points and summarize her information under each point. Did she give the information you predicted?
2. To what other situations could you apply Simmons' hints? Explain.

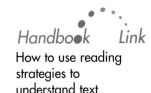

Handbook Link
How to use reading strategies to understand text

Before You Read

Make a list of the ways you think employers could reward employees for good work, reward employees for good effort, and motivate employees toward doing their best. Number the items in order of importance, with 1 being the most important. Explain your top three choices to a partner, and describe how each would motivate you on the job.

THE DILBERT™ PRINCIPLE

by Scott Adams

After You Read

1. Discuss with a partner what the cartoonist is saying about job recognition. How is irony used to convey this message?
2. Look at the list you created before reading. Choose one of the items and use it to create an ironic cartoon about employee recognition.

Handbook Link
How to recognize allusion and irony

Before You Read

Words mean more than their dictionary definitions. They also have connotations, or associated meanings, from our life experience. When we read certain words, we bring our own associations to the word, colouring their meaning for us. In your small group, discuss the gender you associate with each of the words that follow. How do people's life experiences affect how they understand words?

Secretary
Nurse
President
Doctor

Words That Count Women In

by The Ontario Women's Directorate

The Language Barrier

O Canada, our home and native land
True patriot love in all thy sons command ...

Picture two children, a girl and a boy, singing these lyrics. Think of the images formed in their minds. The boy sees countless males like himself, all standing on guard for their country. He feels fully part of the patriotic fervor, a true son of Canada.

The girl is not so lucky. Since our national anthem says nothing about daughters, she can't help wondering whether it applies to her. Can only men be patriots?

"O Canada," the symbol of our democratic spirit, excludes more than half the population. The single word "sons" tells women they do not belong. You could argue that other words express the anthem's point ... [or] that "sons" is just a synonym for "people."

But words create images more powerful than any definition. If you don't choose your words with care, they may send a message you never intended: in this case, that it's a man's world. This song helps perpetuate inequality for all women.

Words most of us use daily do exactly that. "Weatherman" suggests that all weather reporters are male. "Mankind" portrays maleness as the norm for our species and excludes women.

It's a Matter of Clarity

All speakers and writers share the same goal: clear communication. Male-biased words don't meet the challenge. They hark back to a world that no longer exists, a world with no place for women's aspirations. They cause needless doubts and needless offense. Unless you learn to spot them and change them, they'll distract attention from your point.

Some Advice on the "Rules" of Inclusive Language

Changing lifelong habits calls for patience at first, but don't be suprised if your writing improves. Many biased expressions are clichés. Without them, you'll stretch your creativity. A few simple ground rules will get you started.

The Pronoun Puzzle

Until recently, most people didn't see anything wrong with using the generic "he" to refer to both men and women. Women's growing disagreement has inspired some pretty cumbersome proposals for a third person singular pronoun of indeterminate sex. "S/he" makes most readers wince; "he or she" will do in a pinch, but grates with constant repetition.

What's a frustrated writer to do? Try one of three tricks:

Make the sentence plural.

Becoming a doctor can be a lonely experience, one that takes a toll not only on the young doctor, but also on his patients.

changes to

Becoming a doctor can be a lonely experience, one that takes a toll not only on young doctors, but also on patients.

Change "his" to "the."

The member will promptly disclose to his client any interest in a business which may affect the client.

changes to

The member will promptly disclose to the client any interest in a business which may affect the client.

Alternate between "she" and "he."
Whether you're referring to university students, employees or kids at summer camp, this tactic beats constant repetition of "he or she." Just watch out for sex-typed examples. The employee dashing to the daycare centre is not necessarily "she." The youngster in tears over a classmate's teasing might be "he."

In a pinch, change "he" to "one" or "the individual," or use the passive voice. But both techniques, while often recommended, tend to make for stilted writing. Once you get the hang of the others, you shouldn't need them.

One Sex Fits All?

"Some entomologists consider insects to be man's chief competitor, mainly because insects and man both utilize the same things."
— Entomology in Canada:
Career Opportunities

Synonyms for "man" abound (see "Words to the Wise"), so this verbal gaffe is easily fixed. Consider just one possible revision:
Some entomologists consider insects to be humans' chief competitor, mainly because insects utilize the same things we do.

You may wonder why "humans" should be preferable to "man." Similar as the two words appear, they come from different roots — "humans" from the Latin "homo" and "man" from the Old English "mann." Both roots originally meant "human being," but "man" developed its gender-specific connotation as long ago as the 10th century.

"Man" also turns up as a verb. Here's an example from the front page of The *Globe and Mail*:

"We have … found … a declining confidence in our system of parliamentary democracy, and in the politicians who man the system."
— pollster Michael Adams

Is it just male politicians who have fallen out of favour? If not, then why not change "man" to "run"?

Type-Casting

When astronaut Dr. Roberta Bondar made her 1992 space flight, The Toronto *Star* ran this front-page headline:
"Canadian in space does 'housework': Bondar spends hour tidying up shuttle"

A highly skilled physician and scientist, Dr. Bondar was spending no more time on "housework" than her male colleagues on the shuttle. Her efforts really focused on scientific experiments — and had she been male, the male headline writer undoubtedly would have said so.

The *Star* had trivialized a Canadian hero, and readers were outraged. Within a day, more than 150 calls had bombarded the paper. Not for years had it faced such fury.

We don't hear much about Eric Lindros's cooking, or how much time Brian Mulroney spends with his kids. But let a woman step into the spotlight, and reporters suddenly wonder about her cooking schedule and her childcare arrangements. If you've ever introduced a female speaker, you may have made the same blunder. We suggest this guideline: don't mention a woman's domestic life unless you would make the same comment of a man in her position. One more word of advice: don't assume a woman runs a home.

The Beauty Factor

"She's so fresh-faced, so blue-eyed, so ruby-lipped, so 12-car-pile-up gorgeous, 5'5" and 114 pounds of peacekeeping missile."
— *Sports Illustrated*
on figure skater Katerina Witt

Women's looks, like their homemaking, garner needless attention.

A Canadian magazine once published an article by a woman on the Toronto Blue Jays — more specifically, on watching their bottoms under those tight uniforms. She speculated at length on which Blue Jay cut the cutest figure while at bat. In short, she wrote about men the way men always write about women. Angry letters accused the magazine of trivializing baseball.

Two themes stand out in irrelevant descriptions of women. One is sexuality, the other fragility. Here's an example of woman-as-rosebud prose:

"She is a young, elegant woman with the pert appeal of a gamine. But her fragile good looks contradict the power she wields in the fiercely competitive fashion world."
— *Flare* on Fairweather president
Lynn Posluns

"Pert" and "gamine," words only applied to women, shrink the executive's stature. "See how tiny she is," the passage seems to say. "She's not one of those power-hungry women. She wouldn't hurt a fly." Equally belittling — to all women, not just Posluns — is the presumed opposition between power and good looks. Why shouldn't female presidents look good? Does power turn women into drab, grim-faced martinets? In describing a man, one would describe his competence, never his appearance.

As with childcare arrangements, so with looks: if you wouldn't comment on a man's, then don't comment on a woman's.

The Parallelism Principle

"Lyn Goes After Rae"
— The Toronto *Sun*

What's wrong with this headline? It denies a woman, [former] Ontario Liberal leader Lyn McLeod, the same respect it gives a man, [former] Premier Bob Rae. Most news media identify adults by their last names. This practice should apply to men and women alike. To eliminate the bias, just make the headline parallel: either "Lyn Goes After Bobby" or "McLeod Goes After Rae."

Fair's fair. The same principle applies in daily life. If you are addressing men as "Dr." or "Professor," be just as formal with the women in the group. Those who have no titles deserve the courtesy of "Ms." And never call a woman by her first name unless you expect her to use yours.

Parallelism also means that men shouldn't always go first. Vary your style with phrases like "she and he," "hers and his," and "women and men."

Women Writers, Male Nurses: Does It Matter?

Have you ever read an article that identifies an expert as a "woman doctor"? Or heard that someone was treated by a "male nurse"? Many references to gender serve no useful purpose, because they put the emphasis on personal characteristics rather than occupational knowledge and skills.

Don't mention gender unless it is key to understanding the message, as in this headline from The *Globe and Mail*:

"Male secretary ruled sexism victim"

Letter Perfect

If your letter addressed "Dear Sir" ends up on the desk of a vice-president who's a woman, you've committed a major business blunder. Here's how to keep in step with the times:

• Don't be too quick to assume that you're writing to a man. "R. L. Jones" could be a woman … The gender-neutral salutation is "Dear R. L. Jones."

• How to avoid the "Dear Sir" dilemma? "Dear Madam or Sir" is a time-honoured formal solution. Address by title or role, such as "Dear Managing Director," has become increasingly acceptable. Better still, do some research … and find out the name of the person you want to reach.

• Use Ms. salutations instead of Mrs. or Miss.

• Always use a woman's professional title (Judge, Professor) in situations where you would use one for a man. The same rule applies when writing to a man and woman couple: avoid "Mr. and Mrs." salutations unless the couple has indicated a preference for this address. If a woman has kept her birth name, the correct form might be "Dear Jane Jones and David Hodges." If the woman has a professional title, you might write "Dear Dr. Kahn and Mr. De Marco." In any case, wives are not extensions of their male spouses. "Dear Nancy and Tom Cohen" is preferable to "Dear Mr. and Mrs. Tom Cohen."

• Keep your closing simple. Don't sign yourself "Ms." or "Mr." unless you use your initials or have a gender-neutral first name, such as Terry or Chris.

*** GLOSSARY ***
Words to the Wise

The Work World

Inclusive job titles welcome both women and men to a variety of occupations, and help organizations maximize their "people power." Unless there's a specific reason otherwise (like an article profiling women in traditionally male occupations) keep the emphasis on the job, not the gender. Some terms are in transition — "actress" to "actor," "ballerina" to "ballet dancer" — while others, like "police officer," are already well-established.

Non-inclusive	Inclusive	Non-inclusive	Inclusive
actress	actor	ferryman	ferry operator
ad man, advertising man	advertising representative	foreman	foreperson, supervisor
airman, aviatrix	pilot, aviator, flyer	frogman	diver, underwater technician
alderman	municipal councillor	gasman	gas fitter, gas pipe installer
anchorman	anchor, newscaster, announcer	girl Friday	person Friday
assemblyman (manufacturing)	assembler	harbour master	harbour chief, harbour person
assemblyman (politics)	assembly member, legislator	insurance man	insurance agent
		journeyman	trade worker
ballerina	ballet dancer	landlady	landperson, householder, building manager
barmaid	bartender		
businessman	business person, business executive, professional, entrepreneur	lineman	lineperson, lineworker, line installer
		longshoreman	dockhand, shorehand, longshoreperson
career girl, career woman	executive, manager, professional	mailman	letter carrier
cameraman, cameramen	camera operator, camera crew	meter maid (traffic)	parking constable
		meter man (utilities)	meter reader
cleaning lady	cleaner	newsman	journalist, reporter
clergyman	cleric, member of the clergy	papergirl, paperboy	paper carrier
		patrolman	patrol officer
comedienne	comedian, comic	policeman, policewoman	police officer
craftsman	artisan	poetess	poet
draftsman	draftsperson, drafting technician	quarryman	quarrier, quarry worker
engineman	engine operator	repairman	repairer, technician
fireman	fire fighter	saleslady, salesman	sales representative, sales agent
fisherman, fishermen	fisher, fishing crew		

Non-inclusive	Inclusive	Non-inclusive	Inclusive
seamstress	tailor, dressmaker, alterationist	union man	unionist, union member, union organizer
serviceman	service representative, technician	waitress	waiter, server
sideman	side-player, backup musician	watchman	guard, security guard
		weatherman	weather reporter, meteorologist
steward, stewardess	flight attendant		
taxman	tax collector	workman	worker

The Human Family

Generic use of the word "man" will backfire, and have the reverse effect on your audience. Ironically, a politican calling for the "unity of mankind" will be excluding more than half the populace.

Non-inclusive	Inclusive	Non-inclusive	Inclusive
brotherhood	comradeship, community	forefathers	ancestors
		fraternal	warm, intimate
common man	average person, person in the street	fraternal organization	club, society
		Frenchman	the French
countryman	compatriot	man, mankind	humankind, humanity, humans
early man	early people, prehistoric people	modern man	modern society
fair sex, weaker sex	AVOID as it is sexual harassment	rise of man	rise of civilization
fatherland	country of origin, homeland	thinking man	thinking person, thinker
fellowship	camaraderie, friendship	working woman, working man	wage earner, taxpayer

After You Read

1. Discuss in a small group: Why is it inappropriate to use non-inclusive language, such as fireman and male nurse? Why is it particularly appropriate in the workplace to use inclusive language?
2. Think about the language used in your workplace, in a workplace familiar to you, or at school. Re-read this selection to determine if such language falls into the traps mentioned in the article. List any changes or replacement words that could be integrated into the workplace or school.

Handbook Link

How to expand your vocabulary

Before You Read

Through diary entries, letters, and narrative, the novel *The Stone Diaries* tells the story of Daisy Goodwill, whose mother dies in childbirth and whose life takes a series of twists and turns as she is raised by another family, only to lose her adoptive mother at the age of 11.

This excerpt from the novel is set in the early 1900's. Read the description of Barker Flett in the first sentence of the excerpt. List all of the adjectives that describe the young man. From the description, make a guess about his social status, his degree of wealth, and his emotional state. Then read on to find out more about his circumstances.

Childhood, 1916

from *The Stone Diaries*   by Carol Shields

Barker Flett, that tall, gaunt, badly clothed student of botany, sat hunched over his cluttered desk, the angle of his bent head signaling misery. Sighing with vexation, he picked up a steel-nibbed pen, dipped it in the inkwell, and scratched: "My dear Father, I thank you for your letter, though it grieves me to learn of your unwillingness to write to my Mother directly, since I can't help believing that an appeal on your part, if sincerely expressed and softly worded, might encourage her to reflect on her situation and eventually return home." (Here he paused for a moment, staring out at the rain which was rattling against the window.) "In the meantime, I beg you to find it in your heart to make her some small allowance, perhaps one or two dollars a week. As you know, I have had to engage an additional room to accommodate her and the child, and my scholarship income from the College scarcely covers these new and totally unforeseen expenses. There have been a number of doctor's bills also, as Mother has suffered from severe infection following the extraction of her teeth, and the infant has been troubled day and night with what Dr. Sterling calls a tight chest. Perhaps you are aware that your neighbor, Mr. Goodwill, has agreed to provide the sum of eight dollars a month for the child's maintenance. Generous as this is, it barely suffices. I send you, and to my dear brothers as well, my affectionate regards. Barker Flett"

My dear Mr. Goodwill,

Your monthly letter is always welcome, and I thank you most warmly for your Express Money Order, which is much appreciated. I am pleased to write that Daisy continues plump and happy, and her legs are grown strong indeed. My son and I are of the opinion that she will be walking before the month is out. I enclose the photograph you requested. (And again I thank you for sending the necessary money.) You will be able to see for yourself that the photographer has captured the exceptional curliness of her hair, which is of a very pretty color that I have heard described as "strawberry." I am anxious to assure you that, contrary to what you may have heard, the air in Winnipeg is fresh and healthful. In addition, we are fortunate in having a fine big garden next to our house where little Daisy will be able to run about when the summer weather arrives.

With kind regards,
Clarentine Flett

My dear Father,

I have spoken to my Mother as you requested, but I am afraid she is firm in her refusal to return to Tyndall, despite your generous offer to accept her back into the household, even forbearing mention of her sudden leave-taking and long absence from home.

As to your other question, I must regretfully answer in the negative, for I think it would only excite her nerves to receive you here. Her state of mind is relatively tranquil at the moment, and she is much occupied with the garden and with running after young Daisy. We must not, however, give up hope of a future reconciliation.

I regret, also, your decision in the matter of money, which has become, for me, a never-ending source of distress.

Your son,
Barker

My dear Mr. Goodwill,

You will scarcely believe that Daisy is to start her first level at school in a mere ten days. Already she has her alphabet by heart, also Our Lord's Prayer, the Twenty-third Psalm, and a number of simple hymns. She is, moreover, able to recite the common names of all the flower varieties in our garden, of which there are some twenty-five. I am happy to say that these two months of fine weather have improved her chest, as has the regular application of a mullein-leaf poultice at bedtime. As for myself, I keep very well.

Yours faithfully,
Clarentine Flett

Dear Mr. Goodwill,

I thank you for yours of the 28th, and assure you that Daisy is in excellent health. Her school recitation, "A Sailor's Lament," was given with the greatest feeling and enthusiasm.

We were most interested to read of you and your famous tower in last week's *Tribune*. My son, Professor Flett, regarding the tower's rather blurred likeness on the page, grew most curious to see it as it really is, but as you know he never travels anymore to Tyndall since his brothers have gone West.

Yours most sincerely,
Clarentine Flett

My dear Father,

It gives me pain that I must once again apply to you for money. I do beseech you to search your conscience and give a thought to the many years in which you and my Mother lived in harmony, during which time she served most dutifully and lovingly with never any thought of compensation. Our day-to-day situation here is exceptionally insecure at the moment, and I now fear that my decision to purchase the Simcoe Street house, as well as the land that adjoins it, was premature, particularly with the city moving southward, and now talk of war. My actions, I assure you, proceeded from the wish to provide Daisy, who is growing into a fine young girl, with a reliable and respectable home of which she need never feel ashamed. It is true that my Mother does earn some income from the sale of plants and herbs, but the cost of constructing a greenhouse has been considerable. It is also true, as you say, that my own earnings have been augmented by the licensing of the "Marquis" wheat hybrid, but fully three-quarters of these earnings remain the property of the College. I look forward, with hope, to your favorable reply.

You may be interested to know that "Goodwill Tower," as it is known in the city, is much talked of these days, and I am told it draws visitors from all over the region, and even from the United States.

Your son,
Barker

Dear Mr. Goodwill,

This little note will, I hope, bring you the assurance that Daisy is now fully recovered from the attack of measles. It has been a most distressing time, and very tiresome indeed for her to remain so many weeks in a darkened room, particularly as she is by nature an active and healthy child. She was much cheered, however, to discover a photograph of you in the pages of last week's *Family Herald*, standing in front of your tower. "Is that truly my father?" she demanded of me, and I assured her that indeed it was. She became most anxious to pay you a visit, and would talk of nothing else for days, but we believe, Professor Flett as much as myself, that such a visit would cause too much excitement in one so recently recovered from a serious illness.

We remain grateful for your monthly contribution to our household. We manage the best we can on a limited purse, and happily my little garden enterprise is beginning to thrive. It is as if all the world has discovered the happiness that simple flowers can bring to an otherwise dreary wartime existence.

Yours,
Clarentine Flett

Dear Mr. Goodwill,

I thank you most sincerely for your prayers and for your words of condolence. I can tell you truthfully that my dear Mother did not suffer in her final days, having entered into a state of unconsciousness the moment the dreadful accident occurred. Those friends and acquaintances who kept vigil at her bedside found in her repose a source of strength and inspiration. She was laid to rest, finally, amid friends and family, both my brothers arriving from the West in time to pay their respects. Our Father, as you know, remained hardened in his heart to the end, and it is for him we must now direct our prayers. Regarding the young cyclist who struck my Mother down, he has been fined the sum of twenty-five dollars, and I am told the poor fellow is fairly ill with remorse.

I have been thinking much these last days about the question of Daisy, whom my Mother has loved as dearly all these years as if she were her own child — doted on her, in fact. You will agree, I am sure, that it is not in any way desirable for a young girl of eleven years to share a household with a man of my circumstances who has neither a wife nor the means to engage a person who would look after her needs. In any case, it seems I must leave Winnipeg very soon in order to pursue my work with the Dominion Cerealist and his committee in Ottawa. Will you be kind enough to write me the full expression of your thoughts on the subject of Daisy and what we can arrange between us to ensure her future accommodation and happiness.

Yours faithfully,
Barker Flett

After You Read

1. Were your predictions about Barker Flett correct? Did anything you learned suprise you? Share your comments with a partner.
2. Write a response from Mr. Goodwill to Barker Flett. Imagine what he will propose for his daughter Daisy's future. Keep the same formal tone used by Barker and Clarentine. Check your letter carefully to ensure that you have used an appropriate and consistent voice and style.

Handbook Link
How to write a letter
How to revise a draft

Before You Read

This song is about taking over the family business, in this case, fishing. What other jobs are often passed on from parents to children? What factors might "pull" children toward the same line of work as their parents? What factors might "push" them into other jobs or careers?

We'll Carry On

by Jimmy Rankin

If the waves roll rough as in days before
Still we put our boats to sea
The take has been tough
We're counting on more
To make the season pay

It was back in '83
My brothers and me
Laid our poor father in his grave
Even though he's dead and gone
His voice lives on
In the hiss and the pull of the waves

Chorus:
We'll carry on, carry on
Sing these words
Through all the damage done
The old salt would say
I am my father's son
Come hell or high water
We'll carry on

In smokey gray rooms
Beneath bare lightbulbs
The accusations fly
What the hell do they want
They've taken enough
From this way of life once mine

Chorus

It's a merciless scheme
Not a fisherman's dream
The way the tide has turned
For not long before
By these restless shores
A man could his living earn

Chorus

After You Read

1. Re-read your list of push and pull factors. Write to explain which ones are most relevant in this song.
2. Reflect in your reading response journal about what this song says about working together as a family and as a team. Explain how this idea relates to something you have experienced at work, at school, or at home.
3. Explain the pun, "the tide has turned," in the last stanza. Make point form notes about what it describes about the fishing industry.

Handbook   *Link*
How to understand
themes in literature

Before You Read

Consider the poem's title, then read the first line. Predict the poet's point of view about working in a coal mine. Which word in particular in the first line gives you a clue? With a partner, discuss the connotations of this word and how the connotations help you predict what the poem will be about.

COAL BLACK

by Lennie Gallant

There is a ghost that walks this town
His face is tired and coal dust lined
Without a word without a sound
He leads you to the mine
He passes through the barriers there
And leaves you standing hypnotized
Cause you can't follow him down where
The truth has caved in to lies
Father Father tell me how
It was back in an older time
Back where you were young
And lost your brother to the mine
Will some justice give you peace
Ease your mind, let you sleep
In your black tomb buried deep
Do you hear their lines

Chorus:
Digging deeper in my dreams
How far must I go down
Searching this deadly seam
Coal Black - Great big lie
Well who's to bless; who's to blame
Where did you get that alibi
Who was the spark, who fanned the flame
Why did they die

Chorus

Well maybe it's the system
Maybe it's one man
Or maybe it's more than
You can ever understand
But when I hear the ones
Who run for cover from it all
I think about the miner
Running from that fireball
"It's not my fault" "I didn't know"
"I wasn't there" "They were too slow"
"I didn't see" "I didn't hear"
"I'm not responsible" Let me out of here

Chorus

How deep must I go to find the truth

After You Read

1. Discuss with your partner whether your prediction was correct.
2. Create a chart to compare and contrast "Coal Black" with "We'll Carry On." Draw conclusions about the two songs and their content, and give reasons for your answer.

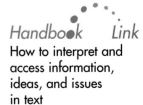

Handbook   Link
How to interpret and access information, ideas, and issues in text

Before You Read

Describe someone you know who has good manners. How does this person speak to others? How does this person act toward others? In your opinion, is it a benefit in our society and at work to have good manners? Discuss this with a partner, then read the essay.

WHY BE POLITE?

by Michael Korda

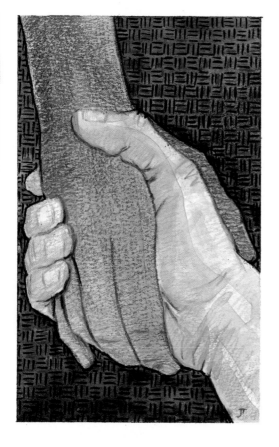

Almost all of us believe that we live in an age of uncouth manners and that things were better in some previous era. For example, the 18th century in England is known as a period of high refinement in social intercourse. We look back with nostalgia to the soft candlelight, the elaborate courtesies, the hand-kissing—unwilling to confront the brutal reality of a century in which duelling to the death was commonplace, and gentlemen were expected to drink themselves under the table.

Manners change. In our day, it is considered good manners to be clean; indeed, we spend billions of dollars on products designed to keep us "fresh." In the 18th century, by contrast, European standards of cleanliness were shockingly low, and women's extravagant coiffures were often infested with lice.

The changeability of manners makes the whole subject difficult to approach. For example, it was not considered bad manners in the 18th century for a man to wear a hat indoors. He would take it off to greet a lady, but then he'd put it right back on.

The reason for this is perfectly plain. In the first place, the hat had long served as a visible mark of status. In the second place, you couldn't draw a sword easily if you were holding a hat in your hand.

There is a lesson here. For the most part, manners are self-protective devices appropriate to the customs of a particular age. These customs invariably derive from some practical need. Thus, on meeting somebody, we commonly shake right hands—a formal custom of no significance now. But in an age when everybody carried weapons, it was a demonstration that one was prepared to converse without a weapon in one's hand. What we think of as "good manners" was merely a way of saying, "I mean you no harm, if you can show me that your intention is the same."

Caution lies behind manners, wherever we look. In days gone by, a host sipped the wine before serving it, not to check that the wine was all right but to prove to his guests that it wasn't poisoned. A wine steward used his silver server to demonstrate his host's goodwill towards his guests. Silver was thought to neutralize poisons in wine.

Why do we let someone older or more important go through the door first? One theory is that in medieval times it was sensible for the strongest man to leave the castle first, since there was always a possibility he would meet armed opponents or the rebellious peasantry waving pitchforks and scythes. Gradually, a certain honour descended upon this position. It was also assumed that the most important person was the strongest, and even if he wasn't, he could hardly deny it.

Manners are society's way of oiling the machinery. If you don't lubricate relationships, tempers rise and people fight unnecessary battles. Besides, it's worthwhile having good manners, if only so that when you drop them for a moment, everyone knows that you mean business.

People with good manners do better in most situations than those without. Most negotiations, for example, are impossible without good manners, which explains why diplomats are famed for their courtesy. The best lawyers, too, are usually people of exquisite politeness. Beware of the man who never raises his voice and always treats you with courtesy—he is probably going for your jugular.

In the 19th century, most of the great gun-fighters of the American West were notorious for their florid good manners, being all too aware that if they let things get out of hand, they would have to draw and shoot. Good manners helped these men survive, since even the best gunfighter could win only so many gunfights before his luck ran out. For the most part, they were not "big-talking men"; they were soft-spoken and courteous. It was said of "Wild Bill" Hickock that the moment he stopped smiling at you, you were dead.

Despite mankind's reputation for violence, most people prefer to avoid confrontation, and avoiding confrontation is what manners are all about. Manners represent the triumph of civilization over barbarism. They are not a demonstration of weakness, but a sign of common sense—mankind's way of saying, "Let's not fight unless we have to." There may be no higher wisdom than that—in diplomacy, in business, in love and marriage, or in the transactions of everyday life.

After You Read

Handbook Link

How to write a memorandum

How to interpret and assess information, ideas, and issues in text

1. In the last sentence, Korda refers to the importance of being polite in business. Write a memo giving four reasons why it is particularly important to be polite in the workplace.
2. As a class, compare the argument in this essay to the points made in "Customers Are Not Always Right" (page 145).

Before You Read

On September 28, 2000, Canada's 15th prime minister, Pierre Trudeau, died. Following is the eulogy delivered by his son Justin at his father's funeral. In his eulogy, Justin tells a story about his father, then reflects on what his father accomplished in his life. At the end, he paraphrases lines from a Robert Frost poem, stating, "He has kept his promises, and earned his sleep."

In your reading response journal, write a paragraph describing your goals in life, and the promises to yourself and others that you hope you will achieve during your life.

A Son's Goodbye

by Justin Trudeau

"Friends, Romans, countrymen…

I was about six years old when I went on my first official trip. I was going with my father and my grandpa Sinclair up to the North Pole.

It was a very glamorous destination. But the best thing about it is that I was going to be spending lots of time with my dad because in Ottawa he just worked so hard.

One day, we were in Alert, Canada's northernmost point, a scientific military installation that seemed to consist entirely of low, shed-like buildings and warehouses.

Let's be honest. I was six. There were no brothers around to play with and I was getting a little bored because dad still somehow had a lot of work to do.

I remember a frozen, windswept Arctic afternoon when I was bundled up into a Jeep and hustled out on a special top-secret mission. I figured I was finally going to be let in on the reason of this high-security Arctic base.

I was exactly right.

We drove slowly through and past the buildings, all of them very grey and windy. We rounded a corner and came upon a red one. We stopped. I got out of the Jeep and started to crunch across towards the front door. I was told, no, to the window.

So I clambered over the snowbank, was boosted up to the window, rubbed my sleeve against the frosty glass to see inside and as my eyes adjusted to the gloom, I saw a figure, hunched over one of many worktables that seemed very cluttered. He was wearing a red suit with that furry white trim.

And that's when I understood just how powerful and wonderful my father was.

Pierre Elliott Trudeau. The very words convey so many things to so many people. Statesman, intellectual, professor, adversary, outdoorsman, lawyer, journalist, author, prime minister.

But more than anything, to me, he was dad.

And what a dad. He loved us with the passion and the devotion that encompassed his life. He taught us to believe in ourselves, to stand up for ourselves, to know ourselves and to accept responsibility for ourselves.

We knew we were the luckiest kids in the world. And we had done nothing to actually deserve it.

It was instead something that we would have to spend the rest of our lives to work very hard to live up to.

He gave us a lot of tools. We were taught to take nothing for granted. He doted on us but didn't indulge.

Many people say he didn't suffer fools gladly, but I'll have you know he had infinite patience with us.

He encouraged us to push ourselves, to test limits, to challenge anyone and anything.

There were certain basic principles that could never be compromised.

As I guess it is for most kids, in Grade 3, it was always a real treat to visit my dad at work.

As on previous visits this particular occasion included a lunch at the parliamentary restaurant which always seemed to be terribly important and full of serious people that I didn't recognize.

But at eight, I was becoming politically aware. And I recognized one whom I knew to be one of my father's chief rivals.

Thinking of pleasing my father, I told a joke about him — a generic, silly little grade school thing.

My father looked at me sternly with that look I would learn to know so well, and said: "Justin, never attack the individual. One can be in total disagreement with someone without denigrating him as a consequence."

Saying that, he stood up and took me by the hand and brought me over to introduce me to this man. He was a nice man who was eating with his daughter, a nice-looking blond girl a little younger than I was.

My father's adversary spoke to me in a friendly manner and it was then that I understood that having different opinions from those of another person in no way precluded holding this person in the highest respect.

Because mere tolerance is not enough: we must have true and deep respect for every human being, regardless of his beliefs, his origins and his values. That is what my father demanded of his sons and that is what he demanded of our country. He demanded it out of love — love of his sons, love of his country. That is why we love him so. These letters, these flowers, the dignity of the crowds who came to say farewell — all of that is a way of thanking him for having loved us so much.

My father's fundamental belief never came from a textbook. It stemmed from his deep love for and faith in all Canadians and over the past few days, with every card, every rose, every tear, every wave and every pirouette, you returned his love.

It means the world to Sacha and me.

Thank you.

We have gathered from coast to coast to coast, from one ocean to another, united in our grief, to say goodbye.

But this is not the end. He left politics in '84. But he came back for Meech. He came back for Charlottetown. He came back to remind us of who we are and what we're all capable of.

But he won't be coming back anymore. It's all up to us, all of us, now.

The woods are lovely, dark and deep. He has kept his promises and earned his sleep.

Je t'aime Papa."

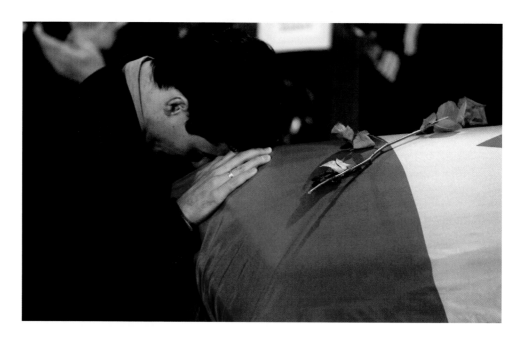

After You Read

1. List the devices that Justin Trudeau uses in his eulogy to achieve a conversational tone. Write to explain whether you think his eulogy is effective, and why.
2. Choose a memorable moment from your childhood. Write it as a speech, paying particular attention to your tone and style. Practise speaking it aloud.

Handbook Link
How to create an effective speaking style

Before You Read

There is an old saying in business that "the customer is always right." But Andrea Janus, who works in a music store, doesn't agree with this. In your opinion, how far should a worker have to go to please the customer? With a partner, write a list of things you definitely should and definitely shouldn't do to make sure that you achieve success with customers. Then write a list of things customers definitely should and shouldn't do when they want service from a store or business.

Customers are not always right

Things get ugly when sales clerk's patience is tested

BY ANDREA JANUS
SPECIAL TO THE STAR

So, it's Saturday, 8 p.m., and what am I doing? Getting ready for that hot date? Funny. Writing the 15-page essay that's due in two days? Nope. I'm cowering in the staff room of the music store where I work, peering through the tiny window in the door to survey the treacherous landscape of CDs where the customers dwell.

Besides the fear of a co-worker crashing through the door and flattening my nose, it is the creature known as the customer that really has me panicking.

Earlier in the day, almost immediately after beginning my shift, the sound of fingers snapping caught my ear.

"Yoohoo, yoohoooooo!" a shrill voice called out.

I at once concluded that some woman, probably wearing a fur coat and 12 pounds of makeup, was looking for the poodle or terrier she had forgotten was tucked into her $8,000 handbag. While I was correct about the first part, the woman I found myself face to face with was not looking for her puppy, but was actually trying to get my attention.

After grabbing my arm with a viselike grip, she asked me if we carry anything by "that famous opera singer." Instead of asking her if she could be any more vague, I suggested Pavarotti and

Domingo, before I hit the jackpot with Andrea Bocelli. When I handed her the CD, she gushed, "Oh, I never liked opera until I heard him sing," and I thought to myself, "And you still don't, honey, because you've actually just discovered Euro-pop. Congratulations!"

If I could teach a course on shopping etiquette, this would be lesson Number 1: The species known as the human being does not respond well to finger-snapping. Kindly reserve that for when Spot attacks the mailman.

Later in the afternoon, a middle-aged man came flying through the front door, wailing that he was double-parked out front (in the middle of rush hour, I might add). In all seriousness, he looked me straight in the eye and told me that he was looking for, "that song, by that guy, you know."

No, I don't know because, being a CD store we, oddly enough, have lots of "songs" by lots of "guys." Any more info for me? "Well, they play it all the time on the radio," he said, adding "I don't remember what station, but the song has the word 'love' in the lyrics.

Ohhhh, that song! I'm being silly today, don't mind me. Sadly, in my job, I meet men like this every day. And I mean every day.

Which brings me to lesson Number 2: Make like Woodward and Bernstein and do your research before you head to your nearest music store. That way you avoid looking like CNN on election night.

Later still, I was juggling a few different customers, when yet another one cut in. (I instantly had a terrifying flashback to a high school dance where this loser tried to pull in a little too close when dancing to that 11-minute nightmare known as "Stairway to Heaven.")

When I asked the man to wait just a moment, he immediately began to curse at me, and then started shoving his way over to one of my unsuspecting co-workers. In the end, everyone got irritated and nobody benefited.

Road rage does not transfer well to a retail environment

Finally, lesson Number 3 — I would put this one on the final exam for sure: Road rage does not transfer well to a retail environment. So, thou shalt not rear-end people in the aisles, yell obscenities at cashiers, or cut in on lineups or salespeople. However, if you plan on driving your Hummer through the front door, just try not to run anyone over.

Now, I know we all have our bad days, and some of us were raised by bears in a cave, however we must remember when we venture out into the real world not to test the patience of the other animals, or things could get ugly.

So play nice when heading out into the habitat known as "the store," and avoid sending a poor sales clerk for a very expensive rhinoplasty.

Well, after getting this off my chest, I'm ready to finish my shift. As for the rest of you, if you have learned anything today, would you mind passing it on to Smokey and the rest of the bear pack? They'd probably be much obliged.

Andrea Janus is a fourth-year student at the University of Toronto, where she is studying English. She works part-time in a Toronto record store.

After You Read

1. Find the three lessons that Janus describes. Re-write them as formal instructions for a guidebook on shopping etiquette.
2. As you re-write the lessons, also record how Janus uses humour, allusion, and irony to make her points.
3. Write each of Janus's three lessons as a heading. Beneath each, describe how you think these lessons apply to working with others, both on the job and in your personal life.

Handbook Link

How to write instructions

How to recognize allusion and irony

Before You Read

Even in team sports there are athletes who stand out. Think of an athlete, either professional or amateur, whom you consider to be great. Describe the skills and attitudes that make this person great. Then compare these skills and attitudes with those that people need to be good at their jobs. Which skills and attitudes are different? Which are the same?

The
STICKHANDLER

by David Solway

Not like the solid defenceman
who, stymied by forecheckers,
can only dump the puck
out to center ice;
or the faithful leftwinger
who diligently patrols his wing
doing what is required of him
& scoring his share of goals . . .

The phenom steals the puck
in his own zone
& skates around his net
deftly evading his check
fakes a pass
& loops across the blueline
(back & forth goes the puck
at the end of his stick
as if magnetized by willpower,
obedient & sure).
Now he is at center, gathering
speed,
   dodges
the tricky rightwinger
trying to cut him off
stickhandles
round the backward-skating referee
& hair flying, 30 miles per hour,
splits the defence.

Nothing protests.
Even the laws of probability
hold their breath
as the stickhandler makes his final deke
& faking a slapshot
backhands the puck
past the wide-eyed goalie
who stands there frozen,
more like an accomplice
than an opponent.

After You Read

1. In your reading response journal, describe the skills of the stickhandler. Define his job. What other positions are mentioned? How do they all work together as a team?

Handbook Link

How to interpret and assess information, ideas, and issues in text

Whether you're applying for a job or already have one, you will need to keep reading, training, and learning. As you begin a job search, you'll read classified advertisements, complete job applications, and have interviews. On the job, you will read texts of all kinds: business cards, business plans, memos, company policies, safety information.

In this unit, you will find these and other workplace texts, as well as literature that shares the experiences of working life.

CONTENTS

Before You Read

In this short story, Geraldine's 15-year-old daughter Carrie-Lynn wants to get a summer job as a waitress, just like Geraldine and her sister Josie did when they were 15. Only now will Carrie-Lynn hear the true story of how hard Josie and Geraldine had to work for their summer wages in 1969, and learn the importance of knowing your rights.

In a small group, discuss what you know about employees' rights, whether at your own job or in general. Include information about hourly pay, overtime pay, vacation pay, weekly hours, and time off.

Summer Wages

by Caroline Woodward

First off, let's put it into perspective, as Josie used to say. I, Geraldine, have worked nine waitressing jobs and have taken the vow never to do it again. Sure, I make those tired old jokes about support hose and roller skates supplied by management but I've got other things I can do for less work and more money. No more shift work either.

I do the books for five businesses right out of my own home. Claim office expenses for one-third of this double-wide trailer under the self-employed category on income tax and I sign off with a nice flourish, let me tell you. It's better that the money comes back to me, hard-working mother of three, than to

the lousy government just lusting to squander it on their corrupt friends or some U.S. kick-ass submarine thing.

But here's the kicker. My oldest, Carrie-Lynn, wants to get a job. Fine. Grade ten, smart as a whip, takes after Ab for brains and Josie for looks, like she used to look before she got into the booze. But the job she wants is waitressing up the highway this coming summer. "Just like you and Aunt Josie did."

I'm building up to spilling the beans on her, sitting her down in the next hour when she gets home and telling it like it is. Was, any-way. She's too innocent and the world is meaner and trickier than it was 1969. I'm going to let loose with the scuzzy side of me and Josie's adventures in Service With A Smileville so she'll clue in and get a decent job. Like being a lifeguard. That's classy and the money is two and a half times minimum wage. She's still got time to get the swim ticket she needs. I'd pay for it, no ifs or buts.

She wouldn't get tips unless she served booze and she's still underage so that's that. The kid's only fifteen now, sixteen in June, runs like a deer, swims like a guppy, brings home ribbons every sports day and swim meet. Lifeguard badge be a cinch for an athletic kid like her.

Getting the damn pool job is another story though. I got to be realistic on that score. Carrie-Lynn doesn't have a high-up Daddy, or Mommy, to pull strings at City Hall. Ab is the *janitor* at City Hall for crying out loud. Plus he invents things like the automated scarecrow. But until he makes some indecent amount of money, people will just laugh at him. "How's it goin', Ab?" "Built a better mousetrap yet, Ab?" And Ab will just miss how entirely mean they are and smile and say he's not that interested in mousetraps, his current project is this or that, keeps me busy, keeps me busy, he says, nodding and smiling at the snickering sons of bees. They don't know who they're talking to. Ab's halfways a genius and he's got the kindest heart in the West, not a mean bone in his body. Me, I'm mean, let me tell you.

Me, I should join the Business and Professional Women's Club, get on the power lunch and business card swapmeet circuit but I'm afraid they'd turn me down. I couldn't take that. It kills me because I'm so proud to

finally get to be a bookkeeper but that might not be enough for them. A chartered accountant and on up is what to be for them. Carrie-Lynn, Carrie-Lynn, that's where you come in.

I started by default, waitressing, because they hired me to chambermaid. It was new then, it's closed now, a gas station and about ten cabins plus a café with a good reputation. Exactly halfways between Fort St. John and Fort Nelson with Pink Mountain looming up out of the muskeg some miles away. The Beatton River began a hundred yards from the café, just a little brown stream coiling around the willows and stunted spruce trees.

Josie was actually thrilled to be a waitress even when she found out there was no uniform, just a long green apron to tie on over her blouse and jeans. Still, she fixed up her hair and

did her nails and worked a full shift an hour after we got there. Petticoat Junction is what the truckers called our place on account of the five young women between sixteen and eighteen that worked there. But by the first of August, Josie and I were the only employees left. The Mister had picked a fight with Henry, the gas jockey whose girlfriend was the head waitress and whose sister was the second cook. The second cook's best friend was the main cook, a farm kid from Tom's Lake who had cooked for her family since she was eleven and that Esther could cook, let me tell you.

All four of them left in a huff because of Henry being fired. They headed back to Dawson Creek and big summer dances with Bim and The Crystal Ship and maybe even Anthony and The Romans. Lucky bums. We didn't realize how much fun July had been until we watched them leave in Henry's souped-up car and the café was suddenly dull. No more Social Centre. Josie and I were on our own with the Mister and the Wife.

The Mister drank at least once every two weeks and was out of commission for three or four days at a time. The Wife was a bible-thumper and an excellent cook but she holed up in one of the motel units whenever he hit the bottle so he wouldn't hit her. Josie and I had orders to leave him be and to bring her meals three times a day. No problem. We avoided him like the plague, sober or drunk.

We never told our parents. We needed the dollar ten an hour and all this booze and sex and violence, just like the TV, only made us feel more grown-up and on our own. We didn't want to worry the folks. Hear what I'm

saying? You got that little smile on.

So. After the big You're Fired! Like Hell I Am, I Quit! We All Quit! episode, Josie and I pretty well ran the place. We'd get up at 5:30 a.m., dash from our unheated shack to the café, get the grill and the coffee on, eat a stack of toast, and go our separate ways. If a tour bus to Fairbanks pulled in, Josie would holler from the back door of the kitchen. I'd set down my toilet scrubber or whatever and run over to ladle out soup and make a bunch more pots of coffee. Josie kept a clean green apron by the door for me so I'd look more or less like a waitress. We'd go flat out getting upward of fifty people fed and watered, answering their dumb questions about where we went to school and how come we didn't have pecan pie and was the soup in the crockpot homemade like the sign hanging over it said?

In July when all five of us had worked, a couple of us could have a break, walk up to the Sikanni Chief airstrip, climb up the old forestry look-out until we lost our nerve around thirty feet up. Henry made it to the top once and so did Josie. It took them forever to get down and I had to run back to cover her shift which pissed me off. It was a whole day off for me and something didn't sit right with me, down on the ground, looking up this ancient creaking tower, and them up there laughing.

Josie and I would hitch the one hundred miles down to Fort St. John every Friday afternoon at four o'clock and on Sunday afternoons we'd hitch back up to work in less than two hours usually. We got rides fast. Two blondes with our thumbs out with no *idea* we were two blondes standing with our thumbs

out on the highway! I can't believe it but no kid of mine would stand out there, male or female, not in these times. Only so many angels on duty per innocent kid.

By mid-August we figured out we were putting in close to eighteen-hour days and then it dawned on us we'd just worked seven days a week for two weeks straight. We were missing the really huge parties at the Old Fort and had romances to tend to. Or we liked to think we did. Pink Mountainview Motel or Pink Elephant Lookout as we called it behind the Mister's back was seriously interfering with our futures, and we each had two hundred dollars clear, a small fortune.

Now listen up. Our Dad phoned us right at a busy lunch spell and told us to quit if we'd had enough, give them a week's notice, come home and have a week off before school started. The Wife came in and gave me a dirty look for being on the phone, my only phone call all bloody summer. So I looked at her, said "Uh huh," when Dad said goodbye, and then I said, "Dead?! Where?" Beat. "Mile 109? Mile 136? Omigosh!" Beat. "Hitchhikers? Have they got the murderer yet?" Beat. "Okay. Yes. Okay. Yes, we will. Bye, Dad."

The Wife pretended she wasn't eavesdropping and scuttled out the door again. Something fell in the garage (closed again) and the sliding door came up and banged down. No Mister though. We waited a couple minutes, cleaning up the last of the lunch specials for a bunch of campers from Idaho and then it was just the two of us.

We got spinny, plunking quarters in the box and dancing to Little Green Bag three times in a row. Dancing like a pair of banshees until another camper pulled in. I settled down and marched out to where the Wife was holed up in Cabin Three and told her through the door that Josie and I had to quit.

I heard the toilet flush. Quit! Flush! Like an exclamation mark. Spent half her life on the can I swear. She opened the door and glared at me.

"There's two weeks left in the season," she says in her snappy boss voice. Her breath reeked of American cigarettes. Took me hours to air out a cabin after she'd holed up in it.

"Our Dad says you owe us four percent holiday pay," I say in my most polite and careful voice.

"But you girls didn't give us two weeks' notice," she says, folding her big huge arms over her big huge bazooms.

"Our Dad says it's the law and you didn't give us notice to work fifteen days straight either." Her mouth makes an O.

I take the plunge and make a decision for Josie and me. "If you give us our pay with the four percent, we won't charge overtime. Our Dad," I say, watching her squinty little eyes, using my most extremely polite voice now that I'm lying like a sidewalk, "Our Dad will come up tomorrow morning for us and I guess he'll talk to you about it if Mister isn't, ahh, around." I raise my eyebrows at her with this last bit.

That did it. She gave me a long, hard look and slammed the door in my face. I started running up to the kitchen, leaping from plank to wooden plank so I wouldn't sink into the mud lake between the cabins and the café.

There were some customers, the geologist guys from the Pink Mountain site, so I held it in until Josie took out their order and came back into the kitchen. I retell the whole exchange with the Wife and we both get so excited our whispers shot up to squeaks and we tried to jump up and down without making noise, her in her wooden clogs and me in my gumboots.

Josie had big dark circles under her eyes and she'd lost fifteen pounds in a month and a half. She was more burnt out than me because short-order cooking and waitressing and night clean-up was all inside work, breathing a steady diet of grill grease and Pine-Sol. At least I could cart towels and linen in the fresh air between cabins. For the first few weeks there was a truck, the Alaska Highway Laundry Express, but then it folded and yours truly used an industrial washer and an outside clothes line about fifty yards long because their dryer had broken down. I liked doing laundry better than making beds and scrubbing toilets.

Outside the air smelled like spruce tea with the late summer mists hanging low and the roots dangling into the little river, steeping it a coppery brown colour. I could hear trucks downshifting miles and miles away, that throaty roar with a silent breath between gears. I stood up on the laundry line perch, singing my head off, pulling wet sheets, towels, pillow slips and kitchen cloths out of my basket and onto the line, or vice-versa.

Back inside I tried to keep my mood light and summery, battling relief and giddiness and drawing a blank when it came to what to do next. I put the apron on to help Josie with night clean-up, strolling over to the jukebox to punch in some Creedence and Three Dog Night and Greenbaum's Little Green Bag, our theme song. The geologists chitchatted about rocks and bone hunters, one of them insisting that this place was smack in the middle of an ice-free corridor during the last glacier age. I poured their refills and kept my ears open because these guys always had the most interesting arguments. Then I heard the Wife giving Josie hell in the kitchen and so did the customers. I set the coffee pot down none too gently and marched back there, do or die.

Josie was looking white and shaky, holding a piece of order pad with some figuring on it.

"You got your hopes up, girlie," says the Wife, standing with her feet splayed apart and her arms hoisted over her bazooms. She launched into a major bullying session with a tired little grade ten waitress. Honestly!

"And what's the problem here?" I snap out in a loud voice that shocks even me. Josie looks at me like we've got one last chance to live and hands over the slip of paper.

"I figured out what I've got coming to me and they won't give it," she says, close to crying.

Josie is very smart with math and so I (no genius) quickly check the end result. I pause just a few seconds. Not for nothing was Drama my best subject.

"Looks right to me," I say in my new loud way, and stare the skinflint down. By this point I am amazing myself!

"I'm paying her for nine hours a day and that includes breaks and meals," she says, looking past me at the heads of the geologists who are lining up at the till. She starts to

move but I jump in front of her, wanting witnesses in case Mister crawls out of his cubbyhole in the garage and things get really weird. The Wife is scary enough but I got to her earlier with the yak about our Dad and the law and I know it.

"This poor kid works more hours than the fourteen a day she's claiming," I say. "She's opened up and closed down this joint for half the summer and she better be paid for it." Then I step aside so she can face the geologists over the cash register. Let the old bag simper and coo about how they like her homemade soup now, the frigging hypocrite!

To make a long story shorter, we got our cheques that night without one word of thanks. By 7 a.m. the next morning we were facing a chilly north wind blowing gravel grit in our faces but in no time flat we were climbing into a big fuel tanker truck. Listening to Buck Owens and Merle Haggard on eight-track stereo. Homeward bound!

It was a deluxe truck with a cabover for sleeping, tons of seat space, tinted windshield, little orange balls across the top that some truckers call Calgary willnots, don't ask me why, and swinging dice cubes in oversized green and white foam stuff. And then there were the naked ladies.

Once I saw them I couldn't stop staring at them out the corners of my eyes because they were cut up into parts and glued onto the dash and the middle of the horn and the ashtray. Mostly breasts, no heads or arms. I was glad the trucker, Al, he said he was, didn't want to talk much because I was sitting next to him. Josie always pulled the shy act when a ride slowed down for us and started whining for the outside seat. The music blared out of four speakers and Al tapped one finger on the wheel but he didn't keep time with the music, just kept the same beat. I had to make myself stop staring at that finger too.

I made myself look out at the scenery rolling by, the miles of stunted muskeg spruce and swamp tamarack giving way to taller spruce and pines and poplars. We passed a jack-knifed rig and a squashed station wagon, burnt to a grey crisp. Ugh. And there was a bunch of wild-looking horses in the ditch, at least twenty of them escaped from who knows where, up to their bellies in good grass, sly and happy-looking the way horses are when they're on the lam.

The sun was pouring into the cab even with the tinted windshield. Al put on sunglasses which made him look even more sinister with his pock-marked jowls and hooked nose, an overweight parrot in a Hawaiian shirt and dirty jeans. He asked Josie to reach into the glove compartment for his pills.

"Gotta speed up my eyeballs," he said. "Hyuh, hyuh. Don't know your ass-pirin from your elbow, do ya, girlie?" Josie's giving him a confused, rabbity look because she can't get the lid of the flat black pillbox open. He asks her to fish two pills out for him. She still can't get the bloody little box open. I could scream.

The inside of the glove compartment is completely papered over with cut up women's crotch shots from magazines. You've got to understand that I'd never seen anything like this filth in my entire seventeen years. This was beyond the regular girlie magazines in the drugstore in 1969 is what I'm saying. I know, it's everywhere today, the TV, everywhere. Makes me puke.

Josie broke a precious fingernail and finally opened the pillbox. Al gulped down two and sucked on an orange he kept up on the dash within reach.

He was really booting it, pedal to the metal, wanting to get to Edmonton by midnight. We roared through the village of Wonowon at eighty miles an hour. That's way over a hundred and twenty kliks to you. Too damn fast. Dogs and gas stations and trailer courts and little Indian kids on trikes blurred by us until a siren drowned out the Buckaroos.

Josie dug into my ribs. When Al cursed and started pumping the air-brakes and downshifting, she mouthed, "Out, out, out." Her face had gone white and every zit she'd ever had sprouted in purplish scar galaxies across her forehead and chin.

When the rig ground to a halt, we jumped out with the big brown suitcase we shared and yelled our thanks. The young constable waved us on and motioned Al down from the truck for their little talk. Josie yanked at the suitcase and my arm at the same time and broke into a run.

"Do you hafta pee or what's the panic?" I yelled. A red stock truck slowed down before I could even catch up to Josie and in it were two young guys with cowboy hats on. When I got closer I could see it was the Wayling brothers, rancher types from near the Blueberry Reserve. I didn't know them except to look at them and that was fine by me. Dark curly hair, cut short except for sideburns, grey eyes, gorgeous noses.

They were, I told Josie later, like Zane Grey heroes minus their buckskin and stallions.

We hopped in the truck and tried our damndest to get them to talk in full sentences for the fifty miles into town. Josie loosened them up with jokes about jogging on the highway to keep the pounds off and I, usually the yappier of us two, sat back and laughed and laughed. Josie was never funnier except they didn't get the one about hippies being living proof that cowboys screwed goats, which was just as well considering their occupation. I don't think they liked girls to swear or talk dirty and Josie figured that out in seconds. She hammed it up about disasters in the café kitchen when the only thing left to cook was freezer-burned hamburger and stale white bread. I bragged about her and Esther turning out fifteen pies at a time, cherry, apple, blueberry, and lemon meringue. Josie flirted with them way worse than I ever did with the geologists. I had the outside seat too, did I mention that? Anyway, it was amazing what a summer of waitressing did for her confidence!

But once we got to Fort St. John, the brothers asked us to go cabareting and that's when they found out we weren't old enough to get into the bar and that was the end of that but it was fun while it lasted. They dropped us off at the end of our block like we asked because we didn't want our folks to see the truck and get ideas and besides, we had to talk.

She told me there was a convex mirror on her side of the window and she'd looked into it and seen a pair of eyes between the curtains of the cabover, staring at her. That was just as we started to barrel through Wonowon. She stared back at the eyes, paralyzed with fright, and then the police siren saved the day. When I asked if it was men's eyes or women's eyes, she said she couldn't tell because of the warping of the mirror. Holy doodle. And here I was freaked out by the dirty magazine scissor work!

We tried not to dwell on it and we didn't tell our folks because the chances of us going further north to, say, Muncho Lake the next summer and earning really decent money would be shot down for sure. See? Not a brain in our heads—or more guts than brains is a better way of putting it.

Look, Carrie-Lynn, I'll spare you my grown-up jobs, nineteen years and up, the classy night spots like the Oil King Cabaret where I pranced around in red polyester hotpants. Sure, laugh. Where I got bonked on the head by a flying beer glass for stepping between my friend Ella and a very hefty, very drunk woman who'd already yanked off Ella's frosted blonde short'n'curly wig. Poor Ella, standing there in her red hotpants suit with bobby pins holding down her greasy brown hair. Don't laugh. A little giggle is all you're allowed. Now that's enough.

You could be a lifeguard. Or go down to the Tourist Information booth. You're smart, you're pretty, you've got a nice personality. Don't leave this godforsaken town until you're eighteen. Promise me that. You got the rest of your life.

Please?

After You Read

Handbook Link

How to create your own voice in writing

How to understand themes in literature

1. This story uses informal language, including slang and clichés, that creates a conversational tone. Analyze the appropriateness of the language and voice in the selection, and describe what would be gained or lost by the use of formal language.
2. Briefly state the theme of the story, and explain whether you think the story's conclusion is an effective one.
3. Discuss with a partner whether you think Carrie-Lynn will agree with her mother's perceptions about work. Do you agree with them? Explain your answer.

Before You Read

Skim the key visuals and links on this page. Like books, Web pages may have "tables of contents," which contain the Web links or buttons that enable you to access the information you need. Where is the table of contents on this Web site? Where might you find it on other sites? Why is this an important design feature of Web pages?

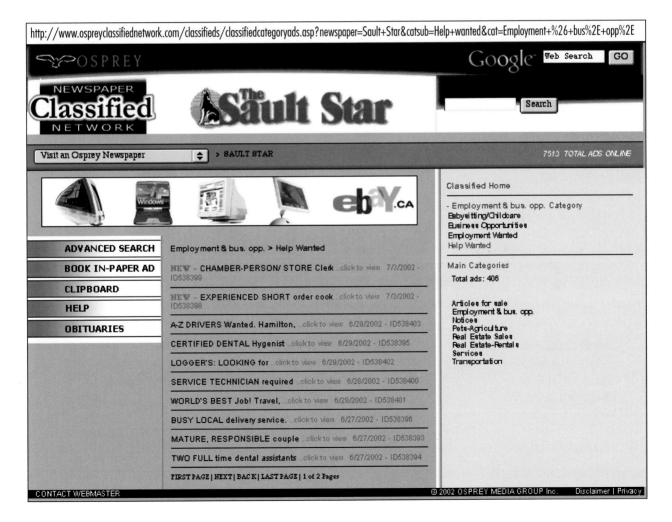

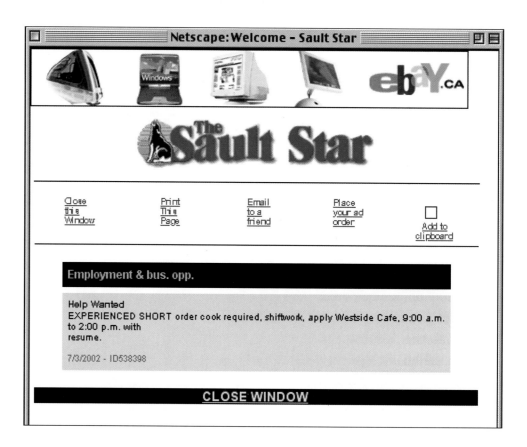

Netscape: Welcome – Sault Star

ebaY.ca

The Sault Star

Close this Window   Print This Page   Email to a friend   Place your ad order   Add to clipboard

Employment & bus. opp.

Help Wanted
EXPERIENCED SHORT order cook required, shiftwork, apply Westside Cafe, 9:00 a.m. to 2:00 p.m. with resume.

7/3/2002 - ID538398

CLOSE WINDOW

After You Read

Handbook Link
How to interpret and assess information, ideas, and issues in text

1. When you place a classified ad, you pay by the word or the line, or pay a price that includes a certain number of words. How does the payment structure affect the organization and vocabulary of classified ads? Cite examples from the classified job ads to illustrate your points.
2. Record the basic information that each job ad must include.

Before You Read

Skim the application form below. What strategy would you use to make sure that you filled in all of the important information? How is the information on this application form like, and unlike, the information you give in your résumé?

Employment Application

We are an equal opportunity employer committed to hiring and having a diverse workforce. All employees are expected to work rotating schedules.

Personal Information

Name _____

Address _____

City _____ Province _____ Postal Code _____

Phone Number _____ SIN _____

Are you eligible to work in Canada?   ☐ yes   ☐ no

Are you under 18 years of age?   ☐ yes   ☐ no

Have you ever been convicted of a criminal offence
for which no pardon was granted?   ☐ yes   ☐ no

If yes, please explain _____

Position desired _____

Hours desired _____ Full time   Part time   Summer

Hours available to work _____

Education

	Name and address of school	Grade or level completed	Did you graduate?	Certificate, diploma, degree received
Secondary School				
College				
University				
Business, Trade, or Technical				

Job Skills

List the skills you have that you think make you suitable for this job. _____

_____

_____

Give an example of a situation where you provided excellent customer service.
Why was your action effective? _____

_____

_____

Have you ever visited one of our locations? Where? Describe your experience. _____

_____

_____

Why would you like to work for our company? _____

_____

_____

Employment History

Please list your current and two previous employers, beginning with the most recent. Please include any volunteer or unpaid experience that you think is relevant to the job for which you are applying.

Name and Address of Employer	Name of Supervisor		Month	Year
Job Title	What were your duties?	Starting Date		
Telephone Number	Why did you leave?	Ending Date		
Name and Address of Employer	Name of Supervisor		Month	Year
Job Title	What were your duties?	Starting Date		
Telephone Number	Why did you leave?	Ending Date		
Name and Address of Employer	Name of Supervisor		Month	Year
Job Title	What were your duties?	Starting Date		
Telephone Number	Why did you leave?	Ending Date		

Have you ever worked for our company before? _____

Do you know someone who works for our company? _____

How did you hear about us? _____

References

List the names of three professional references. You must have known each for at least one year.

Name	Address	How do you know this person, and for how many years?

Pre-Employment Mathematics Test

Please complete the following to the best of your ability.

1. You are working at the cash register. A customer gives you $22.00 for a $16.67 purchase. What change will you give the customer? _____
2. How many 4′ by 8′ sheets of drywall are needed for the walls of a room that is 10′ by 15′ and 8′ high? _____
3. $327.98 \times 1.15 =$ _____
4. $2343.54 + 64.97 + 360.17 + 126.65 =$ _____

I hereby authorize the Company to thoroughly investigate my background, references, work history, and other matters related to my suitability for this workplace. I authorize those listed here to release any pertinent records and I release all employees of such institutions from any claim that arises as a result of this investigation. I authorize that my answers here are truthful, and that any misrepresentation or omission of facts may result in rejection of this application, or, if hired, in necessary discipline or dismissal.

I understand that this application does not constitute a contract or an offer of employment between me and the Company. I further understand that should I be offered a job with the Company, it will be for no specific period, and that my employment can be terminated by me or by the Company at any time without prior notice for any reason.

Date _____ Signature _____

After You Read

Handbook Link
How to prepare a portfolio

1. Based on the information in the job application, list the items you would put in your portfolio to prepare for a job interview with this company.

Before You Read

With your small group, discuss and list the types of questions that a prospective employer is not, under law, allowed to ask you in an interview. Then read the poem to explain why you think the job applicant made the decision she did.

The Interview

by Margie Marks

Good thing I wore a dress today.
I think he liked me.
Was it my eyes? He said I had
beautiful eyes.
I wonder why.
We talked for a while. He asked
irrelevant questions.
I answered them.
We laughed. I chuckled at his old jokes.
He leaned back in his chair and
winked at me.
His eyes followed my dress hem
down to my shoes.
He said I had beautiful eyes.
I refused the job.

After You Read

1. With a partner, role-play this poem. What kinds of questions would be considered irrelevant? How did the interviewee react to these questions? How do you know? Pay particular attention to the body language described in the poem.

Handbook Link

How to create and give effective oral presentations

How to create an effective speaking style

Before You Read

Consider the potentially dangerous equipment you might use every day — for example, in your science lab; technology, Family Studies, hospitality, health care and agriculture programs; at home; or at work. Choose one of those programs or classes as your focus. Imagine that a new student has just entered the class. What are five important safety rules that you would want that person to know?

Young Worker
Awareness Program

http://www.yworker.com/english/ywa_eng.htm

YOUNG WORKER AWARENESS PROGRAM

Home

7 Things You'd Better Know

True Tales of Health and Safety

Health and Safety Quiz

Talk to Us

Free Stuff

Resources

Book the YWA Program

How did you find out about the YWAP site?
- Saw the ads
- Presentation at school
- Friend told me
- Search results
- Other

[Send]

Welcome!

Our goal is to give you the health and safety awareness you need to protect yourself and your fellow workers.

Why?

Because an average of 42 young Ontario workers are injured, made ill, or killed on the job every day. That's over 15,000 each year. Think of it. That's almost 2 young workers injured every hour of every day and every night, seven days a week, and it's often because of *what they didn't know.*

This site contains health and safety information for young workers, their parents, teachers, principals, employers and others. Though the information is specific to the province of Ontario, Canada (the Young Worker Awareness Program is only available to Ontario high schools), others may also find it useful. Health and safety on the job knows no boundaries.

Who is a young worker?

If you're working – part-time or full-time – and you're between 15 and 24 years of age, then you are considered to be a young worker.

What is YWAP?

The Workplace Safety and Insurance Board and its health and safety partners believe that these injuries and deaths could have been prevented.

So we've created the YOUNG WORKER AWARENESS PROGRAM – to give students the information they need to protect their health and safety on the job.

The program is available to any high school in the province of Ontario, Canada. It has two components, a general assembly presentation and a classroom instruction segment. Both the general assembly and classroom components stress student interaction.

Using video and other materials, trained instructors will come to any Ontario high school to deliver this crucial message. Students receive a resource booklet and other information. There is no charge to the student or school for this program.

The program is offered by the <u>Industrial Accident Prevention Association</u>, the <u>Ontario Service Safety Alliance</u> and the <u>Workers Health and Safety Centre</u>, organizations funded by the <u>Workplace Safety & Insurance Board of Ontario</u>.

After You Read

1. List the basic elements of this Web page. Explain whether you think each element is effective, then write a short analysis, commenting on the usability, organization, and look of the page.
2. a. List several statistics from this Web page, then write a paragraph that reflects how you feel about those statistics.
   b. Write a second paragraph suggesting other approaches for dealing with the issue of worker protection.

Handbook Link

How to identify design elements in text

How to describe design and production choices in media

Before You Read

Before you read this article, test your knowledge by answering true or false to the following questions. Then read the article to confirm your answers.

1. Young people between the ages of 15 and 24 are at the highest risk of being hurt or killed on the job.
2. You have the right to refuse to do work that you think is unsafe.
3. People who work in the fast-food industry are at low risk of being hurt or killed on the job.
4. It is the employer's responsibility to train workers in safety procedures.

Learning to
Work Safely

by Rosemarie Bahr

A disproportionate number of young people get injured at work. Students need to learn their rights and to ask questions.

Retired teacher Doug McAndless has examples and stories to illustrate all kinds of risks these Hill Park Secondary School students will face any day on the job.

Yvon Larivière works at Ivaco, making steel products, and is a member of the United Steelworkers. He is one of hundreds of business people, union activists and retired teachers who spend time in classrooms throughout the province making young people aware that workplaces can be dangerous.

In 1999 in Ontario, 16 people between the ages of 15 and 24 were killed on the job. In 1998, it was 18 – 16 young men and two young women.

Every year, more than 15,000 young people are injured on the job. The most common injuries are strains and sprains, damage to soft tissues like cuts, punctures and bruises, broken bones, joint inflammation and burns. Proportionately, more people in this age group are injured and die at work than in any other group.

Bringing Awareness

Doug McAndless tells Barbara Tkach's Grade 9 Introduction to Business students about a woman he knows who, at age 19, can't pick up a cup with her left hand because she has carpal tunnel syndrome. She'd been working part-time as a cashier since she was 14. As he explains that the syndrome, common in people who use computers, involves compressing the nerves in the wrist, half the students flex at least one hand, testing. They can identify with that. They all use computers.

A retired teacher who lives in London, McAndless is spending the day at Hill Park Secondary School in Hamilton, telling students that they need to ask questions and that they have rights when it comes to their health and safety in the workplace.

The class watches a video that features two young workers injured at their job. It reinforces three points: all employees, even part-time students, have the right

to know about the hazards in their workplace, the right to participate in health and safety committees at work and the right to refuse work they think is unsafe.

WHMIS

McAndless shows an overhead of the WHMIS (Workplace Hazardous Materials Information System) symbols and of the symbols that mark hazardous consumer products. He extracts a promise from the students that if they see one of these symbols on anything they need to handle at work, they will go straight to their employer and ask for training on how to use the product.

A few students already have jobs. McAndless asks about hazards where they work and about their training. He has examples and stories to illustrate every situation.

Jane McCormick teaches co-op education at West Hill Secondary School in Owen Sound. During her four years there, they've had McAndless or someone else from the Workers Health and Safety Centre present the Young Worker Awareness Program. "We can read the resource package," McCormick says, "but it is the stories and the interaction that really drive the point home to the students."

She adds, "Most of these kids have part-time jobs, and Doug always asks them if there's a health and safety committee at their work. Ninety-nine per cent of them don't know. A lot of these jobs are in fast food restaurants

and places that are high risk as far as accidents happening. It is incredibly scary, but by far the majority of kids have had zero or minimal safety training from their employer."

Young Worker Awareness Program

McAndless co-ordinates the Young Worker Awareness Program for the Workers Health and Safety Centre (WHSC), a province-wide organization that delivers training programs on workplace health and safety, primarily through union members who are trained instructors.

Presenters of the Young Worker Awareness Program reach more than 36,000 students a year in Ontario. First developed in 1988 by the Workers Health and Safety Centre and the Ontario Teachers' Feder-ation, the program has evolved into a joint project of the WHSC and the Industrial Accident Prevention Association (IAPA), an association of industrial sector companies that also delivers health and safety training programs.

The Young Worker Awareness Program is funded through the Workplace Safety and Insurance Board, formerly the Workers' Compensation Board. Materials and presentations are available in English and French. Both the centre and the association deliver the program. The IAPA uses volunteers from the business community and the WHSC uses retired teachers and sometimes union members.

The presenters, whether they are retired teachers booked through the Workers Health and Safety Centre or business people booked through the Industrial Accident Prevention Association, share a passion for the topic and the well-being of the students.

On the Road

Anne Wilson, a retired elementary teacher in Timiskaming and a past president of the Ontario Teachers' Federation, travels from Gravenhurst as far as Cochrane to deliver the Young Worker Awareness Program. She's one of more than 40 retired teachers recruited by McAndless. Wilson says that all the time she spends on this project will be worth it if it prevents one young person getting injured.

She says, "For the students I think it is an opportunity to have a different face in front of them telling them about something different from what their co-op teacher would be saying. I think many of them remember the examples more than they remember the other stuff. But that's the whole purpose behind the examples, of course."

One example that retired Peel teacher Neil Davis uses is the story of Sean Kells. Sean Kells was pouring a flammable chemical from one ungrounded drum to another when it exploded. It was his third day on the part-time job and he hadn't been told that what he was doing could be dangerous. He was 19 when he died.

A student in one of Davis' classes said that's what she did, pour a chemical from a large drum into smaller ones. "I pressed her," said Davis, "asking what the chemicals were. She didn't know."

Davis asked if they were labelled. She'd never checked. Davis asked how could she do the job when she hadn't considered the safety features. Her response was, says Davis, "If it had been dangerous, he wouldn't have asked me to do it."

Too Trusting

He continues, "They trust mom and dad, they trust their teacher. They transfer that trust to the employer, and that is where things break down because the employer doesn't have the stake in the young person's life and welfare that the teacher does."

Davis, in talking with the students, has learned "there is a tremendous gap between what the law says is supposed to happen and what young people are experiencing in workplaces."

He says, "They leave the session, if nothing else, a little more aware of the fact that all jobs are potentially risky, but that there are rights in the law. If you have the courage to promote them, stand up for them, they will be acknowledged."

Schools also regularly invite presenters from the IAPA. IAPA consultant John VanLenthe has been presenting the Young Worker Awareness Program for more than four years in schools from Burlington to Oakville. He

comments, "We're starting to get through to them that training is important, that they just can't do things without asking questions. They're young, they want to impress the boss. They want to do the job. Getting around the whole mindset about not asking questions is difficult. We as an employer or supervisor have to make sure they have the information."

Ellen Shaeen-Hanright, another IAPA instructor, works at IMAX Corporation as the manager of occupational health and safety. She tells the students, "look out for yourself because it can happen to you. You are ultimately responsible for your safety." She finds that "kids want to talk" and that there's more awareness since recent campaigns about the deaths of young workers like David Ellis and Sean Kells.

Day of Mourning

The story of David Ellis is the subject of a video used in another health and safety program, this one delivered by the United Steelworkers. The 18-year-old was killed in an industrial bread maker on his second day on the job.

The United Steelworkers started the Day of Mourning Young Workers' Health and Safety Campaign in Ontario five years ago. The union decided that a positive way to mark April 28, the international Day of Mourning for workers injured and killed on the job, would be to educate students about workplace health and safety.

In the weeks leading up to April 28, Steelworkers contacted their local schools. The enthusiastic response from teachers and students to presentations by health and safety activists led the Steelworkers to expand the program to the rest of Canada two years ago, and last year, they talked with 30,000 students. Steelworkers now also respond to invitations at any time of the school year.

The content of the Steelworker program is similar to the Young Worker Awareness Program. Presentations and materials are available in French and English.

Passport to Safety

For the last four years, the Greater Peterborough Safe Communities Coalition has been working on Passport to Safety, a pilot project to expand the health and safety training given in schools.

Safe community coalitions have arisen in several communities, stemming from the Safe Communities Foundation. The death at work of 19-year-old Sean Kells in 1994 led his father to set up the Safe Communities Foundation to help prevent any other families from experiencing the same loss. Working with a concept developed by the World Health Organization, communities set up safe community coalitions that develop health and safety programs targeted toward injuries prevalent in their area.

The passport in Passport to Safety is a booklet students get when they take their first health and safety course, which is the Young Worker Awareness Program. They get a stamp in the passport for each additional safety-related course they take to document their safety-related knowledge for potential employers.

Program sponsors hope that employers will give preference in hiring young people who have taken the courses. Some courses are provided by groups like the Red Cross, St. John's Ambulance or the Y. Others are being developed by the Greater Peterborough group. Courses currently being offered to schools in the Peterborough area through this program are the Young Worker Awareness Program, WHMIS, "wear the gear" or using protective clothing and equipment, fire safety, and repetitive strain injuries.

So far, 4,000 Peterborough-area students are registered in the program, meaning they have taken at least the Young Worker Awareness Program, and 2,000 of those have taken at least one additional course.

This ad was created for the Workplace Safety and Insurance Board after 18-year-old David Ellis was killed on the job.

Speaking as an employer, Safe Communities Coalition chair Tom Sayer notes, "It is a great advantage to us to have someone come in and have a basic awareness of safety in the workplace because they are going to be more receptive when I am trying to do my training with them." Sayer is manager of manufacturing at GE in Peterborough.

Employers' Obligation

Sayer says the employers themselves have an obligation to do site-specific training when the student comes into the workplace. "What we are trying to do," he says, "is say there are certain tools that are out there available to you. There is a program called WHMIS and it's the law, everybody has to do it. But they should know that if someone is asking them to work with something that there is a process here that tells them they should be able to get information about it."

The passport program is currently in its evaluation phase. Once that's done, all or parts of the program may be made more widely available.

That would be good news for teachers, as changes to the curriculum place more emphasis on workplace health and safety. For instance, in the new Grade 10 Career Studies, a required half-credit course, students will "demonstrate understanding of how to maintain safety in the workplace and identify employees' and employers' rights and responsibilities."

With so many students working part-time and all students doing 40 hours of community work, it's increasingly important they realize they need to ask the questions to make sure they're safe.

Handbook Link

How to interpret and assess information, ideas, and issues in text

How to describe design and production choices in media

After You Read

1. Confirm your answers from Before You Read.
2. Who is the audience for this article? Discuss with a partner how you know, and list the clues you find to support your answer.
3. With your partner, discuss what you would do if you found yourself in a dangerous situation on the job after being directed to a task by a supervisor.

Before You Read

The following selection describes some of the benefits offered to employees of a company. The package includes fair pay, health benefits, a positive work environment, financial benefits, training and upgrading, and community involvement.

Rank how important each factor is to you in your work, with 1 being most important. Discuss your ranking with a partner or small group. Then explain in a brief paragraph why the first two factors you've chosen are so important to you.

Working
for You

A Package Deal

We're proud to have you as our employee. We expect great things of you, and, in return, we know we're going to have to meet your high expectations of an employer. Don't worry. We think we can do it!

Sure, we're going to pay you well — just compare our salary scale to other companies, and you'll see just how competitive we are — but we know you aren't here just for the money. You want more. You're looking for some important commitments — a guarantee that we'll do our best to help you fulfil your role as employee and to grow and learn in a safe, invigorating environment. We will make that commitment to you, and we'll lay out the details right here in black and white. We are pleased to guarantee you a wide range of important benefits — a package deal — to ensure that you choose to remain a motivated, active part of our team.

Have a look at the pieces that make up this package. Any questions? Let's talk.

Here's to Your Health

Your health, and that of your family, is important to you and to us. We have put the following benefits in place to help you stay well and meet medical or emotional challenges, both while you are working for us and after you retire.

Medical benefits
Dental benefits
Life insurance
Short-term insurance and long-term disability insurance
Vacations
Leaves of absence (for purposes of child care, bereavement, or public
   duty, such as jury duty)
Occupational health services and Wellness program
Staff recreational and cultural activities

The Right Environment

We know how important it is to feel safe and supported at your place of work. That's why we make it a priority to ensure that you have a terrific work environment.

Safe and healthy work facilities
Up-to-date technology and infrastructures
Clearly defined company vision
Culture of open communication and shared purpose

Dollars and Sense

At our company, we do our best to offer you a generous pay cheque, but that's not the only financial reward that will come your way. We invite you to have ownership of the company you work for. That way, when we do well, you see a direct benefit, too. Plus, we offer you ways to save money when you buy company products or services.

Base pay
Profit sharing
Stock purchase
Retirement savings
Employee discount on purchases and products
Daycare discount

Reaching Your Potential

We recognize that we are only successful as a company when you are successful as an employee. We commit to do all we can to help you understand and achieve performance goals, and then to help you aim even higher. We will recognize your achievements and service to the company. When we invest in you, we all win.

Clearly defined performance goals and responsibilities
Regular performance reviews
Annual reports and meetings to keep you in the loop
Recognition programs
Service pins and celebrations
Learning opportunities
Career and professional development
Tuition reimbursement

Lending a Hand

Our company does not stand alone. We recognize and value the local communities in which we function. We feel a responsibility to support them and we are proud to do so in the following ways:

Charitable donations
Business partnerships
Mentoring programs and scholarships for employees' children
Sponsoring of local events
Environmental awards that recognize local environmental initiatives
Seasonal gift and food drives

After You Read

1. Imagine that you work for this company in the Human Resources Department. Choose an excerpt from this policy. In your own words, turn the information into oral instructions to give a new employee on the first day of work.

Handbook Link

How to give oral instructions

Before You Read

In this excerpt from her autobiography, Maya Angelou is determined to get a job as a streetcar conductor in San Francisco, even though no person of colour has ever held that position. She follows her mother's advice to "Put your whole heart in everything you do," but the road is long and hard when you're fighting other people's prejudices.

Think about a time when you or someone that you know may have had to overcome another person's ideas about what you or they could achieve. What steps were taken to achieve the goal? Write a paragraph to describe the situation.

I Know Why THE CAGED BIRD Sings

by Maya Angelou

Later, my room had all the cheeriness of a dungeon and the appeal of a tomb. It was going to be impossible to stay there, but leaving held no attraction for me, either. Running away from home would be anticlimactic after Mexico, and a dull story after my month in the car lot. But the need for change bulldozed a road down the center of my mind.

I had it. The answer came to me with the suddenness of a collision. I would go to work. Mother wouldn't be difficult to convince; after all, in school I was a year ahead of my grade and Mother was a firm believer in self-sufficiency. In fact, she'd be pleased to think that I had that much gumption, that much of her in my character. (She liked to speak of herself as the original "do-it-yourself girl.")

Once I had settled on getting a job, all that remained was to decide which kind of job I was most fitted for. My intellectual pride had kept me from selecting typing, shorthand or filing as subjects in school, so office work was ruled out. War plants and shipyards demanded birth certificates, and mine would reveal me to be fifteen, and ineligible for work. So the well-paying defense jobs were also out. Women had replaced men on the streetcars as conductors and motormen, and the thought of sailing up and down the hills of San Francisco in a dark-blue uniform, with a money changer at my belt, caught my fancy.

Mother was as easy as I had anticipated. The world was moving so fast, so much money was being made, so many people were dying in Guam, and Germany, that hordes of strangers became good friends overnight. Life was cheap and death entirely free. How could she have the time to think about my academic career?

To her question of what I planned to do, I replied that I would get a job on the streetcars. She rejected the proposal with: "They don't accept colored people on the streetcars."

I would like to claim an immediate fury which was followed by the noble determination to break the restricting tradition. But the truth is, my first reaction was one of disappointment. I'd pictured myself, dressed in a neat blue serge suit, my money changer swinging jauntily at my waist, and a cheery smile for the passengers which would make their own work day brighter.

From disappointment, I gradually ascended the emotional ladder to haughty indignation, and finally to that state of stubbornness where the mind is locked like the jaws of an enraged bulldog.

I would go to work on the streetcar and wear a blue serge suit. Mother gave me her support with one of her usual terse asides, "That's what you want to do? Then nothing beats a trial but a failure. Give it everything you've got. I've told you many times, 'Can't do is like don't care.' Neither of them have a home."

Translated, that meant there was nothing a person can't do, and there should be nothing a human being didn't care about. It was the most positive encouragement I could have hoped for.

Maya Angelou

In the offices of the Market Street Railway Company, the receptionist seemed as surprised to see me there as I was surprised to find the interior dingy and the décor drab. Somehow I had expected waxed surfaces and carpeted floors. If I had met no resistance, I might have decided against working for such a poor-mouth-looking concern. As it was, I explained that I had come to see about a job. She asked, was I sent by an agency, and when I replied that I was not, she told me they were only accepting applicants from agencies.

The classified pages of the morning papers had listed advertisements for motorettes and conductorettes and I reminded her of that. She gave me a face full of astonishment that my suspicious nature would not accept.

"I am applying for the job listed in this morning's *Chronicle* and I'd like to be presented to your personnel manager." While I spoke in supercilious accents, and looked at the room as if I had an oil well in my own backyard, my armpits were being pricked by millions of hot pointed needles. She saw her escape and dived into it.

"He's out. He's out for the day. You might call tomorrow and if he's in, I'm sure you can see him." Then she swiveled her chair around on its rusty screws and with that I was supposed to be dismissed.

"May I ask his name?"

She half turned, acting surprised to find me still there.

"His name? Whose name?"

"Your personnel manager."

We were firmly joined in the hypocrisy to play out the scene.

"The personnel manager? Oh, he's Mr. Cooper, but I'm not sure you'll find him here tomorrow. He's … Oh, but you can try."

"Thank you."

"You're welcome."

And I was out of the musty room and into the even mustier lobby. In the street I saw the receptionist and myself going faithfully through paces that were stale with familiarity, although I had never encountered that kind of situation before and, probably, neither had she. We were like actors who, knowing the play by heart, were still able to cry afresh over the old tragedies and laugh spontaneously at the comic situations.

The miserable little encounter had nothing to do with me, the me of me, any more than it had to do with that silly clerk. The incident was a recurring dream, concocted years before by stupid whites and it eternally came back to haunt us all. The secretary and I were like Hamlet and Laertes in the final scene, where, because of harm done by one ancestor to another, we were bound to duel to the death. Also because the play must end somewhere.

I went further than forgiving the clerk, I accepted her as a fellow victim of the same puppeteer.

On the streetcar, I put my fare into the box and the conductorette looked at me with the usual hard eyes of white contempt. "Move into the car, please move on in the car." She patted her money changer.

Her Southern nasal accent sliced my meditation and I looked deep into my thoughts. All lies, all comfortable lies. The receptionist was not innocent and neither was I. The whole charade we had played out in that crummy waiting room had directly to do with me, Black, and her, white.

I wouldn't move into the streetcar but stood on the ledge over the conductor, glaring. My mind shouted so energetically that the announcement made my veins stand out, and my mouth tighten into a prune.

I WOULD HAVE THE JOB. I WOULD BE A CONDUCTORETTE AND SLING A FULL MONEY CHANGER FROM MY BELT. I WOULD.

The next three weeks were a honeycomb of determination with apertures for the days to go in and out. The Negro organizations to whom I appealed for support bounced me back and forth like a shuttlecock on a badminton court. Why did I insist on that particular job? Openings were going begging that paid nearly twice the money. The minor officials with whom I was able to win an audience thought me mad. Possibly I was.

Downtown San Francisco became alien and cold, and the streets I had loved in a personal familiarity were unknown lanes that twisted with malicious intent. Old buildings, whose gray rococo façades housed my memories of the Forty-Niners, and Diamond Lil, Robert Service, Sutter and Jack London, were then imposing structures viciously joined to keep me out. My trips to the streetcar office were of the frequency of a person on salary. The struggle expanded. I was no longer in conflict only with the Market Street Railway but with the marble lobby of the building which housed its offices, and elevators and their operators.

During this period of strain Mother and I began our first steps on the long path toward mutual adult admiration. She never asked for reports and I didn't offer any details. But every morning she made breakfast, gave me carfare and lunch money, as if I were going to work. She comprehended the perversity of life, that in the struggle lies the joy. That I was no glory seeker was obvious to her, and that I had to exhaust every possibility before giving in was also clear.

On my way out of the house one morning she said, "Life is going to give you just what you put in it. Put your whole heart in everything you do, and pray, then you can wait." Another time she reminded that "God helps those who help themselves." She had a store of aphorisms which she dished out as the occasion demanded. Strangely, as bored as I was with clichés, her inflection gave them something new, and set me thinking for a little while at least. Later when asked how I got my job, I was never able to say exactly. I only knew that one day, which was tiresomely like all the others before it, I sat in the Railway office, ostensibly waiting to be interviewed. The receptionist called me to her desk and shuffled a bundle of papers to me. They were job application forms. She said they had to be filled in triplicate. I had little time to wonder if I had won or not, for the standard questions reminded me of the necessity for dexterous lying. How old was I? List my previous jobs, starting from the last held and go backward to the first. How much money did I earn, and why did I leave the position? Give two references (not relatives).

Sitting at a side table my mind and I wove a cat's ladder of near truths and total lies. I kept my face blank (an old art) and wrote quickly the fable of

Marguerite Johnson, aged nineteen, former companion and driver for Mrs. Annie Henderson (a White Lady) in Stamps, Arkansas.

I was given blood tests, aptitude tests, physical coordination tests, and Rorschachs, then on a blissful day I was hired as the first Negro on the San Francisco streetcars.

Mother gave me the money to have my blue serge suit tailored, and I learned to fill out work cards, operate the money changer and punch transfers. The time crowded together and at an End of Days I was swinging on the back of the rackety trolley, smiling sweetly and persuading my charges to "step forward in the car, please."

After You Read

1. The author's confidence and determination help her to attain success. Turn her story about finding her first full-time job into a brief action plan for a job search, up to the part where she fills out a job application.
2. Discuss with a partner or group the lessons that readers can take from this selection. What lessons are particular to those seeking a first-time job? How can these lessons be applied to life in general? To your life?

Handbook Link
How to create an action plan

Before You Read

Skim the features of the workplace memo. How is it like, and unlike, a letter? What are the main differences? What makes this a good form of communication in a workplace environment?

MEMO

Date: June 2, 2003
To: All employees
From: Afua Akande
Re: Upcoming move

As you all know, we will be moving our offices this month. We will be moving by division so that there is as little interruption to our work schedule as possible.

Please carefully read the information below in order to see when your division is assigned to pack files and products, when your boxes will be picked up, and when you will move to the new office space. Each employee is responsible for packing and moving his or her own personal belongings.

	Pack	Box Pickup	Move-In Date
Corporate	June 9	June 10	June 11
Division A	June 11	June 12	June 13
Division B	June 13	June 16	June 17
Sales	June 16	June 17	June 18

Please wear comfortable clothing and shoes to pack. All employees will earn regular pay for their packing day.

If you have any questions or concerns, please call me. I look forward to seeing you all in the new office.

After You Read

Handbook Link
How to write a memorandum

1. In your notebook, outline the basic format of a memo.
2. Write a memo of your own in response to this one.

Before You Read

An annual report gives important information to people who are share-holders in a company or stakeholders in a community or organization. This annual report gives important information to people who live in and around the Grand River, which is an important source of drinking water for many southern Ontario communities. Scan the report to find the key visuals it contains. What important purpose do the visuals serve in the report? Share your observations with a partner.

The **GRAND**

GRAND RIVER
CONSERVATION
AUTHORITY
2000 ANNUAL REPORT

*News for Brantford, Cambridge, Guelph, Kitchener, Waterloo
and Other Communities in the Grand River Valley*

DISTRIBUTION 186,300 COPIES

A Message FROM THE CHAIRMAN

As I have said many times before, "Water will be the issue of the 21st century." Central to our growing concern about water is the whole question of water quality. The Grand River Conservation Authority plays a key role in the protection of water quality in conjunction with its municipal partners in the Grand River watershed. This important water quality work is supported by a portion of the levy (see page 6) that Grand River watershed municipalities provide to the GRCA.

Water quality concerns are also related to economic concerns. If we have good water quality and a healthy environment, we will have a healthy economy. The economy is a subsidiary of the environment. With this connection in mind, it is important to realize that the GRCA carries out its flood control, water quality, and environmental work, all guided by long term planning. We are not planning with just a 5 to 10 year timeline. We are looking ahead at least 50 years. This is not an idle boast. After all, we have been in this business for almost 70 years.

We hope to expand the range of services that we provide in conjunction with our municipalities and the province. Looking to the future, we are currently in contact with senior staff at the Ministries of Natural Resources, Environment, Municipal Affairs, and Agriculture, Food and Rural Affairs. In spite of a temporary downturn in the economy, the future looks bright for the Grand River watershed.

Peter Krause

Peter Krause
Chairman

A Message FROM THE CAO

The past year has been a rewarding one for the Grand River Conservation Authority (GRCA). The watershed management model developed in the Grand River basin has received unprecedented recognition. Internationally, the GRCA received the prestigious 2000 Thiess Environmental Services Award in Brisbane, Australia. Nationally, we received the Red Fisher Conservation Award. Locally, we received an Environmental Sustainability Award in June, recognizing environmental innovation in the Region of Waterloo. In some respects, these awards from our local partners are the most meaningful recognition of all.

The municipalities in the Grand River watershed definitely deserve much of the credit for the recognition the GRCA has received. In Brantford in 1934, eight of these municipalities founded the Grand River Conservation Commission, which later became the Grand River Conservation Authority. The Grand River municipalities have supported our work ever since.

I would like to thank the members of the GRCA General Membership for their support and guidance. I would also like to thank all GRCA staff for their continuing commitment to one of the leading watershed management agencies in the world.

Paul Emerson

Paul Emerson
Chief Administrative Officer

WATER, WATER EVERYWHERE

First of all, let's sort out the different types of water. Rain water, surface water, river water, groundwater, source water — what's the difference?

Let's start with stormy weather, and rainwater. Rain falls with a number of possible destinations. It can become surface water or groundwater.

Surface Water: If rain falls on a lake or a river, it becomes part of those surface bodies of water. If it falls on the ground, and flows into lakes or rivers, it also becomes surface water.

Groundwater: If rain water falls on the ground and percolates into the ground to join water under the ground, it becomes groundwater. Deep and shallow groundwater, aquifers, and water from wells are all known as groundwater.

Sometimes, surface water moves into the ground and becomes groundwater. And sometimes groundwater moves up and becomes surface water — such as spring water.

Source Water: Surface water and groundwater are the two main sources of raw drinking water. In the Grand River watershed about 80% of our drinking water comes from groundwater sources, and 20% from surface water.

Drinking Water: This is the water that comes out of your tap. Unless you're getting your water from a well, it has been treated by the municipality where you live before it reaches you.

Watershed: A watershed is all the land drained by a river or a system of rivers. The Grand River drains or receives runoff from a watershed that is 6,800 sq. km (2,600 sq. mi.)

This issue of The Grand looks at the water quality work that municipalities and the GRCA are carrying out together. This work is important to ensure continuing supplies of water as the communities in the Grand River area continue to grow.

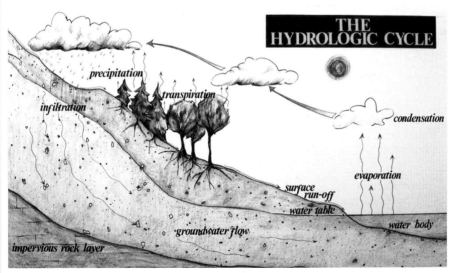

THE HYDROLOGIC CYCLE

What Goes Around, Comes Around

The hydrologic cycle or water cycle seems to be on people's minds more and more these days. The relationship between rain water, surface water, groundwater and drinking water is central to understanding water quality.

WHAT IS THE GRCA SAYING TO THE
Walkerton Inquiry?

In the fall of 2000 the GRCA was invited to appear at the Walkerton Inquiry. Although Walkerton is outside the GRCA watershed boundary, the Authority was the only Conservation Authority in Ontario to receive separate standing at this inquiry. Why?

At that time, the GRCA had just been honoured with the 2000 Thiess Environmental Services Award, recognizing the Authority as the best river management agency in the world. In part, the award was presented in recognition of the GRCA's extensive water quality work in conjunction with its municipal partners.

Dr. Tony Smith of the GRCA was the lead author of a Conservation Ontario paper presented to the Walkerton Inquiry, titled "The Importance of Watershed Management in Protecting Ontario's Drinking Water Supplies." This extensive paper contains a number of important recommendations:

1. The protection of drinking water sources should be recognized as a permanent and integral part of a long-term, secure water supply strategy.

2. The watershed should be recognized as the viable unit for managing water.

3. A provincial integrated water policy should be developed that:
   - Recognizes the principles of watershed management and deals with all aspects of water
   - Builds upon the conservation authority model to advance watershed management
   - Clarifies the role of the provincial government in water management
   - Promotes research into water issues and development of decision support tools to ensure the best science, technology and management practices are shared and available for local application
   - Supports an adequate monitoring program to measure change and adapt policies and programs accordingly
   - Supports the improvement, maintenance and accessibility of resource data for effective local watershed management

4. Adequate and stable source(s) of funding should be established to finance watershed management throughout Ontario.

5. The Province should encourage the Federal Government to develop a national framework for water policy and to strengthen co-operative agreements with provinces under the Canada Water Act.

The Inquiry is still continuing, and at this point it appears that the government of Ontario is committed to improving the protection of the province's water supply.

What Happens Before We
TURN ON OUR TAPS?

The Grand River Watershed

A lot of things happen before we turn on our taps. The municipality where you live tries to ensure the best water quality that it can. Some municipalities take a portion of their drinking water supply from the Grand River system. Most of them take most of it from groundwater supplies. In the Grand River watershed, all municipalities are aware of the GRCA's efforts to help the community where you live in all ways that a Conservation Authority can.

Of course, the GRCA doesn't deliver your drinking water — your municipality does. However, the GRCA is deeply involved in protecting and sustaining the quality of "source" water for your municipality. What types of water quality work? Here are the answers to questions about the water quality work going on where you live.

SHOULD WE STILL CALL THE RIVER THE GRAND?
The Grand River used to almost dry up in the summer. Today GRCA dams add water to the river system and keep the Grand flowing. This added water helps to improve water quality.

WHAT ABOUT THE DRINKING WATER IN YOUR PARKS?
This year GRCA Conservation Areas and Nature Centres will begin to provide treated and tested drinking water to their visitors. Like your municipality, we're trying to make sure there won't be any problems with our drinking water.

WHAT DO TREES HAVE TO DO WITH WATER QUALITY?
Trees slow the rate of runoff to rivers. We've planted over 26 million of them. Slower runoff is often cleaner runoff. Cleaner runoff means better water quality in the river for municipalities that take water from the river.

WHAT ABOUT WATER QUALITY AT THE BEACHES IN YOUR PARKS?
Water samples are taken and tested at least once a week at GRCA beaches during the summer. If there's a problem with the water, the local Health Unit posts the beach as "Unsafe for Bathing."

WHAT DO FISH HAVE TO DO WITH WATER QUALITY?

Fish like clean water. There are 82 different species living in the Grand. They must like the water quality. GRCA Aquatic Resources Staff are helping to make it better, often with volunteers in local communities.

"WELCOME TO DA SWAMP!" WHY DO YOU OWN ALL THAT SWAMP WATER?

Swamps or wetlands hold and filter water. They also recharge groundwater with good quality water as long as these wetlands are protected. So wetlands improve water quality, even if some people still call them 'swamps.'

WHAT HAPPENS WHEN IT RAINS?

Farmers and gardeners are happy. Runoff from the rain replenishes the river, wetlands, and the groundwater under our feet.

I LIVE IN THE COUNTRY. WHAT ARE PEOPLE IN THE CITIES DOING ABOUT WATER QUALITY?

Many cities and their residents are quite concerned about water quality. Municipal sewage treatment plants are being upgraded. In addition, the Region of Waterloo, City of Guelph, and Wellington County have directed millions of dollars toward improving the quality of "rural" water that flows into urbanized areas. It's known as the Rural Water Quality Program — where city and country cousins working together to improve water quality. It may be a first in Canada.

I LIVE IN THE CITY. WHAT ARE FARMERS DOING ABOUT WATER QUALITY?

The great majority of farmers care about their land and the environment. Part of caring about them means working to improve water quality by using environmentally sound farming practices. Thousands of farmers are doing this in the Grand River watershed. Many of them are taking part in the Rural Water Quality Program.

After You Read

1. Answer the following questions in your reading response journal:
   a. What is the purpose of this report?
   b. Who is the audience for this report?
   c. Is the report easy to read? Explain.
2. Find annual reports from other agencies or businesses. In small groups, examine the reports. Create a chart to compare their layout, design, and the type of information shared with the audience.
3. Discuss with a partner whether an annual report is a good tool for informing an audience, and whether annual reports are always credible. Give reasons for your answers.

Handbook Link
How to read a business report

Before You Read

With a partner or small group, talk about a part-time or summer job you've had. Discuss various company policies regarding benefits, sick days, special leave, and overtime pay. How did the policies relate to part-time workers? Summer workers? Who explained company policies to you? As a group, list any unanswered questions you have about employee benefits, and see if you can find answers in the following selection.

EMPLOYMENT INSURANCE

Maternity, parental and sickness benefits

Sickness benefits explained

Sickness benefits apply to situations where you are sick, injured or in quarantine. Benefits are paid for up to 15 weeks if you have had 700 hours of insurable employment in the last 52 weeks, or since the start of your last EI claim.

If you are already on claim for reasons other than illness and while you are on claim you fall ill, then you may qualify with less than 700 hours. Check with your local EI office if this is the case.

As well, you can receive sickness benefits in addition to maternity or parental benefits, but you can't receive more than 30 weeks of maternity, parental and sickness benefits in one benefit period.

You must have a medical certificate telling us how long your illness is expected to last.

While you should apply for benefits as soon as you stop work, sometimes people are too ill to apply right away. If this is the case for you, tell us about it and we may be able to backdate your claim to the time your earnings stopped.

Number of hours of work required

The Employment Insurance system is based on hours of paid work and responds to variations in work situations such as part-time, extended hours and compressed weeks. The principle of the hours system is simple: regardless of whether you work full-time, part-time, as a seasonal worker or on and off throughout the year, the hours that you work and for which you are paid are accumulated toward eligibility for EI benefits. Using hours instead of weeks to calculate eligibility ensures that you are credited for all your paid work time.

This approach applies to overtime, which is calculated hour for hour no matter what the rate of pay. As well, paid leave of any type is insured for the number of hours that normally would be worked in that period, regardless of rate of pay.

To be eligible

- for maternity, parental and sickness benefits, you must have worked a minimum of 700 hours in the past 52 weeks or since the start of your last claim.

- However, if you get sick when you are collecting regular benefits, it is possible to be eligible for sickness benefits with fewer than 700 hours.

Premiums

You will pay premiums on all your earnings up to the annual maximum salary of $39,000. This means that deductions will be made at $2.55 for every $100 of salary until the $39,000 has been reached. After that you will not pay any premiums. For example, if you earn $52,000 a year you will pay premiums on the first $39,000. If your earnings are regular weekly amounts of $1,000 per week, you will pay premiums from January through September but will pay no premiums for the remainder of the year.

Section V

Responsibilities and rights

You have the responsibility to:

- report all work and earnings received while collecting Employment Insurance;
- follow instructions from Employment Insurance staff members;
- report any absences from the country, unless told by Employment Insurance staff member(s) that you don't need to do so.

You have the right to:

- file a claim for Employment Insurance benefits;
- receive help in filing a claim;
- appeal decisions about your benefits which you feel are unjust;
- under the *Privacy Act* you have the right to see any government record which contains your personal information.

Section VI

Employment Insurance Fraud

Protecting the system – With your help

We are determined to protect the EI Fund for honest and deserving Canadians. The wealth of experience of EI personnel and the development of powerful computer tracking and data systems have virtually closed off any possibilities of abuse going undetected for long.

It is your responsibility to help detect and deter EI fraud. Stop abuse before it happens. Disclosure of mistakes or overpayment protects you and the system.

> If you have made a mistake and forgotten to give us information on your status, it is not too late to provide it. Under our disclosure policy we can waive any penalty or prosecution, if the matter is not already under investigation.
>
> Don't let an honest mistake cost you.
>
> For further information, contact your local Employment Insurance office.

Penalties for committing fraud

The penalty for fraud is determined as follows: the maximum penalty is **three times the amount of your overpayment** if the overpayment results from undeclared earnings; **three times the weekly benefit rate** if the fraud is not due to undeclared earnings; or **three times the maximum benefit rate** if you did not qualify for benefits.

After You Read

1. Did your group find any of its answers within the selection? If not, what would be the next steps to take to get those questions answered?
2. Create a radio public service announcement that will inform your audience members about their rights as an employee. Focus on one of the benefits outlined in the brochure.

Handbook Link

How to create an action plan

How to create a radio commercial

Before You Read

In this poem, the man has worked with his machine for many years. Scan the poem for key words that give clues to the man's line of work. Make a list of these words. With your small group, discuss what job you think the man and his machine do. Then read the poem a number of times with a focus on how the man feels about the machine he works with.

The Man and the Machine

by E. J. Pratt

By right of fires that smelted ore
Which he had tended years before,
The man whose hands were on the wheel
Could trace his kinship through her steel,
Between his body warped and bent
In every bone and ligament,
And this "eight-cylinder" stream-lined,
The finest model yet designed.

He felt his lesioned pulses strum
Against the rhythm of her hum,
And found his nerves and sinews knot
With sharper spasm as she climbed
The steeper grades, so neatly timed
From storage tank to piston shot—
This creature with the cougar grace,
This man with slag upon his face.

After You Read

1. Work with a partner to analyze this poem. What is the man's job? How do you know? To your list of words that give clues about the man's line of work, add any words with which you are not familiar. Look them up in the dictionary.

Handbook Link

How to use reading strategies to understand text

How to expand your vocabulary

As we learn throughout life, we keep discovering new things about ourselves. Many people will learn that there are new paths they want to take in work and in life; that they want to explore, expand, or invent new horizons.

In this unit you will read how the enterprising spirit has taken hold of different people, hurtling them into space, onto the stage, or behind the counter of businesses that reflect their passions in life; and you will explore how the walls in front of us can give us the opportunity to find new ways to get beyond them.

CONTENTS

Before You Read

When NASA launched the Hubble Space Telescope in 1990, its scientists learned quickly that no matter how much training a worker has, mistakes still happen. The first photos the telescope sent back to Earth showed a flaw in Hubble's mirror, distorting the images. Since then, through problem-solving and hard work, Hubble has been upgraded and improved and is now sending back stunning images of the cosmos.

Reflect on and write about a time when you discovered a mistake you had made in an important project or task. Describe how you solved the problem, and what work you did to fix it.

New Views of the Cosmos

More than a decade into its mission, Hubble continues to lay bare the beauty of our universe.

by Elesa Janke

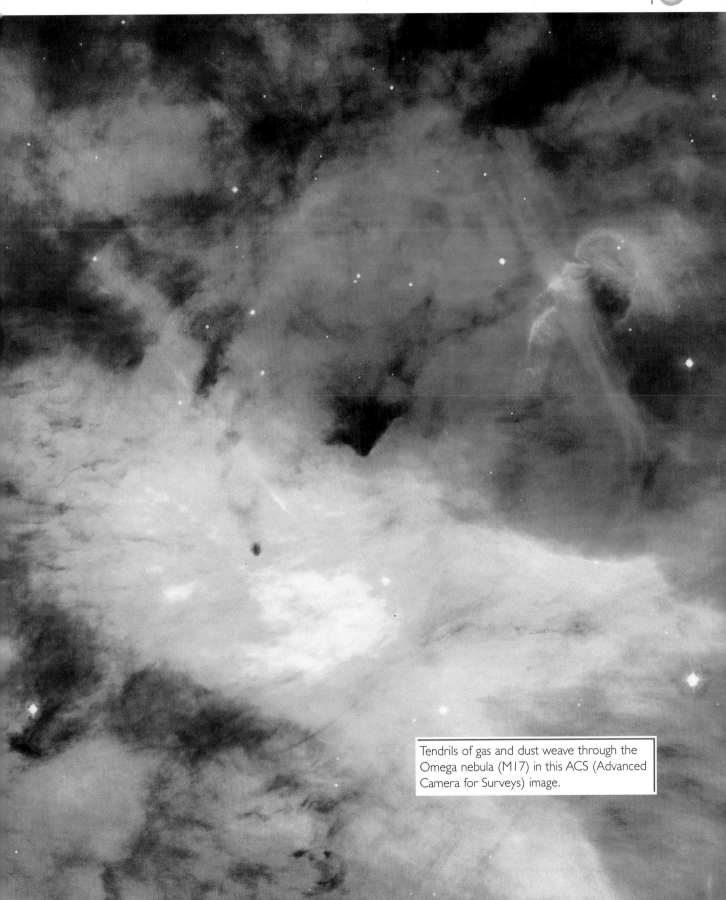

Tendrils of gas and dust weave through the Omega nebula (M17) in this ACS (Advanced Camera for Surveys) image.

NICMOS captured the golden infrared glow from a ring of newborn stars in the heart of the edge-on spiral NGC 4013.

Infrared light from a host of faint young stars pierces the dense dust layers at the tip of the Cone Nebula (NGC 2264).

Since 1990, NASA's Hubble Space Telescope has wowed astronomers and non-astronomers alike with its unprecedented views of the universe, showing us what the cosmos looks like beyond the limited views of earthbound telescopes. But now it seems that the past twelve years of images are only the icing

Although now a second banana, WFPC2 [an earlier Hubble camera] still performs admirably. This 2002 image reveals debris in the Cassiopeia A supernova remnant.

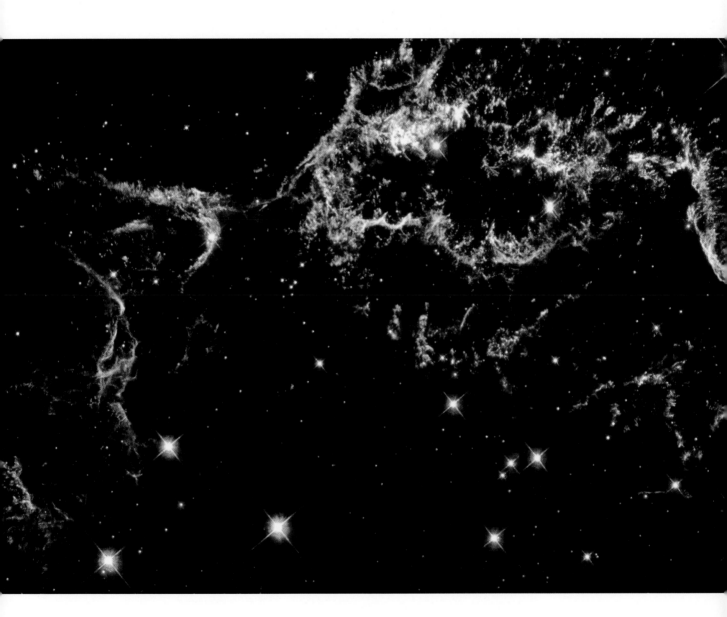

on the cosmic cake. Recently, Hubble's eyesight has improved ten-fold with the addition of the new Advanced Camera for Surveys (ACS). Now, with new images being unveiled on a regular basis, our views of the universe are beginning to expand even beyond the hopes of astronomers.

Another galactic collision formed brilliant star clusters and the long debris tail of the Tadpole (UGC 10214), but this ACS image also captured several thousand background galaxies.

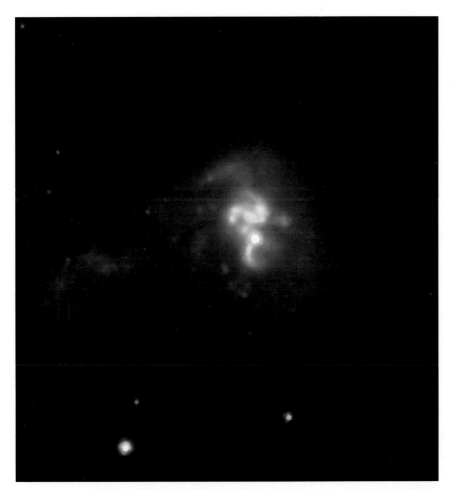

The ACS and NICMOS [Hubble's infrared camera] combined to capture four colliding galaxies, called IRAS 19297-0406.

After You Read

1. Discuss the following questions in a small group:
   a. What is the purpose of this photo essay? Identify the part of the essay that identifies the purpose.
   b. How does the text add to the photos? Explain.
   c. What is the effect of these photos? Explain.

Handbook   Link

How to create a photo essay

Before You Read

With a partner or small group, brainstorm all of the qualities you think someone would need if they want to make it in the music business. Then read about Jaclyn and Cassandra Williams, who released their debut CD in August 2001.

The Era-Banner **ENTERTAINMENT** *Thursday, Sept. 6, 2001*

Singing sisters come home to country

BY STEFANIA RIZZI
STAFF WRITER

It was almost a year to the day Jaclyn and Cassandra Williams took to the stage and made their singing debut in front of a large crowd at the Walkerton Watershed Festival.

Before performing, the two Williams sisters did jumping jacks to calm their nerves and then hit the stage dressed in white knickers, sneakers and matching blue and pink tank tops and jackets.

When the first of two songs started playing, the Newmarket teens began singing. After the last note, the country singers held their breath, waiting to make it or break it.

According to the girls, the round of applause and encouraging shouts they received from the crowd indicated they were a hit.

"Little kids came over and asked us for our autograph. I was like, 'Uh, OK,'" said Jaclyn, 14, the youngest of the two.

Newmarket sisters Jaclyn and Cassandra Williams just released their debut CD.

"I was so confused I didn't know what to do. I wasn't used to (being asked for my autograph) but when we did, it made me feel so good."

The Williams sisters have recently wrapped up recording their debut independent CD, which was released last month at The Lava Lounge in Newmarket.

Recording *The Country Comin' Out in Me* was a dream come true for the girls.

"It's a sense of accomplishment," said 17-year-old Cassandra, appearing relaxed in a pair of dark jeans and blue tank top sitting on a leather couch. "We've been in the studio almost every day, like a full-time job.

"To have it all finished makes you feel like you've done so much and we're so grateful and have so many people to thank for that," said Cassandra, who also plays piano.

Jaclyn and Cassandra have been singing professionally together about a year and a half and have performed across York Region and Ontario, sharing the stage with such popular country acts as Paul Brandt, The Wilkinsons, Marshall Dylon and Sawyer Brown.

The duo, who will be performing at the Newmarket Rodeo this weekend, aspire to international status. Until then, the two Newmarket High School students will stay grounded and focused.

Debbie Dennis, the singing duo's manager, believes the girls have staying power to propel them to the top.

"They fill a void for Canadian country music," said Dennis, who also manages Newmarket rock group Serial Joe.

"There are so many acts out there who want to be like Faith Hill. These girls are not. These girls have married the traditional sound of country music but they still sound new and fresh."

'These girls have married the traditional sound of country music but they still sound new and fresh.'

Although pop and country are vocally driven, Cassandra said she and her sister will remain true to country's original sound.

"They're starting a new trend," said Cassandra, referring to such country/pop artists as Shania Twain and Faith Hill. "Music evolves and they're trying to start a new thing and that's great.

"Country music has a unique style and family atmosphere," said Cassandra, who admires country trio Dixie Chicks' use of such instruments as the banjo.

"You're telling more of a story. That's why I love country ... I can't imagine doing anything else."

For more information, visit www.jaclynandcassandra.com

After You Read

1. What qualities did you list before reading? Do the two sisters have those qualities? What other qualities do they have that helped them succeed?
2. Make a list of what the sisters have accomplished as they strive to attain international status. Do you think theirs is an effective action plan, or is there anything you would add?

Handbook   Link

How to create an action plan

Before You Read

Jarome Iginla, the 2001–2002 NHL scoring champ and a role model for many kids, has realized his dream of playing professional hockey. He needed a number of key qualities and attitudes to help him achieve his dream. Think about the dream that you have for your life. What qualities and attitudes will you need to achieve it? What steps will you have to take to make your dream a reality?

THE REAL-LIFE DREAMS OF JAROME IGINLA

He's the reigning NHL scoring champ and a role model for minority kids. And, JAMES DEACON reports, he's just getting started.

SUMMONING EVERY OUNCE of nerve they've got, three small boys approach Jarome Iginla, hoping to speak with hockey's reigning scoring champ now that practice is over. He's discreetly decked out in civvies — black leather jacket, pale blue T-shirt, faded jeans — but they've spotted him anyway, sitting up in Calgary's Pengrowth Saddledome stands. At first they keep a polite distance, since he's already talking to someone else, but it's clear they're leaking courage the longer they wait. So Iginla excuses himself from his conversation to greet the boys with a broad smile and a big right hand which, one by one, they shake. By then, though, they're

too cotton-mouthed to blurt out a "Hi," let alone what they came to say, so the big guy gets things rolling. "How ya doin'? Have a fun summer?" Iginla asks. A couple of nods. "How's school?" he asks. "What grade are you in?" The biggest boy holds up four fingers.

There's an awkward silence and, finally, one of the boys mumbles the question they came to ask: "Are you playin' tonight?" he wants to know, and all three lean in for the answer. "No," Iginla says, explaining that in preseason games the coaches want to see the rookies more than the vets. "Sorry about that," he says. Disappointed, the boys turn to go, but Iginla stops them in their tracks. "You guys have anything I can sign?" he asks. They

wheel around, happier. "Really?" asks the littlest kid. "Sure," Iginla says, and he proceeds to autograph the scraps of paper they dig out of their pockets. Several thank-yous later, they shuffle off.

Talk about asking for trouble. As soon as he's seen signing things for kids, the professional autograph hounds in the building pounce, thrusting bindered sheets of mint-condition trading cards under Iginla's nose. They don't apologize for interrupting him. They just watch carefully as he signs dozens of cards, calculating, perhaps, what each will soon sell for in card shops and on Web sites. Iginla knew that was the price he'd pay for taking out a pen for the little boys, but he still did it. "It's part of the game," he says.

Not for everyone. Too many pro athletes only smile when the betacams are whirring, and they think their big contracts and athletic gifts entitle them to a free pass on civility. Minnesota Vikings receiver Randy Moss provided the most recent example of extreme jock jerkdom. He nudged his luxury car up to a Minneapolis traffic agent and pushed her down a street last month, eventually knocking her to the ground. The reason? She refused to allow him to make an illegal turn. Didn't she know the rules don't apply to superstars?

No wonder the sports world is starving for guys like Iginla. The people who buy tickets and jerseys invest a lot of emotion in the migrant millionaires who play for the home teams, and it hurts when their heroes turn out to be zeroes. So fans, kids especially, connect with Iginla. Starting his seventh full National Hockey League season, he still seems to have that pinch-me excitement about playing hockey.

About life in general, in fact. He is resolutely decent, a 25-year-old man whose moral compass is directed by strong but discreet Christian convictions, and who appreciates his great fortune rather than bemoaning the inconveniences of fame. He's putting his mother through university so she can pursue a second career. He contributes both his time and his money to Calgary-area charities. He's the nice guy you'd have liked your daughter to bring home if he weren't already engaged to his junior-high sweetheart. Brad Lukowich, a teammate on Iginla's junior team in Kamloops, B.C., once summarized: "If you took the best player on the ice, the best leader in the locker room, the best community guy with the fans, and put them altogether, that's Jarome."

It is fitting then, that his last name means "big tree" in his father's dialect, Yoruba. He needs to be stout because, these days, everyone wants a piece of the muscular right winger who won the NHL scoring title last season — he was the only sniper with 50 or more goals (52). With Joe Sakic and Simon Gagne at the Winter Games in Salt Lake City, he formed Canada's most potent forward line on the men's team that so gloriously won gold. And at season's end, even though the Flames failed to make the playoffs, he was voted the league's most-outstanding player by his peers. He's been inundated with requests from fans, reporters and sponsors (he has deals with EA Sports, Campbell's and General Mills), leaving it to Flames PR director Peter Hanlon to say no: Iginla hasn't learned the word yet.

He is also courted because of his skin colour. His Nigerian-born father, Elvis, is black; his American-born mother, Susan Schuchard, is white. So their son, like Tiger Woods, is a multiracial star in a predominantly white sport and serves as a role model for visible minorities who might feel shut out of the game. Iginla says race never got in the way of his own hockey opportunities when he was a kid in St. Albert, outside Edmonton, but he knew he stood out. Other kids, and their parents, reminded him of that. "I was aware, and others would say to me, that there weren't many black players in the NHL," he says tactfully. "So it meant a lot to me that Grant Fuhr was playing right there in Edmonton, winning Stanley Cups and being an all-star. It meant a lot to see Tony McKegney and Claude Vilgrain. I followed those guys, so I'm glad if I can be a role model — I know what it meant to me."

There's more than the usual pressure on Iginla going into the new season, but he's still his usual exuberant self.

And then there is his multi-faceted role with the Flames, who open the new NHL season this week. They haven't qualified for the playoffs since 1996, and Iginla desperately wants to end that dubious streak. Fans, meanwhile, will be expecting him to justify the two-year pact he just signed with the Flames for a whopping US$13 million, a vast sum for a small-market franchise with a tenuous future. Some argue the Flames paid too much, but their financial woes might have been worse had they tried selling tickets without their star attraction. So on top of everything else, he's central to the team's marketing campaign.

Instead of groaning under the load, Iginla's remarkably cool about it. "There's pressure after signing a big deal, pressure to live up to scoring 50 goals, and the way I look at it is this," he explains. "When I was a kid, I saw Wayne Gretzky doing all the interviews, and Mark Messier and Steve Yzerman. They had all these pressures every year, and they still handled it. So that's what I want to do too, you know?"

A LOT OF PEOPLE were surprised by Iginla's dominance last season. They shouldn't have been. He decided at age 7 he was going to make it to the NHL, after one of his very first games. It soon became clear he was talented, and he succeeded at every level. He won two Memorial Cups for junior-hockey supremacy with the Kamloops Blazers, and the 1996 world junior championship with the national team. Individually, he was named Western Hockey League player of the year in 1995-1996, and was runner-up for NHL rookie of the year the next season.

Iginla wasn't originally chosen to take part in the pre-Olympic camp that Gretzky held in Calgary last year. He was added at the last minute

'IT MEANT A LOT TO ME THAT GRANT FUHR WAS PLAYING RIGHT THERE IN EDMONTON, WINNING STANLEY CUPS AND BEING AN ALL-STAR. SO I'M GLAD IF I CAN BE A ROLE MODEL.'

because Gagne was injured, and the chance to play with that elite group had a profound effect. He'd measured up against the game's best. "You could tell it boosted his confidence," his centreman, Craig Conroy, says. "Jarome's got a great shot, and after that camp, he started to use it more."

To the casual observer, Iginla's talent seems more natural than mechanical, and it's true he's a gifted athlete. But a lot of sweat went into his climb into the elite ranks. He has spent hours training with a former decathlete, Rich Hesketh, to add strength and flexibility to his six-feet, one-inch, 200-pound frame. When he reached the NHL, coaches said his skating ought to be better, so he addressed that. "I approach it like a sprinter, trying to get more explosive," Iginla says of the specialized regimen. Last season, the team needed him to score more, so instead of passing in certain situations, he began to shoot. Bingo, more goals.

Iginla says he's just doing whatever it takes to be a better player and to win. But it's an approach that sometimes makes his dad cringe. Elvis hates that his son sometimes has to fight, and he also knows his son isn't blameless — "As mild as he is off the ice," Elvis says, "Jarome can be very physical and passionate on the ice." Iginla is no enforcer, but he knows a fight can sometimes change a team's momentum. Last week against Edmonton, he and Oilers defenceman Eric Brewer mixed it up a bit. No offence was intended, Iginla says — Brewer's a pal from the Olympic team. If anything, Iginla was sending a message to his teammates to play harder in a tight game with a division rival. "That's part of what happens when our two teams get together," was all he'd say about it.

DURING A PRACTICE at training camp, working on power play drills, Iginla cruised into the slot, took a pass from Conroy and fired a rocket that nailed goaltender Roman Turek squarely in the head. The lanky netminder fell like a bag of cement, but was slowly returning to his feet by the time everyone gathered to see if he was all right. His helmet was badly dented and askew, but his humour was intact. "Is that the best you've got," he shouted at Iginla.

If success ever inflates Iginla's head, his teammates will be right there to let out the air. They call him Iggy — how cutting is that? And they rib him for being a dawdler and for arriving late for buses. "That's because he loves to sleep," says defenceman Robyn Regehr. "He'd sleep 'til two in the afternoon every day if he could."

No one in the locker room doubts that Iginla's the real deal. They talk about his shot and his uncanny knack for getting open in the slot. More than that, though, they talk about character. "He doesn't let his emotions get away from him," Conroy says. "He gets a lot of attention from opposing teams, but he keeps his focus and finds ways to get open." Regehr concurs. "I don't see him as a one-hit wonder at all," he says. "His work ethic is phenomenal, and he's driven — he's always striving to be the best."

His motivation has been the same since he was a kid. Some past coaches tried to turn him into a grinder, a 15-goal and 100-penalty-minutes-a-season player. He didn't bite. "Don't get me wrong," he says. "Playing in the NHL is a dream come true and I'd play any role to stay here. But I always dreamed of getting here and being a scorer, an elite player, a star, to be on a winning team, and win Stanley Cups. I know I'm not there yet, but that's still my goal."

Skeptics doubt he'll reach all those goals in Calgary, where the payroll's barely half of what some teams are spending. In fact, some insiders speculate that if the Flames fall out of contention early this season, they might trade Iginla to a wealthier team for inexpensive prospects. But general manager Craig Button says no such plan exists, and his trade last week to acquire forwards Chris Drury and Stephane Yelle from Colorado for defender Derek Morris and forwards Jeff Shantz and Dean McAmmond indicates he's serious about contending. "We're trying to build a successful team," Button says, "and Jarome's a big part of that."

Iginla's anxious to speed that up after watching other teams compete in the playoffs the last six years. "Maybe people'll judge me by goals and points or whatever," he says. "But to me, what really'd be great is being able to make the playoffs and break that cycle of tough times, and share that with the team." He's so focused on that, in fact, that he and his fiancée Kara Kirkland, a physiotherapist, have not set an exact date for their wedding in St. Albert next spring. His hope is he'll be busy playing into June, and she's used to having hockey dictate their schedules. They've been together since they were 13, give or take the odd rough spot.

HIS FULL NAME IS Jarome Arthur-Leigh Adekunle Tig Junior Elvis Iginla, and it appears in full on his wrinkled old birth certificate. He was two when his parents divorced, so the only life he remembers is one in which he lived with his mother, who worked long hours outside the home as a massage therapist. His father studied law at the University of Alberta and lived elsewhere, and his maternal grandparents, Richard and Frances Schuchard, looked after him when his mother was at work. It was his grandfather, in fact, who took the boy to his first organized hockey tryout.

Back then, he was exhaustingly energetic. "So my mom got me into everything — bowling, tennis, Little League, you name it," he says. At one point he fancied he might grow into a Bo Jackson-type athlete, playing pro baseball, the game his grandfather taught him, as well as hockey. But then he looked at the calendar. "The seasons don't exactly work out," he says, laughing at himself in retrospect. "And really, I wasn't that good of a ballplayer."

Along with sports, he took everything from piano lessons to public speaking classes. "My family's very musical," he says. "On my mom's side, my gramma runs a music school in St. Albert, and my mother's back in school studying to be a drama teacher. Anyway, I used to have some battles. They'd put me into music festivals, and public-speaking things." He blushes at the memory of a shy boy having to perform in front of an audience. "I kept going up 'til junior high, but after that I gave it up."

By then, he was the star of the St. Albert rep team, and was soon drafted to play for the Blazers. It started badly. "It was tough leaving home at 16 years old, and not playing a lot — I was sitting on the bench, playing two shifts a period," he explains. He'd been the star at every level, but now, the dream was in doubt. "I remember talking to my grandpa saying, 'Maybe I should just come home.' But he was like, 'Give it a little longer.' He wasn't saying I couldn't come home, just that I should give it a try. And it did get better."

The story triggers another memory of his family. "I was very fortunate in my situation — I wouldn't change any of it," he says. "Whatever games I had, they'd go and watch, and they were always so positive. I never heard once that I had a bad game from them. I had bad games, obviously, but I had coaches to let me know that." Now, he

appreciates the fact they never pushed him. They knew he loved to play, he says, "and they let it be my ambition."

Left to his own devices, he set high standards for himself, not just in hockey but in life. "What really defines Jarome," Elvis Iginla says, "is his sense of right and wrong. He worries about that a lot, and it spills out into his relationships, his work, everything." That isn't something that concerns some of today's superstars, and Elvis knows that. "I'm happy Jarome's done so well in hockey," his dad adds, "but I am far happier for the person he has become."

After You Read

Handbook Link
How to expand
your vocabulary

1. Write, in your own words, what you think "an enterprising spirit" means. In what ways does Iginla possess that spirit? How does it both empower and motivate him?

Before You Read

List the advantages and disadvantages of starting your own business. Consider the following: money/capital required, work hours, leisure time, risk, being your own boss.

UPFRONT

The BMX clothing Business
by Mark Losey

I can't even begin to count how many BMX T-shirt companies have come and gone over the years. Making T-shirts is a pretty easy way to get started in the BMX industry, but making the company last is not exactly an easy task.

If you're thinking about starting a T-shirt company, this story should give you a good heads up. I called Derek Adams from Little Devil and got the lowdown on how he got his company started, and what's keeping it rolling.

Clothing BMX riders is becoming a big business.

How old were you when you started your clothing company?

I was probably 22. I really started it just because I hated my job, and I wanted to get some quick money to go to contests, and not have to work.

Did it work?

No, it didn't work out. It helped me get to contests, which was my priority. But as far as living the high life off of T-shirt sales, it didn't exactly go that way [laughter].

How did you start out? Did you spend a lot of money on credit cards to get shirts printed?

I actually started with the money that was supposed to go towards my college tuition, which was only about $1,800. I used it to buy silk screening equipment, blank T-shirts, and screens. Then I just taught myself.

Your original plan was to sell them at contests?

Yeah, that's what I did at first. It was tough to even get people to buy them there, because nobody had ever heard of Little Devil. That's the hardest thing to do when you start up; name recognition plays a big role.

Were you working another job at the same time?

I was actually working at a T-shirt printing place. I worked there part-time, and they let me run my T-shirts through their drier to make sure the ink dried well. If you don't have a good drier, all of the ink will fall off the shirt.

How long did it take before you didn't have to do the part-time job anymore?

It started picking up when I realized that if I sold ten T-shirts a week, I'd make the same amount of money I was making at the part-time job. Then I just quit, and spent more time trying to sell the T-shirts. It really started to pick up when I tried to develop a team, and tried to market the team image more. When "Seek and Destroy" came out, it really seemed to pick up into a real business.

And now you have your own retail store.

We were working out of my basement up until about a year-and-a-half ago. Then it just got too big for the basement, and we needed somewhere else to go. Our idea was to either get a warehouse with some ramps, or get a retail store. The first thing we found was a nice retail store, so we went with that. We have an office in the back, and our stock-room is in the basement.

How many people does Little Devil support right now?

Right now it's three full-time people. Around Christmas it was about five, but we had to slim down. You don't do as much business in the winter as you do around Christmas.

Has the company taken away from your riding time?

It originally was a vehicle for me to ride more because I didn't want to work a job. I figured that if I sold T-shirts, I could ride more, and not have to worry about being kept down by the man [laughter]. But it's totally backfired on me. I work constantly, just about nonstop. Hopefully we just secured a warehouse deal that's bigger than we needed, and we're going to put a street course in. We're going to keep the store where it is, and have some- body run that who can concentrate just on the store.

Are the people you work with riders?

One of them is my best friend. He's a skater, but he's really smart, really business-minded, and really trustworthy. The other guy is Anthony Durbano, and he's a flatlander. He just crept in one day, and now he's here to stay.

Do you have any other big plans for Little Devil?

Our video, "Criminal Mischief," is in the editing process now. We spent two years on it, and it's coming together real well. Besides that, really just expanding the line. When I started out, I didn't even know how to print a T-shirt. Now I'm trying to get into more cut-and-sew products, backpacks, and making it a real clothing company.

There should be a lot of cool products coming out this year.

Do you make stuff in-house?

We don't do anything in-house anymore. Once you get to a certain point, unless you want to take on a ton of employees—which is such a pain in the ass—you have to farm your work out and find good people to do it for you. That's really the toughest part. It's a lot about who you know. If you have good people to work with, you have a good end product.

But you still design everything?

Yeah, I still design just about everything myself, with input from my riders and my friends. It's all experimental. We play around with different cuts until we find something we like, and then we make it.

What advice would you give to someone who wants to start a T-shirt business?

My advice would be to do what you like, and to have fun with it. Don't try to take it as a serious business venture at first. Start out the way I did, which was just a side project that I had fun with. If it's something you like doing, then keep doing it. If you don't like it, then it's probably not for you. I really enjoy what I do now. Sometimes I work a lot harder than I ever expected to, but it seems to all be worthwhile in the end. [For me] the riding came first and the business came second. My mom always said that I was going to have to get a real job, and that bike riding would never take me anywhere. It's kind of funny that it did.

After You Read

1. Answer the following in your reading response journal: How did Derek Adams start his T-shirt company? How was he able to expand it? What is ironic about his mother's advice?

Handbook   Link
How to interpret and assess information, ideas, and issues in text

Before You Read

With a small group, make a list of celebrities and athletes who have given their names to businesses to help them sell products. Discuss:
1. What are the advantages to a business of having a famous person or famous name associated with the business?
2. Do you think that famous people should profit from their fame in this way?
3. If you had a product or service to sell, would you want a famous person to promote it? If so, who and why?

Open Ice:
THE *Tim Horton* STORY

by Douglas Hunter

One day in the mid-1950s, [Russ] Gioffrey [the co-owner of Bestway TV & Appliances] remembers Tim Horton walking into his store—this was the original one on Kingston Road at the bottom of Warden. Tim by now had some fame as a Maple Leaf, though he was never someone to make a big deal out of this. The two men discovered they were both from Sudbury, and a twenty-year friendship was born.

By 1958, Bestway had contracted as rapidly as it had expanded. The chain was down to the original store on Kingston Road and a second store on Lawrence, which had moved from its initial site on the north side near Pharmacy to the south side near Warden, fairly close to Tim's house. It became a habit for Tim to drop by the store after Leaf practice on Saturday mornings to have a coffee with the appliance dealer he called Rooskie and shoot the breeze. Their wives became good friends. It seemed that whenever one was pregnant, so was the other.

Gioffrey was in awe of Tim—not as a hockey player, but as a person. "I used to try to model myself after him," he remembers. "I never could. I thought you had to be a saint. He never said a bad word against anyone." They made a point of getting together for lunch at Fran's on Eglinton, and the meal always made Gioffrey feel sorry for Tim. Gioffrey's plate would be clean and Tim's food would scarcely have been touched. Tim was a methodical eater, but his speed wasn't enhanced by the fact that, from the moment he sat down and picked up a menu, Tim was mobbed by diners. "It didn't matter who it was, whether it was a young person or an old person," says Gioffrey. "He always had time for them. *Always.*" Tim's explanation for his tolerance: "These are the ones that like me."

By the summer of 1963 Tim was beginning to have enough money to invest seriously. The Leafs had just won their second straight Stanley Cup, and Tim had finally been rewarded with the recognition his supporters said he had long deserved by making it back onto the All Star team after an eight-season absence, albeit the nomination was, again, to the second-team squad. They decided to put an investment vehicle together, which Dywan (Gioffrey's brother-in-law) would manage. Why not open a store of their own, or his own, and sell directly to the public?

By now, the starter's pistol had been fired in the North American donut-store-franchising race, although the shot had scarcely been heard in Canada. A franchise company was already operating in California, but the Boston area was where most of the action was. Two brothers-in-law [the Hannigans] who'd had a falling out were running rival operations in the south Boston suburbs: Mr. Donut was based in Westwood, while the original chain,

Dunkin' Donuts (founded in 1950), was in Randolph. In 1960, Jim Charade flew to Boston to tour the Mr. Donut operation. He visited their shops and had a look around the training centre. "I was impressed with them and wanted a franchise, but on my way back to Toronto, I thought, Why do I want a franchise? I can do that myself."

Charade believes that he met Tim in the spring of 1963—Dennis Griggs, he says, introduced them when Griggs learned Charade was interested in buying a car, and he is sure he bought a Pontiac from Tim. Griggs has a different version, with which Lori [Tim's wife] agrees. Tim, Griggs says, came into the donut store in the Colony Plaza one day after practice. Although Tim hadn't lived in the neighborhood for more than three years, he still got his trademark brush-cut at Benny's, which was next door to the donut store. (Good old Benny's, at last inspection, was Cyndy and Lynsey Unisex Hairstyling Salon.) "I told him

Tim Horton

what we were doing and I set him up with Jim," says Griggs. "Jimmy was the brains behind it, the one who started the first donut shop, but it was me that got Tim involved. I'm one of the founding fathers."

After Tim Horton did or did not sell Jim Charade a car in May 1963, Charade in turn sold Tim on the idea of going into the restaurant business. Tim appealed to Charade as a partner on several levels. For one thing, they got along. "Tim was a great guy," he says. "He was my best friend." Claudette and Lori also became quite close. And, naturally, there was the matter of capital. Tim was not very well off by any means, but he was comfortable in his finances and what he couldn't kick in directly he could arrange to borrow.

But most important, Tim brought that golden intangible to the business: fame. Jim had read about Gino Marchetti, who had starred with the Baltimore Colts when they won the NFL season championship in 1959 and had started a chain of restaurants called Gino's. That was an intriguing business model for Jim. You had someone the public recognized and admired. Put his name on the restaurant, put him inside it as often as you could, greeting the customers, pressing the flesh. "People always feel you can't just go from sport, if you have a name, into another business," says Charade. "But I thought Tim could do it, if you took care of things and did it well and didn't mess people up and had the right attitude. I took him as a partner for his name, for his autographs. Even if you don't have the product, if you have the name at least you'll get them in the door."

In Lawrence Martin's profile of Tim in a January 1973 issue of *Canadian* magazine, Tim streamlines and even mythologies his business history. His ultimate partner in the donut business, Ron Joyce, becomes an old friend who was on the Hamilton police force when they hooked up, when in fact Tim didn't know him from Adam. Jim Charade has dropped out of the narrative entirely, an inconvenient complication. He is loath to talk about his experience in the hamburger business: "Let's just leave it at that. They flopped." And he offers an unexpected epiphany from his days as a Pittsburgh Hornet. "There was this big, beautiful donut shop on the outskirts of town. I had never really thought of being anything else but a hockey player before, but the first day I walked into that shop, I thought that I would really like to own my own donut shop some day." In 1969 Tim would sum up his venturing into the donut business in a single quip: "I love eating donuts and that was one of the big reasons that I opened my first donut shop. Buying donuts was costing me too much money."

He may well have always harboured a desire to enter the donut business, but when out of the blue Jim Charade presented him with precisely that opportunity, he chose instead the business of drive-in burgers, a business in which neither he nor Charade had any experience. When opportunity knocked, the memory of that fabled donut shop in Pittsburgh obviously did not knock with it. Tim chose to ignore the opportunity of donuts and pursue the business in which the Hannigan brothers were successful. Only Charade seemed

committed to the idea of donuts, licensing Tim's name for his donut enterprise.

• • •

Spencer Brown was a twenty-year-old clerk at a Bank of Nova Scotia branch in Scarborough when he fell in with Tim Horton's would-be restaurant empire in early 1964. The Timanjim burger business was struggling to make its way, and Jim Charade was moving ahead on his plans to open donut franchises under his licensing agreement with Tim.

Griggs and Brown were in Peterborough to investigate possible sites for such a franchise [but the trip] was inconclusive, with no property identified as a definite site.

While on the road back to Toronto, Griggs said to Brown, "Well, we have this place we're just getting ready to open in Hamilton. Would you be interested in going over there?" Brown said he was happy to take a look at it. Brown found a restaurant only a few weeks away from opening, with nobody there to run it. It was at the corner of Ottawa Street and Dunsmure in the city's east end, across the street from the world's first Canadian Tire franchise.

Jim Charade says he had picked Hamilton because Hamilton wasn't Toronto. By then, Mr. Donut had established its first franchises in Toronto, and had none in Hamilton. Country Style had also come to Toronto in 1963. In Hamilton there would be no competition. Ironically, Jim Charade was scrupulously avoiding establishing franchises in the city in which the Tim Horton name was best known.

Charade had found this old Esso Station on Ottawa Street. The property was owned by a Ukrainian fellow in Kitchener, who agreed to build to suit and would ride into town on his bicycle—a round trip of seventy miles—to keep tabs on the project. They wound up with a bleach-white building with a purple interior for about $200 a month.

The restaurant was stocked with used equipment, and Brown tore up his arm on the lava rock in the wall left over from the service station days, but he liked what he saw. They agreed to a down payment of $1,500 and a royalty rate that escapes Brown. (It was probably the standard 2 per cent.) He went to his uncle and borrowed every penny of the down payment, quit his job at the bank and headed for Hamilton. The Tim Horton Donut Drive-In Restaurant opened with little fanfare in April 1964, one month before Spencer Brown's twenty-first birthday.

Before it opened, Jim Charade passed an entire night counting cars on Parkdale Avenue to the east. It was the main commuter route for the steelworkers pouring out of the city's industrial northeast at the end of every shift, making their way up the escarpment to their homes in the new suburbia in the city's southeastern section. "I watched the traffic at three a.m., four a.m., because it was going to be open twenty-four hours. I thought, I've got to be crazy. But there was nothing to compare it to." He hoped that once people got to know the restaurant, they would make the detour to stop in at the end of their shift to meet, talk and eat donuts.

Brown stayed at the YMCA for a week, then found a room close by the store as he went to work. If Tim Horton didn't know a donut from a hockey puck, Brown didn't know a donut from a tire—as he puts it, they were both round and had a hole in the middle. Tim Horton, for that matter, was nowhere to be seen. Brown didn't even meet him until he'd been open for a week. Charade sent down his Scottish baker to help him get going. Brown was on the cutting edge of fast food, and he was about to help ignite a franchise revolution.

As it turns out, Charade could not have picked a better city in which to launch the first franchise. The city's blue-collar denizens

A new franchise is born.

literally ate up the concept. "It went super well," says Brown. "It was busy, busy, busy. For a kid that had been making about forty dollars a week in the bank, all of a sudden I'm making four hundred a week." At the end of a long day, he would keel over on a bag of flour in the kitchen, sleep for a few hours, then start all over again.

It was a long way from what Tim Hortons would become. Although coffee was on the menu, it was a very American drink at the time, in Canada something served in the home after dinner. Tea was the hot beverage of choice. Charade recalls that coffee contributed about 20 percent of revenues then, when today it's responsible for about 60 percent. But in donuts the men involved in the first franchise found a product that challenged the simile "Sold like hotcakes." The first Tim Hortons franchise was going great guns with a wide variety of donuts. "The big things were jelly and condiment-filled donuts," says Brown. The donut was pumped with goop and the outside sugared. "It was a really big deal: Venetian filled, jelly filled—apple and spice was a big seller—and honey dipped.

Cake donuts were the only type people knew, and we didn't sell much of those. We had peanut crunch, macaroon, coconut crumble, you name it. We really tried hard to have at least forty different varieties there at any one time." Brown ordered tins of fillings from suppliers and went to work with Charade inventing a cultural phenomenon. "You ordered what you needed from a supplier for that week, and sometimes we had to order a second shipment because we were really selling a lot of product. It was terrific. It just went gangbusters." A dozen donuts were sixty-nine cents; two bits got you a cup of coffee and a donut. It was a snack break tailor-made for the bleary-eyed men off shiftwork: straight caffeine and sugar.

They didn't even sell off day-olds at a special price. "We'd put things in the proofer and keep them warm at 5:30, 6:00 a.m., before the shift changed at Dofasco. We'd walk by the counter with a tray of donuts that were probably about twelve hours old, saying, 'They're hot, excuse me, they're hot.' People would yell, 'I'll take six,' 'I'll take four.' We never had anything left over."

After You Read

1. Discuss the following questions with a partner:
   Why does the well-known hockey player decide to create a donut shop? What does he contribute to the business? Would you describe him as enterprising? Who was the target audience for the business? Why was the business so successful? Discuss and explain whether these success factors apply today.

Handbook Link
How to interpret and assess information, ideas, and issues in text

Before You Read

The following is a folk tale told by the Ashanti people of Africa. Folk tales are stories that have been passed down from generation to generation because they preserve values and truths that are important to the people who tell them. Folk tales often have supernatural elements in them that make us see the everyday world with different eyes.

In this story, everyday objects begin to talk. Before you read, imagine what your shoes/your pen/your wristwatch might say to you if they/it could talk. Write a brief description of the conversation between you and your chosen object.

Talk

AN *ASHANTI* TALE

Once, not far from the city of Accra on the Gulf of Guinea, a country man went out to his garden to dig up some yams to take to market. While he was digging, one of the yams said to him, "Well, at last you're here. You never weeded me, but now you go around with your digging stick. Go away and leave me alone!"

The farmer turned around and looked at his cow in amazement. The cow was chewing her cud and looking at him.

"Did you say something?" he asked.

The cow kept on chewing and said nothing, but the man's dog spoke up. "It wasn't the cow who spoke to you," the dog said. "It was the yam. The yam says leave him alone."

The man became angry, because his dog had never talked before and he didn't like his tone besides. So he took his knife and cut a branch from a palm tree to whip his dog. Just then the palm tree said, "Put that branch down!"

The man was getting very upset about the way things were going, and he started to throw the palm branch away, but the palm branch said, "Man, put me down softly!"

He put the branch down gently on a stone, and the stone said, "Hey, take that thing off me!"

This was enough, and the frightened farmer started to run for his village. On the way he met a fisherman going the other way with a fish trap on his head.

"What's the hurry?" the fisherman asked.

"My yam said, 'Leave me alone!' Then the dog said, 'Listen to what the yam says!' When I went to whip the dog with a palm branch the tree said, 'Put that branch down!' Then the palm branch said, 'Do it softly!' Then the stone said, 'Take that thing off me!'"

"Is that all?" the man with the fish trap asked. "Is that so frightening?"

"Well," the man's fish trap said, "did he take it off the stone?"

"Wah!" the fisherman shouted. He threw the fish trap on the ground and began to run with the farmer, and on the trail they met a weaver with a bundle of cloth on his head.

"Where are you going in such a rush?" he asked them.

"My yam said, 'Leave me alone!'" the farmer said. "The dog said, 'Listen to what the yam says!' The tree said, 'Put that branch down!' The branch said, 'Do it softly!' And the stone said, 'Take that thing off me!'"

"And then," the fisherman continued, "the fish trap said, 'Did he take it off?'"

"That's nothing to get excited about," the weaver said. "No reason at all."

"Oh, yes it is," his bundle of cloth said. "If it happened to you you'd run too!"

"Wah!" the weaver shouted. He threw his bundle on the trail and started running with the other men.

They came panting to the ford in the river and found a man bathing. "Are you chasing a gazelle?" he asked them.

The first man said breathlessly, "My yam talked at me, and it said, 'Leave me alone!' And my dog said, 'Listen to your yam!' And when I cut myself a branch the tree said, 'Put that branch down!' And the branch said, 'Do it softly!' And the stone said, 'Take that thing off me!'"

The fisherman panted, "And my trap said, 'Did he?'"

The weaver wheezed, "And my bundle of cloth said, 'You'd run too!'"

"Is that why you're running?" the man in the river asked.

"Well, wouldn't you run if you were in their position?" the river said.

The man jumped out of the water and began to run with the others. They ran down the main street of the village to the house of the chief. The chief's servant brought his stool out, and he came and sat on it to listen to their complaints. The men began to recite their troubles.

"I went out to my garden to dig yams," the farmer said, waving his arms. "Then everything began to talk! My yam said, 'Leave me alone!' My dog said, 'Pay attention to your yam!' The tree said, 'Put that branch down!' The branch said, 'Do it softly!' And the stone said, 'Take it off me!'"

"And my fish trap said, 'Well, did he take it off?'" the fisherman said.

"And my cloth said, 'You'd run too!'" the weaver said.

"And the river said the same," the bather said hoarsely, his eyes bulging.

The chief listened to them patiently, but he couldn't refrain from scowling. "Now this is really a wild story," he said at last. "You'd better all go back to your work before I punish you for disturbing the peace."

So the men went away, and the chief shook his head and mumbled to himself, "Nonsense like that upsets the community."

"Fantastic, isn't it?" his stool said. "Imagine. A talking yam!"

After You Read

With a partner, discuss the following:
1. Find examples of irony, personification, humour, and repetition. What do they add to the folk tale?
2. Discuss the values and truths you think are shared in this tale, and explain how they relate to your personal life and your life on the job. What universal message do you think they have?

Handbook   Link

How to recognize allusion and irony

How to understand themes in literature

Before You Read

List two or three games, pastimes, or toys that were your favourites when you were younger; or list those that are favourites of a younger sibling or family member now. Share your list with a partner or small group. Discuss what you think those games teach us about ourselves, about others, and about life.

Talking Toys
Speak Volumes about
Gender Stereotypes

by David Staples

For those who blather about feminists having no sense of humor, I offer the Barbie Liberation Organization.

The BLO is waging a witty, sneaky, and subversive campaign. I wish I had thought it up.

The BLO has 150 members: feminists, anti-war activists, business people, lawyers. The common thread is most of them are parents.

The group is based in New York. There are six operatives in Canada, two in Western Canada.

The group's plan is simple: buy Teen Talk Barbie and Talking G.I. Joe dolls, then switch the voice boxes. The altered dolls are then placed back on store shelves and resold to unsuspecting kids.

In the end, blonde, curvaceous Barbie has an evil laugh and makes machine gun noises. She says things like: Eat Lead, Cobra!; Attack!; No escape for the guilty!; Vengeance is mine!; Dead men tell no tales!

Meanwhile, muscle-bound G.I. Joe says: Will we ever have enough clothes?; I love to shop with you; Let's plan my dream wedding; Ken's such a dream.

"Our methods are clearly tongue in cheek, but our message is not," says a BLO spokesman, who goes by the code name of G.I. Joe.

"Our message is that these dolls perpetuate gender-based stereotypes. And we think that is tied into some greater societal problems, especially a thing like G.I. Joe, which encourages kids to act in a violent way.

"A lot of people really don't think about what these toys are saying unless it appears to them in a way they're not expecting it."

Joe says the BLO launched its campaign last August [1993]. It was pushed to act after the brouhaha over Teen Talk Barbie saying, "Math is hard."

After purchasing the dolls, operatives send them to group headquarters in New York City, spokesman Joe says.

"Corrective surgery" is then performed on the doll. Using a screwdriver, Barbie is split in half. G.I. Joe has to be cut in half by a small saw. The circuits are removed from the chest, then switched.

Plastic surgery must be done to make the dolls appear untouched. The entire operation takes between three and six hours, Joe says. So far, 330 dolls have been reprogrammed.

The doll makers, Mattel and Hasbro, have said the group is wasting its time, but haven't threatened legal action, Joe says.

Most kids are pleased with their altered dolls and don't return them to the stores. "We think we're actually delivering a superior product," Joe says. "It's actually an educational product in ways that the old product wasn't. It will bring attention to this idea of gender-stereotyping."

Since my wife Gillian and I had a baby boy, Jack, last April, I've been thinking more and more about gender stereotyping. Some people say no matter what you do, testosterone-filled boys will be rambunctious and loud, while testosterone-free girls will be sweet. I'm not so sure. My son is loud and rambunctious, but he's also sweet.

Do my wife and I encourage loud and rambunctious behavior? If we have a little girl some day will we treat her the same? Are we afraid of Jack being too sweet? Would we ever dress him in pink? Are we just a bit too glad that he's a great, big boy for his age and that he likes to hoot and holler and pound the floor like a madman, rollicking in his jolly jumper?

And is any of this worth getting worked up about?

I don't have the answers. But the use of BLO's clever campaign is it didn't get my back up, it got me thinking.

The BLO could have done something stupid and criminal, like break into a toy store, trash the place and splash red paint on all of the Barbies. It could have shouted slogans and declared all men are brutish Rambos. What I like is the nonviolence, subtlety and humor of the BLO's clever campaign.

I'm also happy to report there have been few casualties during the doll surgery.

"We've only lost one patient," Joe says. "The Barbie sustained a broken neck."

After You Read

1. Discuss the following questions with your classmates:
   a. What are the goals of the BLO? Do you believe that they are successful in attaining their goals?
   b. What is gender stereotyping?
   c. List other examples of gender stereotyping.

Handbook   Link
How to interpret and assess information, ideas, and issues in text

Before You Read

Look quickly at each of the business cards below. Which one appeals to you the most? Choose and list a few effective adjectives to describe the design of the card. What impression do you get about the business based on the card design?

Two Guys and a Plow
For all your snow removal needs

Timothy Fairbanks	Roger O'Neal
555-2323	555-8794

Angélique Laplante Custom Woodworking

27 Raymond Lane
Kirkland Lake, ON
P2N 3R3

705 555 3784

Ellen Nguyen
Tax Analyst
Taxation Centre

123 Main Street
Sudbury, ON
P3A 5C1
(705) 555-6738
e.nguyen@sudtax.ca

Rivers Photography

Winston Rivers, Photographer

RR#3
Sturgeon Falls, ON
P2B 1M7

The Corner Store
... gifts for your home

7503 Heron Road
Sudbury, ON
P3A 5C3

555–1157

Walter and Olivia
Morischuk, Proprietors

After You Read

1. Discuss with a partner or small group how the design of business cards can leave the reader with an impression of a person or organization. Identify together what you believe people look for on a business card.

Handbook Link
How to identify design elements in text

Before You Read

A business plan is written to provide key information to investors or other stakeholders in an enterprise. Read the heading titles in this executive summary of the Business Plan for Northern Spirit Gallery. What important information does each section of the report provide? Why is it a good idea to write a business plan?

BUSINESS PLAN
Executive Summary

Business Description

Northern Spirit is a new retail business venture due to begin operations in September 2003. The store sells Aboriginal handicrafts, art works, and jewellery to serve the thriving tourist settlement of Moose Bay and surrounding area. Our goal is to showcase the talent of the local Aboriginal community.

Ownership and Management

Northern Spirit is a sole proprietorship that is owned and operated by Caroline Crow. Ms. Crow has extensive experience in the tourism industry, having worked as a sales clerk at the Moon and Feathers Native Gallery in Curve Lake and Sales Manager at Hudson Bay Trading in Northern Inlet, Ontario. Ms. Crow holds a Retail Management Diploma from Moose Bay College.

Key Initiatives and Objectives

The objective of Northern Spirit is to attain and maintain a position as the major source of North American Aboriginal art in Moose Bay. Currently, a retail art gallery is not present within 30 km of Moose Bay. The retail gallery is scheduled to open in September 2003. A short term loan of $15 000 is needed for the gallery to acquire inventory when it opens. Also, an operating loan of $1000 is required to maintain cash flow during the first year. Negotiations with five well-known local artists have taken place and a tentative contract to supply art and jewellery for the store is in place. These contracts will be finalized as soon as the gallery becomes approved for bank financing.

Marketing Opportunities

Ms. Crow's personal experience in the retail art sectors has been favourable. The Aboriginal craft market is a growing industry, and the market for local handicrafts is strong and is expected to grow within the next 10 to 20 years.

With the population of Moose Bay expected to increase by 20% according to a recent regional growth study, and increased tourist opportunities provided through the improvement of the Trans-Canada Highway, the Northern Ontario Tourism Association estimates that the market for Aboriginal crafts has the potential to reach in excess of $200 000 by the end of 2003.

The key market segments for Moose Bay are North American tourists who travel along the Trans Canada Highway. A market study by Valenton and Associates Ltd indicates that 55% of those who purchase Aboriginal crafts are retired couples whose household income ranges from $45 000 to $75 000 per year. Another large market is skilled labourers from the nearby Domtar Forest Products Company in the settlement of Sally's Cove.

Competitive Advantages

With no other gallery showcasing Aboriginal art and handicrafts for 200 km, Northern Spirit is in a unique position to capture the majority of Aboriginal art sales in the greater Moose Bay area. The company believes that there is a wealth of local talent in the Moose Bay area that has not been exposed to other retailers and distributors and, by showcasing these talents, Northern Spirit can consistently maintain a competitive position as the leading gallery for Aboriginal art for the growing tourism industry. The gallery will be complementary to the growing range of retail and service stations that serve the greater Moose Bay area.

Marketing Strategy

The major target market is greater Moose Bay District residents and the vacationers and seasonal tourists who travel through the Trans Canada Highway during the peak months of June to September. Since the major industries in the area are forest products and mining, families that are involved in these industries are also targeted. Northern Spirit will attempt to carry a wide range of inventory that will appeal to all ages, ranging from school-age children to retirees. Local folklore and legends will be reflected in the myriad of product offerings which will include soapstone carvings, etchings, jewellery, acrylic paintings, and sportswear. No mass-produced inventory from other suppliers will be carried by Northern Spirit.

During its first year of operations, Northern Spirit will be advertising in the *North Bay Nugget* and *Sally's Cove Times*. A colourful brochure showing samples of inventory has been completed and has been placed in the Northern Getaways travel booklet and at major kiosks and hotels within a 100-km radius of Moose Bay. Currently plans are underway to prepare a Web site, as well as a "meet the artist" day, which will be hosted by Northern Spirit during the annual Pow Wow.

Summary of Financial Projections

We project strong revenues in 2003 due to the steady influx of U.S. visitors travelling through the greater Moose Bay area during the previous two years. The healthy U.S. economy and strength of the U.S. dollar should result in a very profitable year for Northern Spirit. Northern Spirit predicts revenues in the order of $200 000 in its first year of operation, due to its position as the only gallery in the greater Moose Bay area. The recent increase in employment in the Moose Bay area, predicted by the pulp and paper and mining industries to grow steadily over the next two years, will be beneficial to Northern Spirit.

After You Read

Handbook Link

How to read a business report

How to use reading strategies to understand text

1. Create a three-column chart to summarize the information in the business plan. Label the columns Report Subheading; Turned into a Question; Answers Found While Reading. Record your information in the appropriate column.
2. Compare the structure of this report to the structure of "The Grand River Conservation Authority 2000 Annual Report (pages 183–188)." Identify their similarities and differences.

Before You Read

This booklet is organized to help you find the information you need easily and quickly. Skim the excerpt. What feature of the text would you use if you wanted to get information about starting a small business? Use this text feature to find information on another topic that interests you. Then share what you've found with a partner.

Printing and distribution cost: 26¢

Important information on over 130 services Keep for easy reference

Government of Canada Services

For You

Government of Canada   Gouvernement du Canada

Canada

1 800 O-Canada
(1 800 622-6232)

www.canada.gc.ca
TTY/TDD: 1 800 465-7735

Table of contents

1 800 O-Canada
(1 800 622-6232)

www.canada.gc.ca
TTY/TDD: 1 800 465-7735

Canada

Introduction

Every day, millions of Canadians like you rely on the great number of essential services provided by the Government of Canada – from weather forecasting, food inspection, and emergency response, to coast guard protection and passports – often without giving them a second thought.

The Government of Canada offers you many other specific services, including:

- product safety and health information for new parents;
- programs for young adults planning their careers;
- step-by-step support to start up a business;
- tips and personal safety information for Canadians travelling abroad; and
- guides to help citizens explore Canada's extensive and diverse parks, museums, and historic sites.

This guide can help you find out more about the Government of Canada services that may be of interest to you, your family, and your friends.

Using the Guide

The services are grouped by subject area and shown in **bold text**.

Web site addresses are also included in most cases. If you don't have Internet access at home, you can use a computer at any public library or community centre. Through the Connecting Canadians initiative, the Government of Canada and its partners have helped connect all of Canada's public libraries to the Internet.

1 800 O-Canada
(1 800 622-6232)

www.canada.gc.ca
TTY/TDD: 1 800 465-7735

Canada

Youth

The **Youth Employment Strategy** (www.youth.gc.ca/YES) can help you get the experience, knowledge, skills, and information you need to prepare for and participate in the labour force.

The **Young Entrepreneur Financing Program** is aimed at giving start-up entrepreneurs between the ages of 18 and 34 a solid foundation for building a new business. Visit the Web site at www.cbsc.org and click on "government programs and services," then follow the search instructions.

The **Canada Student Loans Program** (www.hrdc-drhc.gc.ca/student_loans) provides grants and loans to more than 350,000 post-secondary students every year.

The **Youth Resource Network of Canada** (www.youth.gc.ca) is the number one Web site for all the facts on work experience opportunities, starting your own business, career planning, and job-search strategies.

Campus Worklink (www.campusworklink.com) is a comprehensive career database and employment resource specially designed for university and college students, recent graduates, and the employers seeking to hire them.

Citzine (www.citzine.ca) is an interactive, youth-oriented Web site that promotes awareness of Canadian citizenship, history, and identity.

3

Smashed provides information on drinking and driving, and offers tips on how to take effective action to prevent impaired driving. The publication is available in print, and online under "public safety" and then "road safety" at www.tc.gc.ca

Quit4Life (www.quit4life.com), a teen smoking cessation program, will give you the knowledge you need to help you stop smoking.

Cadets Canada (www.cadetscanada.org) helps youth develop leadership skills and encourages them to become physically fit and active citizens – all within an environment that stimulates an interest in the Canadian Forces.

Junior Canadian Rangers provides a structured youth program that promotes traditional cultures and lifestyles in remote and isolated communities in northern Canada.

Citizenship and Immigration Canada Welcomes Foreign Students and **Studying in Canada: A Guide for Foreign Students** are two useful publications available in print, and online under "visitors" and then "studying in Canada" at www.cic.gc.ca

4

Finding a job

Jobs.gc.ca provides information and online applications for challenging career opportunities at all levels within the Public Service of Canada.

Human Resource Centres provide information on employment programs, including special services for youth and people with disabilities. To find the office closest to you, visit www.hrdc-drhc.gc.ca and click on the map of Canada.

The **National Job Bank** (jb-ge.hrdc-drhc.gc.ca) is a comprehensive online database of thousands of jobs, and work or business opportunities available across the country.

The **Electronic Labour Exchange** (ele.hrdc-drhc.gc.ca) is an Internet job-matching service that connects you with potential employers at the click of a button.

Employment Insurance benefits (www.hrdc-drhc.gc.ca/ei) may be paid to people who have lost their job and are looking for a new one. These benefits may also be available to people who cannot work because of illness or maternity, or because they are caring for a newborn or newly adopted child.

Canada WorkInfoNet (www.workinfonet.ca) is a unique Web site that can help you plan and carry out your job search. It covers everything from résumé writing to interview techniques, and from potential employment opportunities to starting your own business.

5

Young Canada Works (www.pch.gc.ca/YCW-JCT) gives young people the opportunity to work at heritage institutions, national parks, and national historic sites, as well as in other interesting locations at home and abroad.

Canadian Forces Recruiting Centres provide information about basic eligibility for the many interesting jobs available in the Canadian Forces at www.recruiting.dnd.ca

SkillNet.ca is Canada's fastest growing network of job and career information Web sites. More than 40,000 employers use this network as a quick and effective way to advertise full-time, part-time, and summer job opportunities.

6

1 800 O-Canada
(1 800 622-6232)

www.canada.gc.ca
TTY/TDD: 1 800 465-7735

Canada

Small business

The **Guide to Government of Canada Services and Support for Small Business** offers a wealth of information on federal services for small business. It is available in print and online at www.strategis.gc.ca (click on "business support and financing," then on the title on the right-hand bar).

Canada Business Service Centres (www.cbsc.org) are your single point of contact for information on government services, programs, and regulations for business.

Strategis (www.strategis.gc.ca) provides comprehensive business information online to help you find partners, discover new technologies, and explore growth opportunities.

$ources of Financing (www.strategis.gc.ca/sources) is your online database of financial providers for small- and medium-sized businesses, as well as a source of useful resources to help build your financing knowledge.

The **Canada Small Business Financing Program** (www.strategis.gc.ca/csbfa) can help you get a head start in financing your own business.

The **Business Development Bank of Canada** (www.bdc.ca) provides financial and consulting services to Canadian small businesses, particularly those in the technology and export sectors of the economy.

7

Team Canada Inc (www.exportsource.gc.ca) is your essential one-stop shop for information on export and trade.

Export Development Corporation (www.edc-see.ca) helps Canadian businesses export and invest in 200 markets worldwide by providing financial and risk management services, including export credit insurance, financing, and guarantees.

Self-Employment Assistance for Employment Insurance recipients and the **Youth Entrepreneurship Program** are two great ways to help you create your own job and business.

Small Business Information Seminars (www.ccra-adrc.gc.ca/business) provide information on your responsibilities regarding customs, income tax, and GST/HST, as well as the services available to you.

Contracts Canada (www.contractscanada.gc.ca) provides businesses with information on how and what the Government of Canada buys. The site also provides a link to the **MERX**™ (www.merx.cebra.com) database of current Government of Canada bidding opportunities.

The **Trade Commissioner Service** Web site (www.infoexport.gc.ca) can help you identify foreign business opportunities, learn more about target markets, or get in touch with employees in 133 offices around the world.

8

1 800 O-Canada
(1 800 622-6232)

www.canada.gc.ca
TTY/TDD: 1 800 465-7735

Canada

After You Read

1. Use the table of contents to get initial information about each of the following: planning a vacation, buying a new home, information for Native Canadians, attaining employment insurance benefits, upgrading your education, seeking a student loan, advising your grandparents about their pensions, and attaining employment insurance benefits.

Handbook Link
How to use and create a table of contents

Before You Read

Before you read this online information guide, choose one of the following topics and write a brief opinion paragraph about it. Then share your paragraph with a partner.

- It's important to know your rights as a tenant because…
- It's important to know your rights as a landlord because…
- I'd prefer to own my own home because…

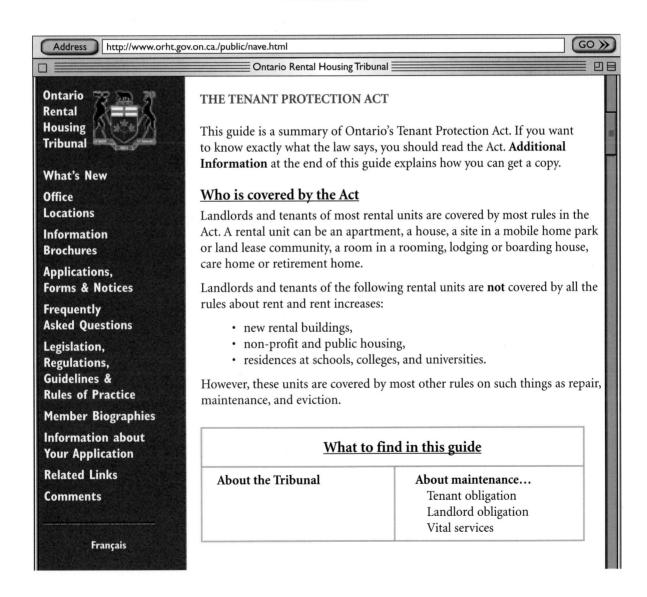

Address http://www.orht.gov.on.ca./public/nave.html   GO »

Ontario Rental Housing Tribunal

Ontario Rental Housing Tribunal

What's New

Office Locations

Information Brochures

Applications, Forms & Notices

Frequently Asked Questions

Legislation, Regulations, Guidelines & Rules of Practice

Member Biographies

Information about Your Application

Related Links

Comments

Français

THE TENANT PROTECTION ACT

This guide is a summary of Ontario's Tenant Protection Act. If you want to know exactly what the law says, you should read the Act. **Additional Information** at the end of this guide explains how you can get a copy.

Who is covered by the Act

Landlords and tenants of most rental units are covered by most rules in the Act. A rental unit can be an apartment, a house, a site in a mobile home park or land lease community, a room in a rooming, lodging or boarding house, care home or retirement home.

Landlords and tenants of the following rental units are **not** covered by all the rules about rent and rent increases:

- new rental buildings,
- non-profit and public housing,
- residences at schools, colleges, and universities.

However, these units are covered by most other rules on such things as repair, maintenance, and eviction.

What to find in this guide	
About the Tribunal	**About maintenance…** Tenant obligation Landlord obligation Vital services

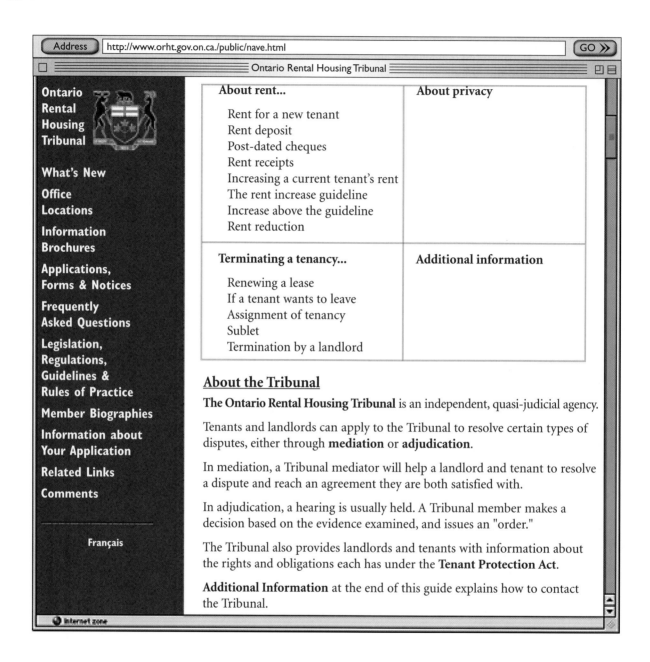

Address http://www.orht.gov.on.ca./public/nave.html   GO »

Ontario Rental Housing Tribunal

Ontario Rental Housing Tribunal

What's New

Office Locations

Information Brochures

Applications, Forms & Notices

Frequently Asked Questions

Legislation, Regulations, Guidelines & Rules of Practice

Member Biographies

Information about Your Application

Related Links

Comments

Français

About rent...

Rent for a new tenant
Rent deposit
Post-dated cheques
Rent receipts
Increasing a current tenant's rent
The rent increase guideline
Increase above the guideline
Rent reduction

About privacy

Terminating a tenancy...

Renewing a lease
If a tenant wants to leave
Assignment of tenancy
Sublet
Termination by a landlord

Additional information

About the Tribunal

The Ontario Rental Housing Tribunal is an independent, quasi-judicial agency.

Tenants and landlords can apply to the Tribunal to resolve certain types of disputes, either through **mediation** or **adjudication**.

In mediation, a Tribunal mediator will help a landlord and tenant to resolve a dispute and reach an agreement they are both satisfied with.

In adjudication, a hearing is usually held. A Tribunal member makes a decision based on the evidence examined, and issues an "order."

The Tribunal also provides landlords and tenants with information about the rights and obligations each has under the **Tenant Protection Act**.

Additional Information at the end of this guide explains how to contact the Tribunal.

Internet zone

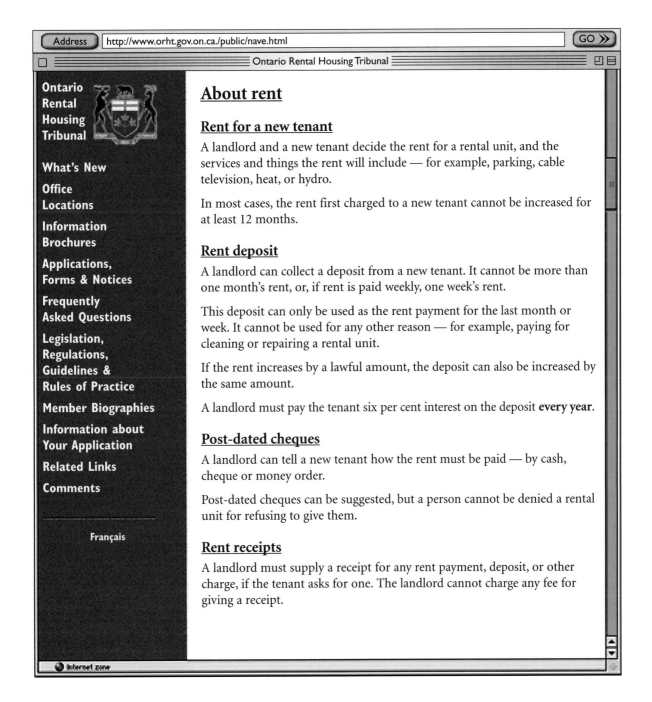

Address http://www.orht.gov.on.ca./public/nave.html GO »

Ontario Rental Housing Tribunal

Ontario Rental Housing Tribunal

What's New

Office Locations

Information Brochures

Applications, Forms & Notices

Frequently Asked Questions

Legislation, Regulations, Guidelines & Rules of Practice

Member Biographies

Information about Your Application

Related Links

Comments

Français

About rent

Rent for a new tenant

A landlord and a new tenant decide the rent for a rental unit, and the services and things the rent will include — for example, parking, cable television, heat, or hydro.

In most cases, the rent first charged to a new tenant cannot be increased for at least 12 months.

Rent deposit

A landlord can collect a deposit from a new tenant. It cannot be more than one month's rent, or, if rent is paid weekly, one week's rent.

This deposit can only be used as the rent payment for the last month or week. It cannot be used for any other reason — for example, paying for cleaning or repairing a rental unit.

If the rent increases by a lawful amount, the deposit can also be increased by the same amount.

A landlord must pay the tenant six per cent interest on the deposit **every year**.

Post-dated cheques

A landlord can tell a new tenant how the rent must be paid — by cash, cheque or money order.

Post-dated cheques can be suggested, but a person cannot be denied a rental unit for refusing to give them.

Rent receipts

A landlord must supply a receipt for any rent payment, deposit, or other charge, if the tenant asks for one. The landlord cannot charge any fee for giving a receipt.

Internet zone

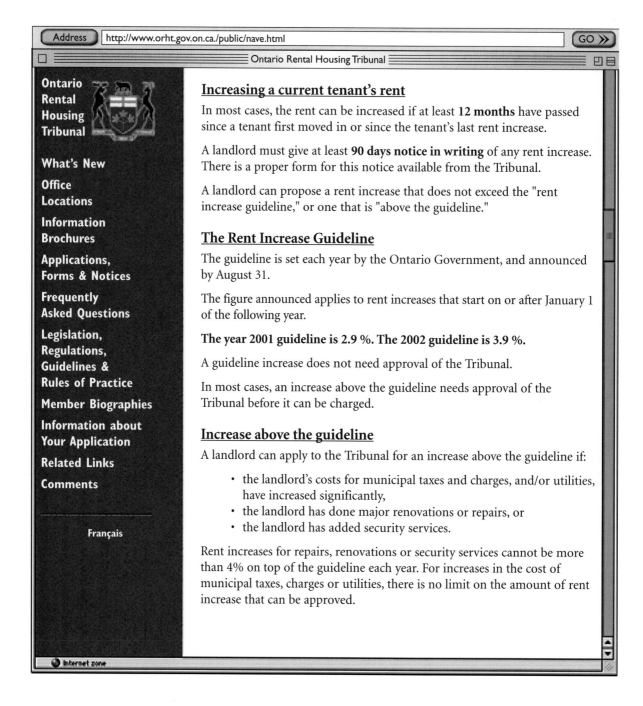

Address http://www.orht.gov.on.ca./public/nave.html   GO »

Ontario Rental Housing Tribunal

Ontario Rental Housing Tribunal

What's New

Office Locations

Information Brochures

Applications, Forms & Notices

Frequently Asked Questions

Legislation, Regulations, Guidelines & Rules of Practice

Member Biographies

Information about Your Application

Related Links

Comments

Français

Increasing a current tenant's rent

In most cases, the rent can be increased if at least **12 months** have passed since a tenant first moved in or since the tenant's last rent increase.

A landlord must give at least **90 days notice in writing** of any rent increase. There is a proper form for this notice available from the Tribunal.

A landlord can propose a rent increase that does not exceed the "rent increase guideline," or one that is "above the guideline."

The Rent Increase Guideline

The guideline is set each year by the Ontario Government, and announced by August 31.

The figure announced applies to rent increases that start on or after January 1 of the following year.

The year 2001 guideline is 2.9 %. The 2002 guideline is 3.9 %.

A guideline increase does not need approval of the Tribunal.

In most cases, an increase above the guideline needs approval of the Tribunal before it can be charged.

Increase above the guideline

A landlord can apply to the Tribunal for an increase above the guideline if:

- the landlord's costs for municipal taxes and charges, and/or utilities, have increased significantly,
- the landlord has done major renovations or repairs, or
- the landlord has added security services.

Rent increases for repairs, renovations or security services cannot be more than 4% on top of the guideline each year. For increases in the cost of municipal taxes, charges or utilities, there is no limit on the amount of rent increase that can be approved.

Internet zone

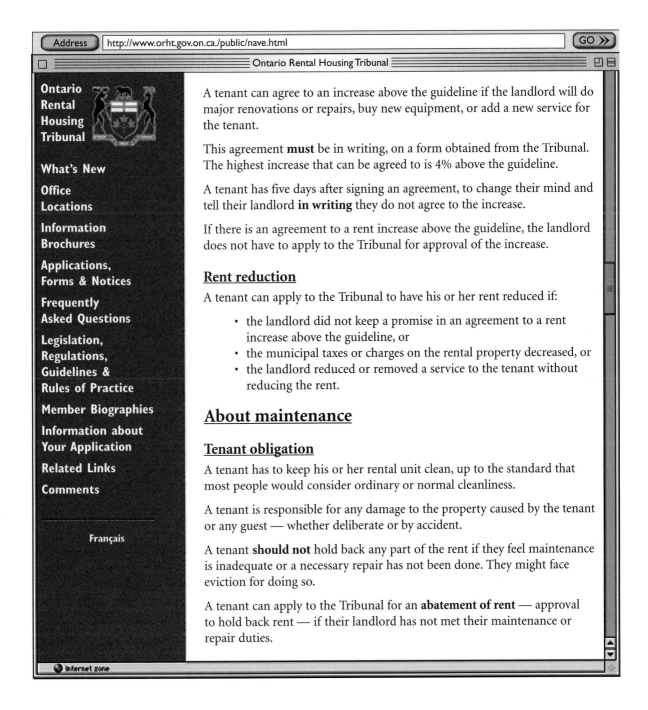

Address http://www.orht.gov.on.ca./public/nave.html GO »

Ontario Rental Housing Tribunal

Ontario Rental Housing Tribunal

What's New

Office Locations

Information Brochures

Applications, Forms & Notices

Frequently Asked Questions

Legislation, Regulations, Guidelines & Rules of Practice

Member Biographies

Information about Your Application

Related Links

Comments

Français

A tenant can agree to an increase above the guideline if the landlord will do major renovations or repairs, buy new equipment, or add a new service for the tenant.

This agreement **must** be in writing, on a form obtained from the Tribunal. The highest increase that can be agreed to is 4% above the guideline.

A tenant has five days after signing an agreement, to change their mind and tell their landlord **in writing** they do not agree to the increase.

If there is an agreement to a rent increase above the guideline, the landlord does not have to apply to the Tribunal for approval of the increase.

Rent reduction

A tenant can apply to the Tribunal to have his or her rent reduced if:

- the landlord did not keep a promise in an agreement to a rent increase above the guideline, or
- the municipal taxes or charges on the rental property decreased, or
- the landlord reduced or removed a service to the tenant without reducing the rent.

About maintenance

Tenant obligation

A tenant has to keep his or her rental unit clean, up to the standard that most people would consider ordinary or normal cleanliness.

A tenant is responsible for any damage to the property caused by the tenant or any guest — whether deliberate or by accident.

A tenant **should not** hold back any part of the rent if they feel maintenance is inadequate or a necessary repair has not been done. They might face eviction for doing so.

A tenant can apply to the Tribunal for an **abatement of rent** — approval to hold back rent — if their landlord has not met their maintenance or repair duties.

Internet zone

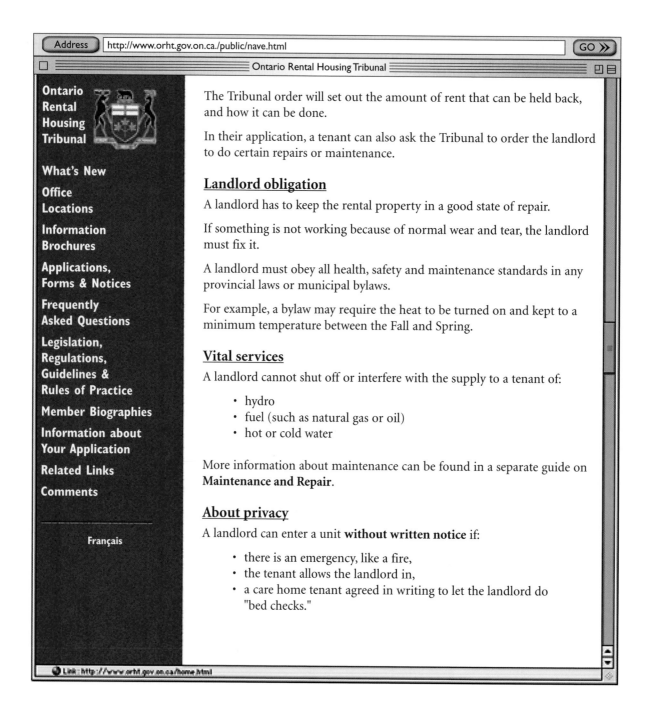

Ontario Rental Housing Tribunal

Ontario Rental Housing Tribunal

What's New

Office Locations

Information Brochures

Applications, Forms & Notices

Frequently Asked Questions

Legislation, Regulations, Guidelines & Rules of Practice

Member Biographies

Information about Your Application

Related Links

Comments

Français

The Tribunal order will set out the amount of rent that can be held back, and how it can be done.

In their application, a tenant can also ask the Tribunal to order the landlord to do certain repairs or maintenance.

Landlord obligation

A landlord has to keep the rental property in a good state of repair.

If something is not working because of normal wear and tear, the landlord must fix it.

A landlord must obey all health, safety and maintenance standards in any provincial laws or municipal bylaws.

For example, a bylaw may require the heat to be turned on and kept to a minimum temperature between the Fall and Spring.

Vital services

A landlord cannot shut off or interfere with the supply to a tenant of:

- hydro
- fuel (such as natural gas or oil)
- hot or cold water

More information about maintenance can be found in a separate guide on **Maintenance and Repair**.

About privacy

A landlord can enter a unit **without written notice** if:

- there is an emergency, like a fire,
- the tenant allows the landlord in,
- a care home tenant agreed in writing to let the landlord do "bed checks."

Link: http://www.orht.gov.on.ca/home.html

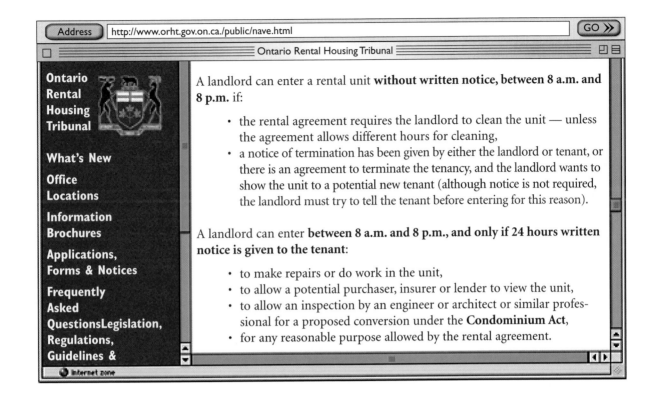

Address | http://www.orht.gov.on.ca./public/nave.html | GO »

Ontario Rental Housing Tribunal

Ontario Rental Housing Tribunal

What's New

Office Locations

Information Brochures

Applications, Forms & Notices

Frequently Asked QuestionsLegislation, Regulations, Guidelines &

Internet zone

A landlord can enter a rental unit **without written notice, between 8 a.m. and 8 p.m.** if:

- the rental agreement requires the landlord to clean the unit — unless the agreement allows different hours for cleaning,
- a notice of termination has been given by either the landlord or tenant, or there is an agreement to terminate the tenancy, and the landlord wants to show the unit to a potential new tenant (although notice is not required, the landlord must try to tell the tenant before entering for this reason).

A landlord can enter **between 8 a.m. and 8 p.m., and only if 24 hours written notice is given to the tenant**:

- to make repairs or do work in the unit,
- to allow a potential purchaser, insurer or lender to view the unit,
- to allow an inspection by an engineer or architect or similar professional for a proposed conversion under the **Condominium Act**,
- for any reasonable purpose allowed by the rental agreement.

After You Read

1. Imagine that you and a friend are going to rent an apartment together. Write instructions to follow that summarize the most important points you need to be informed about before you sign your lease.

Handbook Link

How to write instructions

How to use reading strategies to understand text

Before You Read

Focus on a wall, with no doors or windows, in your classroom. Observe it carefully. Write a brief paragraph describing the wall: what it's made of, its texture, its shape, its strength, its colour, its size. Create two or three similes that express what walls are like. Then read the poem and compare your vision to the poet's.

Where There's a
WALL

by Joy Kogawa

Where there's a wall
there's a way through a
gate or door. There's even
a ladder perhaps and a
sentinel who sometimes sleeps.
There are secret passwords you
can overhear. There are methods
of torture for extracting clues
to maps of underground passages.
There are zeppelins, helicopters,
rockets, bombs, battering rams,
armies with trumpets whose
all at once blast shatters
the foundations.

Where there's a wall there are
words to whisper by loose bricks,
wailing prayers to utter, birds
to carry messages taped to their feet.
There are letters to be written —
poems even.

Faint as in a dream
is the voice that calls
from the belly
of the wall.

*Faint as in a dream
is the voice that calls
from the belly
of the wall.*

After You Read

1. Reflect on what the poet says about overcoming obstacles. Write to explain how that idea applies to your life, and how that idea applies to humanity in general.
2. Imagine what you think "the voice that calls/from the belly/of the wall" is saying. Write a poem to share your thoughts.

Handbook Link

How to understand themes in literature

How to write a poem

Acknowledgements

Every effort has been made to find and to acknowledge correctly the sources of the material reproduced in this book. The publisher welcomes any information that will enable it to rectify, in subsequent editions, any errors or omissions.

"The Dilbert Principle" by Scott Adams. United Features Syndicate. Reprinted by permission.

"I Know Why the Caged Bird Sings" from *I Know Why the Caged Bird Sings* by Maya Angelou, copyright © 1969 and renewed 1997 by Maya Angelou. Used by permission of Random House, Inc.

"Me as My Grandmother" by Rosemary Aubert is reprinted from *Two Kinds of Honey* by permission of Oberon Press.

"Learning to Work Safely" by Rosemarie Bahr, from Ontario College of Teachers *Professionally Speaking*.

"The Wealthy Barber" by David Chilton. Courtesy David Barr Chilton, Author & President, Financial Awareness Corporation.

"Government of Canada Services for You" © Her Majesty the Queen in Right of Canada. All rights reserved. Communications Canada, 2000. Reproduced with the permission of the Minister of Public Works and Government Services, 2002.

"Talk: An Ashanti Tale" from *The Cow-Tail Switch and Other West African Stories* by Harold Courlander and George Herzog. Copyright © 1947, 1974 by Harold Courlander. Reprinted by permission of Henry Holt and Company, LLC.

"My TV" by Gisèle Danis. Courtesy of Gisèle Danis, VR News-Chum Group.

"The Real-Life Dreams of Jarome Iginla" by James Deacon. Reprinted by permission of *Maclean's* Magazine.

"All I Really Need to Know I Learned in Kindergarten" from *All I Really Need to Know I Learned in Kindergarten* by Robert L. Fulghum, copyright 1986, 1988 by Robert L. Fulghum. Used by permission of Villard Books, a division of Random House, Inc.

"Coal Black" by Lennie Gallant. Reprinted by permission of Lennie Gallant.

"The Grand River Conservation Authority 2000 Annual Report." Courtesy of the Grand River Conservation Authority.

"How to Quit Smoking in Fifty Years or Less" by Peter Gzowski. From *Addicted: Notes from the Belly of the Beast*, Lorna Crozier and Patrick Lane, Eds.

"The Rez Sisters" by Tomson Highway. Reprinted with permission from *The Rez Sisters*. Copyright 1998 by Tomson Highway. Published by Fifth House Ltd., Calgary, Canada.

"Mother to Son" by Langston Hughes. From *The Collected Poems of Langston Hughes by Langston Hughes*, copyright 1994 by The Estate of Langston Hughes. Used by permission of Alfred A. Knopf, a division of Random House House Inc.

"Maternity, parental and sickness benefits." Human Resources Development Canada. Reproduced with the permission of the Minister of Public Works and Government Services Canada, 2002.

"Open Ice: The Tim Horton Story" from *Open Ice: The Tim Horton Story* by Douglas Hunter. Copyright © Douglas Hunter, 1994. Reprinted by permission of Penguin Books Canada Limited.

"New Views of the Cosmos" by Elesa Janke. Published in *Astronomy's Explore the Universe*, 9th Edition 2003. Kalmbach Publishing Co., Waukesha, WI.

"Customers Are Not Always Right" by Andrea Janus. Reprinted courtesy of Andrea Janus.

"Why We Crave Horror Movies" by Stephen King. Reprinted with permission of Stephen King. All rights reserved. Originally appeared in *Playboy* (1982).

"Where There's a Wall" by Joy Kogawa. Reprinted by permission of Mosaic Press.

"Why Be Polite?" by Michael Korda. Reprinted in *Essays, Patterns, and Perspectives*. Ed. Judith Barker-Sandbrook. Toronto: Oxford University Press, 1992.

"The Survival of the Fittest" by Stephen Leacock. Reprinted by permission of Nancy K. Winthrop, copyright holder.

"The BMX Clothing Business" by Mark Losey from *BMXonline.com* Magazine, published by Times Mirror Magazines.

"The Interview" by Margie Marks. Reprinted by permission of Marjorie Marks.

Analyzing the "Tween" Market. Reprinted by permission of MediaWatch.

"Finding and Keeping a Sense of Accomplishment and Worth" by Cheryl Nafziger-Leis. Published in the Kitchener-Waterloo *Record*.

"Words That Count Women In" by the Ontario Women's Directorate.

"In My Hands" from *In My Hands: Memories of a Holocaust Rescuer* by Irene Gut Opdyke with Jennifer Armstrong, copyright © 1999 by Irene Gut Opdyke with Jennifer Armstong. Used by permission of Alfred A. Knopf, an imprint of Random House Children's Books, a division of Random House, Inc.

"A Day No Pigs Would Die" from *A Day No Pigs Would Die* by Robert Newton Peck.

"The Man and The Machine" by E. J. Pratt. Copyright holder unknown.

"One Ocean" by Betty Quan. Copyright © 1994 by Betty Quan. First broadcast on CBC-Radio.

"The Tenant Protection Act." Copyright © The Queen's Printer for Ontario, 2002. Reproduced with permission.

"We'll Carry On" by Jimmy Rankin. Reprinted by permission of Song Dog Music Co. Ltd. © Song Dog Music Co. Ltd. 2001.

"Singing Sisters Come Home to Country" by Stefania Rizzi. Courtesy of The *Era-Banner*.

"The Sault Star — Classified Advertisements Online." Courtesy of *The Sault Star*.

"The Metamorphosis of Lesra Martin" by Lynne Schuyler. Reprinted with permission from the December 2000 *Reader's Digest*.

"Childhood: 1916" extracted from *The Stone Diaries* by Carol Shields. Copyright © 1993 by Carol Shields. Reprinted by permission of Random House of Canada, a division of Random House of Canada Limited.

"Pros, Peers Share Youth Job-Search Secrets" by Barbara B. Simmons. Reprinted by permission of Barbara Simmons.

"The Stickhandler" by David Solway. Reprinted by permission of David Solway.

"Talking Toys Speak Volumes about Gender Stereotypes" by David Staples. Reprinted with permission of The *Edmonton Journal*.

"Who, Then, Is a "Canadian"?" by Suwanda Sugunasiri. Professor Suwanda Sugunasiri teaches at the University of Toronto. He is the founder of Nalanda College of Buddhist Studies and was a columnist for the *Toronto Star*.

"A Son's Goodbye" by Justin Trudeau. Copyright © 2000, Justin Trudeau.

"Adversity" by David Trupp. Reprinted by permission of the author.

"Television Viewing: The Human Dimension" by Charles S. Ungerleider and Ernest Krieger. From *Television and Society* by Charles S. Ungerleider and Ernest Krieger. Published by Irwin Publishing, 1985.

"In a year when so much was taken …". Courtesy of the United Way of Greater Toronto.

"I Volunteer." Reprinted by permission of Volunteer Canada (www.volunteer.ca).

"Summer Wages" by Caroline Woodward from *Disturbing the Peace* by Caroline Woodward. Published in 1990 by Polestar, an imprint of Raincoast Books.

"Young Worker Awareness Program Web Site." Courtesy of WSIB.

Illustrations

page 2: June Lawrason, pages 6, 9: Jocelyne Bouchard, page 11: Shelagh Armstrong-Hodgson, page 14: Nicholas Vitacco, pages 17, 20: William Kimber, page 29: Vesna Krstanovic, pages 51, 53, 54: Shelagh Armstrong-Hodgson, page 74: Donna Guilfoyle/ArtPlus Limited, pages 99, 101: Jay Turner, pages 104 - 107: Daniel Ferguson, page 109: Alisa Belshaw, page 102: June Lawrason, pages 110, 111: Scott Adams copyright © United Features Syndicate, pages 113-115: John Etheridge, pages 119-122: Joe Weissmann, page 128: Jay Turner, page 136: Sacha Warunkiw, pages 137, 138: David Shaw, pages 143, 145, 147: Lisa Rotenberg, page 155: Chum McLeod, pages 163-165: Daniel Ferguson, pages 175, 177: Courtesy of The Grand River Conservation Authority, pages 184-185: Alisa Belshaw, page 220: Ken Suzana, page 223: Susan Todd, page 225: Cindy Jeftovic, page 230-232: Farida Zaman, pages 246-247: Alisa Belshaw

Photographs

page 2: Corbis, page 22: Corbis, page 26: Courtesy of Gisèle Danis, VR News-Chum Group, pages 35, 37, 40, 43, 46: Courtesy of Irene Gut Opdyke and Random House Inc., page 48: Corbis, page 58: Reprinted by permission of Alex Waterhouse Hayward, page 65: Peter Parsons/CP Photo Archive, page 76: Boris Spremo/CP Photo Archive, page 77: Ross Allard/CP Photo Archive, page 110: Adalberto Rios Szalay/Sexto Sol/PhotoDisc, pages 124–126: Andrew Vaughan/CP Photo Archive, page 131: Ryan Remiorz/CP Photo Archive, page 134: Paul Chiasson/CP Photo Archive, page 150: Corbis, page 158: Ontario College of Teachers *Professionally Speaking*, page 161: Courtesy of WSIB, page 169: © Mitchell Gerber/CORBIS/MAGMA, pages 173-174: Courtesy of the Grand River Conservation Authority, page 196: Corbis, pages 198-199, 202: NASA, ESA, and the ACS Science Team, page 200 top and bottom: NASA, ESA, and the NICMOS Science Team, page 201: NASA and the Hubble Heritage Team (STScI/AURA), page 203: The ACS and NICMOS Science Teams, page 204: Heidi Reidner, pages 207, 209: Sandy Nicholson, page 213: Murray Mitchell/CP Photo Archive, page 217: PhotoDisc, page 218: O-Pee-Chee/Hockey Hall of Fame